Guadalupe in New York

Guadalupe in New York

Devotion and the Struggle for Citizenship Rights among Mexican Immigrants

Alyshia Gálvez

NEW YORK UNIVERSITY PRESS
New York and London

NEW YORK UNIVERSITY PRESS
New York and London
www.nyupress.org

Library of Congress Cataloging-in-Publication Data

Gálvez, Alyshia.
Guadalupe in New York : devotion and the struggle for citizenship
rights among Mexican immigrants / Alyshia Gálvez.
p. cm.
Includes bibliographical references and index.
ISBN-13: 978-0-8147-3214-4 (cloth : alk. paper)
ISBN-10: 0-8147-3214-3 (cloth : alk. paper)
ISBN-13: 978-0-8147-3215-1 (pbk. : alk. paper)
ISBN-10: 0-8147-3215-1 (pbk. : alk. paper)
1. Mexican Americans—New York—New York—Religion. 2. Mary,
Blessed Virgin, Saint—Devotion to—New York—New York.
3. Guadalupe, Our Lady of. 4. Citizenship—United States. 5. United
States—Emigration and immigration. 6. Civil rights—United States.
7. Emigration and immigration—Religious aspects—Christianity. I. Title.
BR563.M49G35   2009
305.868'7207471—dc22   2009026863

New York University Press books are printed on acid-free paper,
and their binding materials are chosen for strength and durability.
We strive to use environmentally responsible suppliers and materials
to the greatest extent possible in publishing our books.

Manufactured in the United States of America
c   10 9 8 7 6 5 4 3 2 1

p   10 9 8 7 6 5 4 3 2 1

Arrival of *La Antorcha Guadalupana*, outside
Saint Patrick's Cathedral, December 12, 2002

For Carlos, Lázaro, and Elías.
My best friends, the loves of my life.

Contents

List of Figures		xi
Acknowledgments		xiii
1	Introduction	1
2	On Citizenship, Membership, and the Right to Have Rights	16
3	Los Comités Guadalupanos and Asociación Tepeyac: Their Formation and Context	31
4	Our Lady of Guadalupe: The Image and Its Circulation	72
5	El Viacrucis del Inmigrante and Other Public Processions	107
6	La Antorcha Guadalupana/The Guadalupan Torch Run: Messengers for a People Divided by the Border	140
7	Conclusion: Citizenship for Immigrants	167
	Appendix: A Note on Methodology and the Use of Pseudonyms	193
	Notes	197
	References	211
	Index	227
	About the Author	237

List of Figures

Arrival of *La Antorcha Guadalupana,* outside Saint Patrick's
Cathedral, December 12, 2002   v

The Shrine to Our Lady of Guadalupe outside Our Lady
of the Rosary Parish   2

Image of the Virgin of Guadalupe, outside Saint John Parish,
Mott Haven, Bronx, New York   41

Mexican couple emerges onto the street outside of Saint John
Church after being married   47

Banner of Asociación Tepeyac, 2000   61

Josefa's new home, near Atlixco, Puebla, Mexico, 2002   69

Statue of Our Lady of Guadalupe for sale on Fourteenth Street,
photograph by Eileen O'Connor   73

Woman holds flowers as an offering before Saint Juan Diego in
Saint Bernard Parish, 2005, photograph by Eileen O'Connor   74

The lintel near the image of Our Lady of Guadalupe at Saint
John Parish   97

Viacrucis del Inmigrante, Broadway, lower Manhattan, 2003   108

Flyer for *El Viacrucis del Inmigrante,* April 9, 2004   109

Malenny, an altar girl, participated in Saint John's Viacrucis,
in the Bronx   122

Parishioners playing roles of Jesus and the Roman soldiers in the
Viacrucis at Our Lady of the Rosary parish, April 18, 2003   128

Viacrucis del Inmigrante, lower Manhattan, April 2003   135

Participants in *El Viacrucis del Inmigrante,* lower Manhattan   136

Poster for the Antorcha Guadalupana, 2002   145

Launch of the Torch Run. Luz María, widow of a   148
    victim of September 11, 2001

Torch run passes through Zapotitlán Salinas, Puebla, Mexico, 2007   150

The Torch passes through Progreso, State of Puebla,   157
    photograph by Joel Merino, Antorcha 2007

La Antorcha Guadalupana arrives to Saint Patrick's Cathedral,   168
    December 12, 2003

Dancers celebrate the arrival of the torch outside Saint Patrick's   169
    Cathedral, December 12, 2003

Participants in the Torch Procession enter Saint Patrick's   170
    Cathedral, December 12, 2008

Child dressed like Juan Diego being carried into Saint   171
    Patrick's Cathedral

Man holding sign asking for legalization outside Saint Patrick's   172
    Cathedral, December 12, 2003

Participant holding sign at *El Viacrucis del Inmigrante,*   184
    lower Manhattan, 2003

Demonstration for general amnesty, midtown Manhattan,   186
    October 2000

Acknowledgments

This book would not exist without the significant contributions of the research participants, colleagues, mentors, friends, and family who cared enough about the project and about me to ensure its existence. In spite of their efforts, the errors and faults of this book that undoubtedly remain are mine alone.

It is impossible not to think of those who have passed away in the period encompassed by the research and writing of this book—each loss is a sad marker in the trajectory of the project and my life: Jocelyn Solís, William Roseberry, Foster Buckner, Jr., Lowell Livezey, and Sarah Hannah. I also cannot but mention the new lives who burst onto the scene and inevitably put everything into perspective, most especially my sons Lázaro and Elías, as well as their cousins and my friends' children.

For making this book possible, I thank the organizations within which and individuals with whom I conducted this research. While they did not always fling their doors open for me, their eventual openness, respect, and enthusiasm about my project were all the more precious for having been gradually earned. Too many people to name took time out of their busy lives to orient me, allow me to tag along with them, and answer my pesky questions. Among those who went out of their way to be helpful, I must make special mention of María Zúñiga, Manuela Fuentes, Father John Grange, Joel Magallán, Luz María Magaña, Esperanza Morales, Teresa García, and Jocelyn Solís. Jocelyn's overbrimming enthusiasm was matched only by her powerful intellect, making her untimely loss all the more tragic and a particularly sad punctuation mark in the time period and community this book describes.

Like a fairy godmother, Judy Hellman dropped into town at just the right moments over the course of several years. She demonstrated enthusiasm for the project before even I was sure what it was about and then gave me wise counsel on its development all the way to press; I am very thankful to her. Diana Taylor, Faye Ginsburg, and Thomas Abercrombie have provided constant support, guidance, and countless opportunities for learning and growth (not to mention material sustenance!) from the very beginning. Courses with and mentorship by Linda Green at Columbia University and Rolf Foerster at La Universidad de Chile inspired me to become an anthropologist. William Roseberry deeply impacted my perspective on the discipline, as well as its relationship to history, and moved me by generously serving as reader on my masters' thesis in the last months of his life. Bambi Schieffelin, Robert Smith, Lok Siu, and Joel Magallán helped me plant the initial germ of an idea that would become this book. Renato Rosaldo arrived at New York University as I was leaving, but I will be forever grateful for the incredible generosity he showed me and his eagerness about this project. I am particularly indebted to him for his attention to this as a piece of writing, not just writing up. I am thankful to Fred Myers for introducing me to Jennifer Hammer at New York University Press, and to Jennifer for her passion for the project and meticulous attention to its realization in its current form. I also thank the no longer anonymous reviewers, Miguel Díaz-Barriga and Joseph Palacios, whose constructive advice made revision far less agonizing than it might have been.

Material support for the research contained herein came from the Social Science Research Council's Program on Philanthropy and the Nonprofit Sector, the Wenner-Gren Foundation, and the National Science Foundation. The SSRC in particular provided support in the form of multiple grants as well as the opportunity for fellowship with other scholars at important junctures. During the writing and revision of this book, I had the good fortune of holding a two-year teaching fellowship at New York University's Center for Latin American and Caribbean Studies (2005–2007). There, I was exceedingly fortunate to co-teach with George Yúdice and benefit from his bottomless knowledge. Also at CLACS, I was fortunate to work with, know, and receive lots of help from Maritza Colón, Patricia Oscategui, Ana María Ochoa, Carolina Fermín, and Thomas Abercrombie. Masters' students and graduate assistants at New York University who not only suffered my obsessions in my courses but did everything from hunt down library books to debate transnationalism and immigrant rights with me are Eva Blom Raison, Eileen O'Connor, and Catherine Reiland. Catherine in particular has been a joy to work with on this and a half-dozen other projects, even reading the entire manuscript for me at a crucial moment.

During the writing of this book, I benefited from invaluable opportunities to present portions of this book and receive extremely helpful suggestions from extraordinary colleagues. These opportunities included a faculty seminar in the City University of New York's Center for the Humanities on the "Sacred and the Secular" funded by the Mellon Foundation (2008–2009), working groups and many activities at New York University's Center for Religion and Media and Hemispheric Institute of Performance and Politics, as well as a University Seminar on "Religion in New York City" at Columbia University. Other helpful opportunities for feedback included lectures I was invited to deliver at Bard College, Fordham University, and la Universidad Autónoma de la Ciudad de México.

I was aided in research and writing by the very fine assistance of several individuals. Elizabeth Capone-Newton (Capone-Henríquez) assisted me in demographic research and also was an excellent sounding board for ideas in their early stages. José Carlos Luque Brazán transcribed many, many hours of interviews and also offered tireless support. Sari Lapin Mayer selflessly pored over the final manuscript from start to finish and gave many astute suggestions. Thanks are also due to my colleagues in Latin American and Puerto Rican Studies at Lehman College, including Laird Bergad, Milagros Ricourt, and Licia Fiol-Matta, as well as other colleagues and friends: Juana Ponce de León, Liliana Rivera-Sánchez, Ulla Berg, Miguel Díaz-Barriga, Tomás Eloy Martínez, Courtney Bender, Milton Machuca, Kathleen Coll, Ayala Fader, Nara Milanich, Carlos Decena, Kristen Norget, Nicholas DeGenova, Nina Siulc, Christina Díaz, Leslie Martino, Marian Ronan, Carlos Encina, Camila Vergara, Kathryn Tomko-Dennler, Arlene Dávila, Marcy Schwartz, Linda Kintz, Irene García, Sherine Hamdy, Orlando Lara, Susanna Rosenbaum, Elizabeth Kipper, Sergio Cortés, Alison Lee, and Leigh Binford for their helpful advice and camaraderie at important moments.

I am grateful to my family and those friends who are like family for their unwavering and unconditional support: my parents: Kathy and Eric Blond; grandmothers: Margaret Buckner and Rosemary Matrejek; as well as Blanca García; Cybele Lyle; Kelly Collins; Bob O'Hagan; Elizabeth, Mikhail, and Sophia Shishkov; Alison Ritz; Denis Pareja; Lucila Martínez; Sergio, Veronica, and Francisco Rodríguez; and Alexandra Atkin. I wish that my father, David Clawson, and grandfather, Foster Bucker, could have witnessed the publication of this book—I know they would have been especially proud. I must make special mention of Alicia Carmona and her family, who have been a constant source of encouragement and friendship for a decade. Proofreading this manuscript is only Alicia's most recent act of generosity. Finally, I thank my husband Carlos and two sons, Lázaro and Elías, for their love, and to them this book is dedicated—words do not serve to express my love and thanks.

1

Introduction

Desde el cielo una hermosa mañana,
Desde el cielo una hermosa mañana,
La guadalupana, la guadalupana, la guadalupana bajó al Tepeyac .
Suplicante juntaba sus manos y eran mexicanos su traje y su faz.
Su llegada llenó de alegría de luz y armonía todo el Anáhuac.
Junto al monte pasaba Juan Diego y acercóse luego al oír cantar.
A Juan Diego la Virgen le dijo, este cerro elijo para hacer mi altar.
Y en la tilma entre rosas pintada su imagen amada se dignó dejar.
Desde entonces para el Mexicano
Ser guadalupano es algo esencial,
En sus penas se postra de hinojos y eleva sus ojos hacia el Tepeyac.
    —*"La Guadalupana,"* devotional song
    for Our Lady of Guadalupe[1]

Turning down a quiet, residential street toward Our Lady of the Rosary Parish early on a weekend morning, it is possible to imagine that one is not in the Bronx or New York City at all, but somewhere more quiet and peaceful. When the air is clear and the temperature is warm, and the window boxes, yards, community gardens, and trees are full of leaves and flowers, it is possible to find a certain resemblance between this place and other very different places, here and "home," for some who nurture nostalgia for somewhere other than this city. It was just such an August morning when I arrived at Our Lady of the Rosary Parish to talk with Marco. I found him tending to the image of Our Lady of Guadalupe which is just outside the rectory. He swept around the feet of the Virgin and the sidewalk in front of her shrine. He discarded the wilted flowers left as offerings along the image's enclosure and emptied then refilled the vases with water, placing them carefully within reach of the sidewalk. He

The Shrine to Our
Lady of Guadalupe,
outside Our Lady of
the Rosary Parish

remarked that if he did not do this regularly, people would simply throw
flowers at the Virgin's feet in offering, and he would later have to remove
the decaying stems. He cleaned the glass enclosing the image of the Virgin, and picked up gum wrappers and other bits of litter that had found
their way into the area. Before he left, he deposited his own flowers into a
vase, crossed himself and kissed his fingers.

For many observers, there is nothing less remarkable than someone
from Mexico engaging in devotional practices to that country's patron
saint, Our Lady of Guadalupe. That Marco was in the Bronx tending
to the Virgin's shrine is not, in itself, noteworthy in this age of accelerated migration from Mexico to the United States. When these practices
actually surface to the level of commentary in migration literature, they
are often described as a retention of cultural and religious identity from
"home": Guadalupan devotion, *guadalupanismo*, is the most salient, well
known, and widespread aspect of religiosity in Mexico, so it is logical that
it would continue in the diaspora. Further, there is a centuries-old history
of Guadalupan devotion in the region now known as the Southwestern
United States, further cementing its centrality in U.S. understandings of
Latino religiosity. Historians of migration and of religion have chronicled

the deployment of national devotions in the project of immigrant incorporation in the United States, by which assimilation is measured and charted by the insertion of "Old World" beliefs and rituals into the frame of civil religion. As assimilationist paradigms have been revised, and in some cases, rejected, the attention to religion perhaps became a proverbial baby thrown out with the bathwater, receding from centrality in analyses of immigrant insertion in the United States. Only in the last few years have religious practices, modes of congregation, and devotion again been observed to be both transformed and transforming in the migration experience, and immigration studies and religious studies have come together (see Hondagneu-Sotelo 2007; Alba, Raboteau, and DeWind, 2009; Vásquez and Marquardt 2003, among others).

While the devotional practices centered on Our Lady of Guadalupe engaged in by Mexican immigrants in New York City may seem familiar to some observers, they occur in a unique historical moment of massive and accelerated migration, militarization of the border, stagnation of immigration laws, and worldwide struggles for rights by those displaced by globalization. They occur in New York, a city that has been site of many kinds of immigrant mobilizations over more than a century, but never any precisely like these. Every year on December 12, thousands of Mexican immigrants gather for the mass at Saint Patrick's Cathedral in honor of Our Lady of Guadalupe's feast day. They kiss images of the Virgin, carry framed portraits in expectation of a bishop's blessing, and wear traditional costumes associated with the story of the Virgin's apparition; and they also carry signs asking for immigration reform, chant "¡*Sí, se puede!*" [Yes, we can!] just like protestors do at marches, and display Mexican and U.S. flags. It is through Guadalupan devotion that many undocumented Mexican immigrants are finding the will and vocabulary to demand rights, immigration reform, and respect. In these practices and in the places that they make Guadalupan through their activities, not only is their faith transformed into a platform for making claims to rights, but they transform themselves, becoming emboldened in their struggle to provide for their families and build their lives in the city with dignity.

This book is about New York–based Mexican immigrants who envision community, develop modalities of collective organization, reimagine their own identities, and turn these to the task of broadening their rights—all in the idiom of devotion to the Virgin of Guadalupe. All of this is happening in parish-based confraternal social organizations called *comités guadalupanos,* Guadalupan Committees, which together are linked in a network called *Asociación Tepeyac de New York*. Members of these organizations join together *as immigrants* and in defiance of the undocumented status many of them share. As such, they develop a mode of *being*, of situating oneself with respect to the state and society in the United States and in the broader multinational globalized sphere that neither assumes assimilation nor the seamless maintenance of ties to the homeland. Instead, it is an activist, enfranchised identity, as globalized as the capitalist economic forces which prompted their migration in the first place, uniquely dedicated to the transformation of life in the present, not in the nostalgic past of "home" nor in the imagined future of return or legalization in the United States.

This transformation has implications for notions of citizenship. While much writing on immigration assumes that citizenship is a condition that begins after the bestowal of the juridical attributes of belonging, I argue in this book that Mexican immigrants are engaging in political, activist activities which enhance their sense of well-being in material, lived, and symbolic ways even while their juridical status remains unchanged. This kind of citizenship—broader, more performative, and more agential than the strictly juridical classification of citizens—is necessary to all other rights projects, both in the realm of formal citizenship and in other areas of social life. Mexican immigrants' involvement in such activities, and perhaps more importantly, the disposition which enables such engagement, is not easily measured quantitatively in votes cast, dollars raised, petitions circulated, or meetings attended. While such dispositions may not register on formal surveys of political activities, it is no less important and real for the people involved. Indeed, it is their engagement and willingness to stand up for themselves and other members of the community they have created that will have the biggest impact on their quality of life in the United States. Legalization of their immigration status, if and when it comes, will be joyfully welcomed, but they are no longer holding their breath. Historically in the United States, as well as in many other immigrant-receiving nations, citizenship has not been defined exclusively as juridical membership in the nation-state the way it increasingly is today. Rather, citizenship has had broader meanings referring to notions of belonging, rights, responsibility, and a disposition toward civic engagement. Coherent within these meanings, the activities of members of the comités guadalupanos and Asociación Tepeyac constitute an important model of citizenship in the here and now, even as these immigrants struggle for access to the juridical realm of membership in the nation-state.

Not simply another piece of baggage brought—sealed and intact—by migrants into new locales, religiosity is only recently coming to be understood as a space for new kinds of collective and individual identities. Religion offers a privileged lens for examining immigration, as immigration does for religion, and both offer insight into U.S. society and its treatment of newcomers as well as the newcomers' perception of and adaptation to life in this country. Sociologists of religion have been at the forefront of this wave of attention to the intersection of religion, immigrants, and civil society (see Alba, Raboteau, and De Wind 2009; Ebaugh and Chafetz 2000; Hondagneu Sotelo 2007; Kniss and Numrich 2007; Palacios 2007; Warner and Wittner 1999; Wood 2002; and Zolberg and Casanova 2002) and this book enters into conversation with such perspectives while incorporating anthropological research methodologies and perspectives on transnationalism, devotional practice, citizenship, and personhood.

Religiosity—and by that I mean the whole complex of practices, beliefs, devotions, and modes of social organization and relations between and among practitioners as well as between laypeople and specialists— is a vector for collective and individual transformation. It provides ways for immigrants to contextualize, signify, and actively redefine their place in the United States and it transforms their understandings of who they are, where they come from, and most importantly, the rights and treatment they feel they deserve. Therefore, it is not safe to assume that as immigrants become more deeply embedded in the receiving country and are distanced in time and space from "home" that the role of religiosity in their lives will wane. We also cannot attribute religiosity's persistence solely to participation by immigrants in transnational social networks that compress the sensation of distance from their communities of origin and perhaps enable them to sustain the festive calendar of their hometowns. Instead, there is something far more vital and transformative that occurs when Mexican immigrants engage in devotional practices dedicated to Our Lady of Guadalupe in New York City.

Each December since 2002, Asociación Tepeyac and its member comités have organized a binational torch run, *La Antorcha Guadalupana*, in which a living flame has been carried by relay runners, over land, from the Basilica of Guadalupe in Mexico City to Saint Patrick's Cathedral in New York. The runners wear shirts that read "Messengers of a people divided by the border" and advocate for immigration reform at the same time that they pay homage to their patroness. As the runners make their way south from Mexico City to the *Mixteca* region from which many

Mexicans in New York hail, then up the eastern seaboard, they draw people into the streets who walk or run along with the torch and two enormous paintings of Our Lady of Guadalupe and Saint Juan Diego, witness to her apparition. People come out of their homes and workplaces to kiss and touch the images and the torch, acquiring a bit of the residue of the Basilica, epicenter of Guadalupanismo, even while they find themselves in Anniston, Alabama; Charlotte, North Carolina; or Newark, New Jersey. An organizer told me that the torch connects Guadalupanos in Mexico and the United States who are not themselves able to travel. These nodes of Guadalupanismo are like a string of pearls, he said, forged by devotion and activism. The pearls evoked by the antorcha's organizer are like an amulet, protecting and linking Mexican immigrants in the United States as a collective and also giving individuals reassurance and a sense of protection as they face new challenges.

Argument

Immigrants involved in comités guadalupanos and Asociación Tepeyac are redefining their rights, citizenship, and identities by renegotiating the symbols of faith and nation, mobilizing the space of the church, and participating in activities normally reserved for citizens. They do these things with very material aims such as immigration rights, social services, and political and economic equity, and less material aims such as expanding notions of the rights to which they feel entitled, and their sense of solidarity and community with other Mexican immigrants. This argument challenges existing theorizations of the role of religion in the lives of immigrants in the United States, of their relationship to conceptualizations of citizenship, and of the nature of immigrants' political engagement.

Mexican immigrants in New York City who participate in these organizations often name their main connections to each other as national identity, faith in the Virgin of Guadalupe, and undocumented migration status. While there are many who consider themselves members of the Mexican community and who participate in these organizations yet do not subscribe to one or more of these identities, these nevertheless constitute the primary modes of identification linking members of these organizations and those they consider to be their constituency. Analysts of Mexican migration might *expect* Guadalupanism, immigration status, and Mexican national identity to provide important idioms of collective identity for a

Mexican immigrant population in the United States. Nonetheless, I argue that these three vectors of identity are revalorized and made to serve different and powerful purposes in the experience of migration in a process that is, at the same time, a process of community formation. The term "vector" implies both magnitude and direction. Guadalupanism, migration, and national identity are commonalities shared by many Mexicans living in New York, but they are not static attributes. They are dynamic, lived, and changing sets of practices and meanings. Scholars of transnationalism and migration have, commendably, developed vivid metaphors for movement, frequently favoring the use of terms like *circuits* and *flows* to describe the movement of people, ideas, practices, values, goods, and capital, between sending and receiving communities. Some of these metaphors have been developed as a critique of earlier studies of immigration for their assimilationist bias, in which migration is a teleological ray, starting in one place and aspiring toward another in a unidirectional fashion. In such models, features such as language and religion were as static as luggage, carted along but not changing, and eventually abandoned. Here, we attribute dynamism to aspects of identity which are both transformed and transformative by viewing them as vectors.

The undocumented Mexican immigrants involved in comités guadalupanos and Asociación Tepeyac come to interpret, through their participation in these organizations, their "illegality" in moral terms, as a failure of larger economic structures beyond their control that cause human suffering and can only be remedied both through recourse to Our Lady of Guadalupe and activism in her name. The revalorization of Guadalupe in the context of what liberation theologians would call structural sin—racism, inequality, poverty, exclusion, or exploitation—cannot be taken for granted. How should we trace the ways that Guadalupanism comes to provide language for a project of rights acquisition and empowerment? I would suggest that it is not through a broad statement or doctrine developed by the Church or by a charismatic activist or group of activists attempting to "politicize" Guadalupan devotion, but rather emerges from the everyday experiences of Mexican immigrants as they go about their business of going to work, keeping their families together, participating in church activities, and sweeping shrines to the object of their devotion.[2]

Of course, there are significant numbers of Mexicans in New York who do not participate in these or other organizations (such as Casa México, Casa Puebla, small business collectives and so on), or whose memberships in voluntary associations are limited to soccer leagues and hometown clubs. However, participation in los comités guadalupanos and in the Asociación Tepeyac differs in providing two self-conscious projects: the building of a Mexican community and the promotion of its members' rights as Mexican immigrants through the idiom of Guadalupan devotion. This agenda differs from other community-building projects centered upon a shared status as workers, as Latinos, or as migrants from a particular town or state, such as that which occurs in other organizations. Also, as I will show, individual variance from the modes of identification asserted by the comités guadalupanos and Asociación Tepeyac is often subsumed into a collective discourse that asserts them.

Sweeping

In the ethnographic vignette above, we focused on a single devotional practice, one that is not picturesque, but, rather, mundane: sweeping. Dating at least to Early Modern Spain, sweeping and other housekeeping in a shrine to the Virgin Mary has been considered a profound devotional practice. Philip II, perhaps the most powerful sovereign of his age, was known to regularly sweep the shrine at Guadalupe in Extremadura (Christian 1981; see also Altman 1989; and Starr-LeBeau 1996). As he swept, he asserted both his power over his subjects and his humility to the Virgin Mary, on the stage of such dramatic turning points in Spain's history as the resolution of the *Reconquista* and launch of the Conquest.[3] In Mesoamerica, prior to Spanish arrival, sweeping had different but similarly profound meanings. At the end of a 52-year bundle of years, the Mexica [Aztec] century, all dwellings were swept, all refuse brushed away, all pottery, utensils, and brooms broken, and then all fires were extinguished, to await the lighting of the New Fire in the chest of a sacrificial victim. That fire was subsequently delivered by relay runners carrying torches to every corner of the empire, assurance that the sun would again rise and life would continue (del Paso y Troncoso 1979).

In the process of compiling the Florentine Codex, Mexica informants told Fray Bernardo de Sahagún their origin myth, albeit with vocabulary already colored by Iberian religiosity (e.g., the notion of penance): their principal deity, Huitzilipochtli, was conceived when his mother, Coatlicue, who already had 401 children, was sweeping, and a feather flew into her womb, implanting his fetus:

In Coatepec, on the way to Tula,
    there was living,
    there dwelt a woman
    by the name of Coatlicue.
    She was mother of the four hundred gods of the south
    and their sister
    by name Coyolxauhqui.
And this Coatlicue did penance there,
    she swept, it was her task to sweep,
    thus she did penance
    in Coatepec, the Mountain of the Serpent.
    And one day,
    when Coatlicue was sweeping,
    there fell on her some plumage,
    a ball of fine feathers.
    Immediately Coatlicue picked them up
And put them in her bosom.
    When she finished sweeping,
    she looked for the feathers
    she had put in her bosom,
    but she found nothing there.
    At that moment Coatlicue was with child. (Sahagún 1950: 44)

In Mexico, from the colonial period forward, tasks like sweeping the local chapel have historically been the responsibility of participants in the extensive cargo system, sometimes called *la mayordomía,* in small rural towns in which power in the community is managed through the hierarchical and collective distribution of labor and goods (Chance 1985).[4] Today, in towns across *la Mixteca,* the region that overlaps Puebla, Oaxaca, and Guerrero states, with so many residents now living in New York City and other U.S. locations, the roles associated with the upkeep of the chapels and the devotional images are often fulfilled, against custom, by women and elderly men. Because participation in the mayordomía remains a basic requisite for retaining access to communally held land (Rivermar Pérez 2003), such tasks are neglected only at significant cost. Even though sweeping might seem instrumental— maintaining the chapel in hopes that a saint will return the favor, or fulfilling a communal obligation in exchange for benefits—it is much more than that. Sweeping has become a poignant indicator of change: a repetitive, mundane, and at the same time profound practice for marking time and attempting to compensate for the absence of those who have left.

Change happens thousands of miles away, as well: I could see it as I watched Marco, sweeping a shrine dedicated to Our Lady of Guadalupe in the Bronx. As he moved the broom to and fro, enjoying the pleasant weather and the peaceful street, Marco asserted himself as the Virgin's legitimate caretaker, possessing keys to the rectory, fulfilling his appointed task cheerfully and reliably. As he would tell me in interview, he is someone who has found a familiar and gratifying task in his new hometown, and with his broom, stroke by stroke, he contradicts the dominant image of Mexicans in New York living a disenfranchised, fearful, virtually clandestine existence. The meditative back and forth of the broom also contradicted the impression many Mexicans have of their countrymen in the United States: forgetting who they are and where they came from, forgetting their mother, the Virgin of Guadalupe. And even while Marco's personal life was in a shambles, he told me it was his work at the parish, among other devotees to Guadalupe, that remained stable and fulfilling. It was precisely this kind of mundane but meaningful activity which gave him a way to be, a role and identity that contradicted the instability of other areas in his life and lent meaning to his very presence in this city. While this is not a book about sweeping, it is in small, individual devotional acts as well as spectacular collective ones engaged in by immigrants that we can learn more about the ways that they make a place for themselves in a new city and draw from that a sense of how they see themselves and the rights they feel they deserve.

In devotional practices like sweeping, leaving flowers at the Virgin's feet, or organizing her feast day celebration, most participants do not set out to resist or revise what they assert are the appropriate ways to pay homage to Our Lady of Guadalupe, and yet to ignore the transformations implied in these practices would be to miss their significance. In the chapters that follow, I trace how devotional practices to the Virgin of Guadalupe among Mexicans in New York, in multiple circumstances and settings, are a way that individuals and groups transform themselves, form communities of practice, and come to understand themselves as more deserving of rights and dignity than their status as undocumented immigrants usually entails.

Research Setting

The Mexican population in New York City is 289,755, according to U.S. Census data for the most recent year available, 2007; a growth of 57.7 percent since 2000 (Limonic 2008). The Census itself estimates an undercount for New York City of 7.9 percent (Smart Girl Technologies 2002: 5), which, if Mexicans were undercounted at the same rate, would make the Mexican population 312,655. Because Mexicans are probably undercounted at a higher rate, a reasonable estimate is probably around 350,000–400,000. According to Joel Magallán, executive director of Asociación Tepeyac, there are as many as a half million Mexicans in New York City, a full 50 percent of them undocumented. While activists have an interest in larger numbers which might help convince others of the urgency of their claims, the discrepancy in numbers can also be interpreted as a function of undocumented migration in which, from the moment of border crossing, immigrants attempt to circulate and live undetected by a state that would deport them. Official estimates by government agencies such as the Census miss entire segments of the population, including those who live clandestinely in illegal housing such as sub-basements or who share an apartment among as many as two dozen people, situations in which, even if a census worker does knock on the door, full disclosure does not behoove those inside.[5]

Analysts classify migration by Mexicans to New York as accelerated (Cortes 2003; Binford, cited in R. Smith 2001: 281; Rivera Batiz 2002: 4; Rivera Sánchez 2004), doubling in the 1990s, and again since 2000, with the majority of this community having arrived only after the mid-1990s (Bergad 2007; Limonic 2008). Of all Latino groups, Mexicans have the highest percentage of immigrants among them, 63–70 percent (U.S. Census 2006; Rivera-Batiz 2002: 5), an indication of the recentness of migration and the still nascent second generation. Analyzing the phenomenon of migration only from the state of Puebla, which until 1995 sent the clear majority of Mexican immigrants to New York City, there was a 26-fold increase in the rate of international migration (which is virtually all to the United States) from 1980 to 2000; and between 1995 and 2000, the number multiplied five times more (Cortes 2003). At the same time, migration expanded to include other parts of La Mixteca, as well as more migrants from Mexico City's periphery (especially Ciudad Nezahualcóyotl), and other states.[6]

Many scholars have argued against facile and mechanistic assessments of the "push" and "pull" factors influencing migration (Guarnizo and M. P. Smith 1998; Mahler 1998; R. Smith 1995, 2005). They ask, for example, if a nation experiences an economic crisis, why isn't there a still higher rate of migration and why do members of communities in particular areas tend more often to seek solutions to economic problems through migration than others (see R. Smith 2005)? Keeping this in mind, it is possible to attribute the accelerated migration of people from communities in La Mixteca to a combination of multinational, national, and local economic and political factors which made earlier modes of subsistence in the region less fruitful at the same time that the flow of migrants to a newer destination deemed to offer greater economic opportunities reached sufficient mass to enable greater numbers of people to participate. Massey argues that each cohort of migrants makes it easier for those who succeed them by lowering the costs and risks associated with migration (1999; also Durand and Massey 1992). This contributes to a snowball effect in which migratory flows that began with a trickle come to impact virtually every household in many rural Mexican hamlets.

In Mexico, the application of neoliberal policies of structural adjustment, the North American Free Trade Agreement, and the devaluation of the peso, which precipitated an economic crisis in 1994, had a disproportionately negative impact on poorer and rural economies.[7] The influx of cheap rice, wheat, and corn from the United States further battered Mexican farmers and the local farm economy. But these events were perhaps only the final straw, given that in 1986–87, a series of events triggered what has been called "the migration syndrome" in La Mixteca region, including a crisis in regional agriculture and increased demographic pressure (Marroni 2003). Indeed, a greater proportion of the people I interviewed in the course of my study migrated to New York between 1989 and 1995 than during any other time period.[8]

The two comités guadalupanos included in this study are located in the Bronx. The Bronx is the borough of New York City with the third largest population of Mexicans, after Brooklyn and Queens, but it is the one that has experienced the steepest growth in its Mexican population in recent years, 92.5 percent since 2000 (and an impressive fivefold increase since 1990) versus an average of 33.5 percent for the other four boroughs this decade (Bergad 2007). Brooklyn received larger numbers of Mexican immigrants earlier than the other boroughs, but the growth of the Mexican population there has tapered off in this decade. While slightly more than half of the Bronx's foreign-born population has naturalized, the Mexican immigrant population is composed overwhelmingly of new arrivals who have had few opportunities to regularize their immigration status. Generally speaking, the more recent an individual's immigration, the more likely he or she is not naturalized. For those Mexicans who arrived to New York before 1980, 22 percent are naturalized citizens, while for those who arrived after 2000, the number is less than 1 percent. In the Bronx, 39 percent of the total number of Mexicans in the borough arrived since 2000, an additional 40 percent arrived since 1990: in other words, four out of five have been here less than two decades (Bergad 2007).[9]

Because of the disproportionately recent growth of the Mexican population in New York City, constituted in large part by undocumented young people who migrated prior to having finished secondary school or established a vocation in their place of origin, there is a tendency among scholars, Mexican government officials, activists, and service agencies to generalize and associate this profile with all Mexicans in New York. Further, organizations like Asociación Tepeyac tend to emphasize the severe needs and high numbers of people in that category for whom poverty, exploitation, and disenfranchisement are primary concerns. Nonetheless, there are many thousands of Mexicans in New York City who are neither undocumented nor especially vulnerable to the problems and circumstances suffered by recent immigrants. Current research by scholars in the region is beginning now to fill one gap in this area with a focus on the very different issues facing the second generation of Mexicans in New York City as they work to fulfill the aspirations their parents had for them when they migrated (Smith 2005; Cortina 2003).

This book focuses on a relatively small proportion of the overall Mexican population in New York City: those people who were members of comités guadalupanos or associated with Asociación Tepeyac from 2000 through 2003. I have continued to follow the organizations in an intermittent fashion until the present and there are individuals with whom I have maintained close contact. This book does not seek to characterize, describe, or analyze the Mexican population as a whole, although many of the issues, concerns, and perspectives presented in this book by individuals, in meetings, and by community leaders, are relevant to a much larger number of people (immigrants, undocumented immigrants, Mexicans) than those whose experiences I focus upon directly.

Research for this book was conducted from 2000 to 2008, including 18 months of full-time research from May 2002 to October 2003.

Methodologies, discussed further in the next chapter, included participant observation, structured and unstructured interviews, photo elicitation, and focus groups. In all, I interviewed approximately 60 people formally (all of them adults, with slightly more women than men) and enjoyed informal conversations and *convivencia*[10] with many more, in addition to regularly attending comité guadalupano meetings and most events the comités and the Asociación organized. Participants were recruited and participant observation occurred in three key sites: los comités guadalupanos, or Guadalupan Committees, of Our Lady of the Rosary and Saint John parishes, located, respectively, in the University Heights and Mott Haven neighborhoods of the Bronx, as well as Asociación Tepeyac de New York, located on Fourteenth Street in Manhattan.[11] Together, los comités guadalupanos and Asociación Tepeyac constitute the largest membership-based network of Mexicans in New York.

Asociación Tepeyac is the most well-known community organization dedicated to Mexicans in the city, with its leaders often serving as prominent and visible spokespeople and advocates for Mexicans in New York in Spanish and English-language media in the United States and in Mexico, with elected officials, and vis-à-vis other community organizations, foundations, and service providers. The two comités on which I focused my attention formed under very different circumstances. While Saint John's comité was among the first confraternal parish organizations to be founded by early immigrants from Mexico in the 1980s, more recent immigrants from rural Puebla state founded el comité guadalupano of Our Lady of the Rosary Church with help from Asociación Tepeyac in 1998. Observing the daily practices and interactions of these three entities with each other and other comités, the archdiocese, the press, and other social groups, I traced the flow of ideas between a larger umbrella organization charged with agenda setting and discursive production, and local sites of participation. Situating myself in three sites simultaneously provided a fruitful basis for comparison and for judging the currency of the discourses of guadalupanismo, or faith in Guadalupe, within and outside the sphere of Tepeyac.

Organization of the Book

The remaining chapters focus on the formation of los comités guadalupanos and Asociación Tepeyac and the different activities in which these
groups engage. The second chapter outlines the theoretical framework
that structures our analysis and also describes the methodology of the
study and demographic characteristics of Mexicans in New York. The following chapter recounts the founding of the two comités guadalupanos
that were the focus of the research and the umbrella organization that
links them, Asociación Tepeyac. The three subsequent chapters focus on
three distinct modes of Guadalupan devotion engaged in by members of
these organizations. The first, discussed in chapter 4, is about the image
of Our Lady of Guadalupe and its ability to serve as a beacon to Mexican immigrants in New York City, as well as its circulation. I focus in
part here on *la misión guadalupana*, the practice of carrying an image of
Our Lady of Guadalupe from home to home, one of the most common
practices among comités guadalupanos around the city. La misión is frequently one of the activities least known to outsiders but most important
for the members of the comités, not only for marking members and potential members as part of the community but also a means by which the
group makes claims over a specific local territory. The second practice,
described in chapter 5, is the performance of the Stations of the Cross, or
el Viacrucis, which occurs on Good Friday each year. Parish-based and
citywide performances of the Stations of the Cross differ in their purposes
and intent, serving both as a means in which groups negotiate their roles
vis-à-vis each other and map parish bounds but also for the comités to rehearse their groupness against imagined outsiders. Chapter 6 examines *La
Antorcha Guadalupana*, or Guadalupan torch run, organized annually by
Asociación Tepeyac, in which a flame is brought overland from the Basilica of Guadalupe in Mexico City. Finally, the concluding chapter analyzes
these practices and the ways that they assert a platform for community
formation based on Guadalupan devotion, Mexican national identity, and
being undocumented. In sum, the practices of the members of los comités
guadalupanos and Asociación Tepeyac forge a space in which participants
imagine themselves to have rights in a context that not only denies them
their rights and citizenship, but even their humanity.

2

On Citizenship, Membership, and the Right to Have Rights

While the immigrants involved in the comités guadalupanos and Asociación Tepeyac frequently relate everyday experiences of discrimination based on race, language, and ethnicity, their first collective project is to develop a space in which they come to understand themselves as worthy and deserving of rights. Only after that task is complete can their claims toward the surrounding society for justice, and for their very humanity, be forceful and credible. They begin first with the task of asserting their own personhood, their right to have rights (Arendt 1994). These assertions are at once political, civil, social, and cultural. They are, to borrow anthropologist Aihwa Ong's phrasing, a process of self-making and being made (1996: 738), within communities of similars as well as within the larger nation-state. The comités guadalupanos represent a premier space for these processes.

This book seizes on theories of citizenship that acknowledge the agency of those excluded from the fruits of "first class citizenship"; some of these are grouped under the heading "cultural citizenship." If juridical citizenship is the beginning and end of our discussions of rights, we overlook the centuries of history in this country and in pluralistic democracies elsewhere during which equal or greater weight has been placed on civic disposition, engagement, and other behaviors associated with being a "good citizen." Such an impoverished view of citizenship would make all but a small fraction of practices, electoral behaviors (voting), and duties (such as enlisting in the armed services) fall out of the purview of analyses of citizenship. Instead, we must reinvigorate our understanding and definition of citizenship to be comprehensive of behaviors and attitudes accessible to those who hold a nation's passport and also those who do not. As such, we may begin to examine the implications of struggles for rights within the context of rough exclusion that undocumented status implies. In a decade in which an average of 500 migrants per year have died crossing the border, Democratic and Republican members of the U.S. Congress have voted overwhelmingly in favor of the construction of a border fence, and nursing mothers have been detained awaiting deportation 900 miles from their babies,[1] undocumented immigrants do not have the luxury of making claims for rights they are supposed to already have, a basic premise of much of the work on cultural citizenship. However, they do use cultural and religious idioms to assert their worthiness for the rights of citizenship, and thus their efforts can be viewed as acts of cultural citizenship.

In what ways do Mexican immigrants in New York make a space for themselves in their new city and negotiate competing visions of human worth and belonging? The numerical majority of Mexicans in New York are immigrants who entered the country without inspection, and thus are frequently called undocumented immigrants, or, less humanely, "illegal aliens." These terms link their very personhood to their precarious legal status and a fundamental lack: of documents authorizing their presence and employment, and of juridical citizenship in one or more nation-states. Nonetheless, they subscribe to and are ascribed by others, membership in other kinds of collectivities and the attendant rights and obligations those memberships entail. These offer competing visions of belonging and human value that encompass a range of meanings far broader than the very narrow definition of citizenship commonly used in immigrant-receiving nations today. Most basically understood as membership in a polity, citizenship in the United States has historically referred to residence in a territory and abstract notions regarding the attitudes and dispositions associated with (good) citizenship. Only recently has it been limited so strictly to the category of juridical belonging in the nation that it often is used to signify today. As immigration restrictions and border enforcement have expanded, citizenship has been more rigorously defined in legal terms over the last several decades, and the legal terms have been seized upon by those who would restrict the rights of non-citizens living within the nation-state.[2] Legal scholar Linda Bosniak has eloquently described this as "an effort to reinvigorate, or revalorize, the legal status of citizenship in this country—either by making citizenship count for more, by making it harder to obtain, or both" (1998: 26).

Just as states grant citizens rights, citizenship is the means by which the state is granted citizens (Verdery 1998: 293, paraphrasing Brubaker). However, the existence of non-citizens in a polity "poses a special challenge"

(Bosniak 1998: 32) to the nation and nation-building projects, whether they are seen to threaten the basis of the nation's own charter myths of inclusion (Schuck and Smith 1985) or inject those myths with new vigor (Honig 1998, 2001). Anthropologist Phyllis Pease Chock asserts that the semantic and semiotic struggle over the meaning of the very term "citizen" depletes its lived meaning: "renegotiations of 'citizen' ignore people's struggles to make lives and connections for themselves" (1994: 50). Sociologist T. H. Marshall's notion of "social citizenship" is a crucial precursor to contemporary theories on cultural citizenship: "the whole range from the right to a modicum of economic welfare and security to the right to share to the full in social heritage and to live the life of a civilized being according to the standards prevailing in the society," or a citizen's guarantee of rights in spite of capitalist inequality (Marshall 1950: 72).[3]

Anthropologists Arjun Appadurai and James Holston similarly view citizenship as a dynamic negotiation, often brimming with violence or its potential, between subjects and states: "Citizenship concerns more than rights to participate in politics . . . it concerns the moral and performative dimensions of membership that define the meanings and practices of belonging in society" (Holston and Appadurai 1999: 14). Drawing on this conceptualization, anthropologist Miguel Díaz-Barriga describes "structures of belonging" as a "visceral experience," part of "wider structures of feeling that are conditioned by modes of production and power" and in which feelings of "belonging" might be fostered or denied as part of hegemonic practice (2008: 136). Immigrants stretch notions of citizenship from the inside and the outside of the nation, bringing into question issues of polity and sovereignty with their incursions into national territories, and joining other ethnic or cultural minorities to challenge the nation-state's criterion of inclusion from the inside (Koopmans and Statham 1999: 656).

Renato Rosaldo, anthropologist and pioneer of the Latino Cultural Studies Working Group, which led to the book *Latino Cultural Citizenship* (Flores and Benmayor 1997), argues that vernacular understandings of citizenship ranging from full to second-class citizenship are not to be found by looking in a dictionary—or presumably a civics textbook—but only through "the art of listening attentively to how concerned parties conceive, say, equality and well-being" (Rosaldo 1997a; also 1999). In that book, the authors frame cultural citizenship largely as a process of empowerment, regardless of whether it materially or juridically alters participants' status; it is "a broad range of activities of everyday life through which Latinos and other groups claim space in society and eventually claim rights" (1997: 15). For cultural studies scholar Toby Miller, cultural citizenship is "the maintenance and development of cultural lineage through education, custom, language and religion, and the positive acknowledgement of difference in and by the mainstream" (2001: 2). Thus, cultural citizenship is an assertion of rights, even in the face of discrimination and exclusion.[4] Yet, within approaches like this we can see that one shortcoming of "cultural" expressions of citizenship is that they can be acknowledged, even endorsed, by states without any obligation to back them up with political, economic, or social rights (see Abercrombie 1992). Is the effort to assert rights through idioms of culture valuable in and of itself even if juridical rights are deferred? Is the assertion of a collectivity composed of individuals deserving of rights and willing to claim them a necessary step toward all other rights projects? This book asserts that the answer to both questions is a resounding "yes."

While the Women's Suffrage and the Civil Rights movements, in contemporary U.S. imaginings, are assumed by some to have resolved the issue of disenfranchisement and reasserted citizens' birthright access to certain rights, race, gender, religion, class, and ethnicity are held by others to continue to undercut access to those rights (Flores and Benmayor 1997; Ong 1996, 1999; Verdery 1998; Yuval-Davis 1997). Thus, on top of the juridico-legal limitations on lawful permanent residents' (LPR) and other immigrants' access to the rights, protections, and privileges of citizenship, some scholars hold that as long as these minorities are seen as ethnically marked, not white, under the logic of "racialized constructions of difference" (DeGenova 1998), they will never be full citizens (see Chávez 2001, 199; Ong 1996).

If we follow this line of reasoning, rather than celebrating cultural citizenship, we should lament it as the futile effort of transnational subjects to reconfigure or refuse their place in new global capitalist orders. Ong defines cultural citizenship as "the cultural practices and beliefs produced out of negotiating the often ambivalent and contested relations with the state and its hegemonic forms that establish the criteria of belonging within a national population and territory" (1996: 738). She traces transmigrants' engagement in modes of "flexible citizenship": "the cultural logics of capitalist accumulation, travel and displacement that induce subjects to respond fluidly and opportunistically to changing political-economic conditions" (1999: 6). She asks, "What are the mechanisms of power that enable the mobility, as well as the localization and disciplining, of diverse populations within transnationalized systems?" (1999: 11). Ong urges us to take into consideration not only how "the little routines and scenarios of everyday life are embodiments and enactments of norms, values, and conceptual schemes," but also how they are "a form of cultural politics embedded in specific power contexts" (1999: 5). This is "cultural citizenship as subject-making": "self-making and being-made by power relations that produce consent through schemes of surveillance, discipline, control and administration" (Ong 1996: 737). For Ong, transmigrants engage in flexible strategies to access the rights and privileges of membership in multiple polities, but always within the constraints of political economies of power and authority. While they may evade certain mechanisms of state domination, they are never completely free of them.

Other scholars have forwarded alternative understandings of the effects of globalization and transnational practices on the notion of citizenship. Sociologist Yasemin Soysal uses the example of guest workers in Europe to advance a category she calls "postnational citizenship," which "confers upon every person the right and duty of participation in the authority structures and public life of a polity, regardless of their historical or cultural ties to that community" (Soysal 1994: 3). Anthropologist Lok Siu synthesizes the expressive culture and juridico-legal strands of cultural citizenship to see actors strategically making claims within the nation while also positing membership in a supranational diaspora (Siu 2001: 8, 2005). In our age of increasingly mobile populations responding to the global flows of capital, the bounded nation-state is no longer the exclusive referent for citizenship. Instead, Soysal argues, "human personness constitutes the normative basis of an expanding citizenship, [it] has become an imperative in justifying rights and demands for rights, including those of nonnationals in national polities" (1994: 42; also Jacobson 1996: 9). Personness, in turn, is a category upheld by multinational entities including the United Nations and international human rights organizations.[5]

Our point of departure in each of these approaches is an understanding of the ways that individuals negotiate their belonging and, by extension, their rights and responsibilities in a polity; a process that articulates personhood while also producing collectivities. In the most liberal versions of citizenship, the only relevant collectivity is that of the nation of equals. In the rather less idyllic reality of most pluralistic democracies, the promise of equality is often pursued by the activism and vigilance of collectivities of minorities that defend individuals who experience less than "first class" citizenship. By tracing the formation of these collectivities, we can discern the articulation of vectors of identity and attendant under-standings of the roles and responsibilities of individuals and the rights due them. Any individual may enjoy membership in multiple collectivi-ties which are engaged or latent, depending on the circumstances.

Looking at the range of memberships that are more operational than "belonging," less bureaucratic than "citizenship," we can see that there are many competing visions which imply both rights and entitlements, obli-gations and privileges. These memberships are given weight and nuance by the vectors of identity discussed above: Guadalupan devotion, Mexi-can national identity, and undocumented immigration status. In this way, some of the ties that ground, protect, and also constrain immigrants as they make their lives in New York City become lighter and others more resistant. Some of these memberships are ascribed, some actualized through communities of practice, some aspired to, and others ideational. But perhaps all of them are engaged to a greater or lesser degree in an immigrant's decision to leave her or his place of origin and begin a new chapter of life somewhere else. These memberships also impact their deci-sion whether or not to partake in civil society in home and host locales, to worship in the same or different ways in each place, and influence the perennial question of whether to stay or go back "home," among a host of other factors.

The first of the collectivities is the most primal, and usually the one that prompted their migration: membership in a family. Two of the most commonly cited reasons for migrating are to seek access to higher wages to provide for family members left behind or to reunite with family mem-bers who have already migrated. Both of these reasons, and the narratives immigrants tell which reference them, give primacy to the bonds of fam-ily and imply that self-sacrifice is often necessary to enable the stability and sustenance of the larger family unit. In this vision, the pull of com-munity, country, profession, and even, or perhaps especially, to one's own self-fulfillment are secondary to one's obligation and affective ties to kin. In turn, kin groups often—although of course not always—provide the most intimate and reliable sense of belonging, assistance, affection, and support, and are frequently described by the immigrants with whom I conducted research as "the *only* people you can really trust."

Another membership is that of workers, centered on the dignity of work and worker: the laboral contributions immigrants make to the U.S. economy enabled by their flexibility and responsiveness to global capital flows and neoliberal restructuring of markets. In this vision, honest, hard work is in itself offered as a justification for demands for fair wages and working conditions, decent treatment, and a measure of personal prosperity. This "sweat equity" is argued by some workers to be strength for a claim for the extension of political membership in the nation-state in which they labor. This vision resonates with classical liberal notions of human worth in which "individuals have natural and inalienable rights, appended to them based on their status as individuals[;] . . . individual entitlements that are to be protected from coercion by collectivities" (Williams 2007: 19). In this formulation, property holders are free to exchange commodities in the market (including personal labor) (ibid.). However, the borders of the nation-state artificially constrain the exchange of commodities in an ever more globalized market, by disabling the free and legal encounter of those who would sell and those who would buy the labor of immigrants. Thus, current migration restrictions run contrary to the free market principles that are seen by many to be not only at the heart of the U.S. economy, but its very creed.

Indeed, another competing vision related to this one is the historical notion of liberal citizenship, a function of an individual's right to "participate in society unfettered by illegitimate external constraints" (Williams 2007: 28). While this vision of citizenship is viewed by many as the basis of the United States' social contract, the premise of its democracy and the Bill of Rights, or what Parker calls "the rich delights of membership, empowerment and inclusion" (2001: 584), it also implies, by the same logic, potential denial of membership, marginalization, and exclusion.

Nonetheless, even while undocumented immigrants are juridically excluded from the fruits of political membership in the nation-state, many of them subscribe to these liberal notions of individual freedom to pursue life, liberty, and happiness. Some seek just that through migration, seeing their willingness to strike out, struggle against the odds, and start anew in a different country as the fulfillment of the promise of individual potential and self-worth. Even while they seek the full benefits of membership in the nation-state through their activism for immigration reform and their own efforts to *arreglar papeles*, or regularize their immigration status, they are not immune to the rhetoric of individual rights and liberty and its appeal, even as their lived reality may negate such utopian visions.

A contrasting vision may be offered by the notions of membership more commonly found in the rural villages of La Mixteca Baja, the region that overlaps parts of the states of Oaxaca, Guerrero, and Puebla from which many immigrants in New York hail. While the Mexican Revolution guaranteed all Mexicans membership in the nation-state on quintessentially liberal, egalitarian terms, the terrain on which the guarantee of the rights attendant with citizenship is claimed is frequently eminently local. In many migrants' home towns, at least until the early 1990s, much land was organized by the *ejido* system of communal ownership, granted to rural communities by the land reforms of President Lázaro Cárdenas in 1934. Thus, property ownership, the cornerstone of citizenship in the early United States, in post-Revolutionary Mexico was organized communally with rights distributed through membership in a collective. In this way, to state it in overly simplified terms, the rights that in the United States have historically accrued to individual property owners, in Mexico have sometimes been granted to the collectivity. While the collectivity is not the only repository of rights in Mexico in the Revolutionary period, and especially not since, it is an important one.

This association of membership and land contributes to the popular notion of *arraigo*, or rootedness, a term commonly used to refer to the measure of one's bond to place. This linking of presence and work to a particular piece of land and community, along with patron saint festivals, extended patrilocal families (who build their homes and live on the same parcels of land), and other features of life in rural hamlets make communal responsibility and reciprocity arguably more powerful discourses of citizenship for many Mexican immigrants than notions of individual liberty. This has been the subject of anthropological attention: John Monaghan has looked at it in conjunction with the notion of "modes of sociability" in Mixteca towns (1994), as has Kristen Norget, who describes the practices of friendly gift-giving, sharing of labor, and reciprocity referred to as *tequios* and *guelaguetzas* as a means of "foster[ing] an ethic of neighborhood collectivism and a sense of neighborhood cohesion" in the case of Oaxaca's popular neighborhoods (2006: 63). Of course, in the colonial period, indigenous peoples' settlement was organized around parishes with labor, evangelization, and residence bound together within specific geographic distributions (see Celestino and Myers 1981; Jackson 1999). The promotion of *cofradías*, confraternal societies dedicated to a patron saint, reinforced connections between people, place, faith, rights, and entitlements in important ways. We see that some such local ties have endured to the present and that these ties may have buffered rural people from some of the effects of neglect by the federal government, political violence, and corruption which characterized the PRI's (Partido Revolucionario Institucional) monopoly on power for 71 years, from 1929 to 2000.

As a result of recent efforts under neoliberal governance to dismantle the legal codes governing communal land ownership, many rural people have turned to their neighbors, extended family, and confraternal networks more than ever. It is evident why local attachments and collective reciprocity have continued to be powerful in the present.

While these competing ideas may seem irreconcilable, most immigrants I talk to reference more than one of them when they narrate their migration histories. Personal narratives have a knack for integrating contradictory social discourses and juridical categories, and for lending coherence to a life story which might, without the ordering power of narrative, appear as a series of coerced or circumstantial events. In the United States in the twentieth century, immigrant stories were frequently folded into larger societal discourses about assimilation and assimilability. Today, in part because of the closure of many formerly existing paths to assimilation as well as more proactive recognition that migration is not simply or even mainly about "becoming American," narratives are increasingly complex and draw meaning from sources in home and host locales. Narrative can make meaning out of the alienating experiences of migration (Carmona 2008; Delgado-Gaitan 1994; Ochs and Capps 1996; Raison 2007; Rosaldo 1989). Life stories "emphasize retrospective intelligibility by demonstrating how later events were conditioned, occasioned or facilitated by earlier ones" (Gallie, cited in Rosaldo 1989: 132). Further, narrative has been called a "socially symbolic act" and the basis for "the political unconscious" (Frederic Jameson, cited in Stevens-Arroyo and Díaz-Stevens 1998: 50). As such, the stories a group tells about its collective and individual experiences shape interpretations of their circumstances. Thus, a migrant like Marco, who is mentioned at the start of this book, references narratives of individualism, striking out on his own to follow a dream; of family obligation, seeking a better living for his family; and finally, of communitarianism; in telling his story of migration to and residence in the Bronx. New relationships and experiences can challenge, reinforce, or modify the narrative tropes and unique experiences immigrants use to construct their stories. The comités guadalupanos offer one site in which narratives are formulated, rehearsed, and retold as part of an individual and collective process of assertion of rights and dignity.

Narrative is an important part of oral history and plays an important role in ethnographic research: moreover, it is what frequently emerges in open-ended "life history" interviews, but also in the testimony members of the comités guadalupanos offer each other when recruiting a friend to come to a meeting, arguing a point before the group, or speaking to the media or the crowd at a demonstration. However, narrative is, by definition, a verbal art and as such is not sufficiently comprehensive as a frame for our analysis here. We also examine the performative aspects of many of the activities of the comités guadalupanos and Asociación Tepeyac. These include the feelings and engagement of participants in these organizations which they sometimes struggle to verbalize but which are evident in their actions; persistent involvement; even their posture, and which can be perceived by attentive observation. In these sites, some of the most memorable and meaningful moments are those that offer an opportunity for cohesion among competing notions of personhood, a reconciliation of immigrants' past lives, present realities, and the trauma of border crossing. When such cohesion is achieved, we can see that a community has been formed. That community may be lasting and self-evident. Alternatively, it may slip quickly from view but be readily recreated at the next event. Or, participants may constantly struggle for, but never quite achieve, a sense of community, striving for a feeling they name but cannot quite accomplish. In this book, I trace the different modalities by which Mexican immigrants who participate in the comités guadalupanos and Asociación Tepeyac work to form an enduring community and to build on its platform an assertion of their collective and individual rights.

In the comités guadalupanos and Asociación Tepeyac's activities, immigrants find very compelling ways to insert their own, often harrowing, migration stories, into a context which acknowledges their sacrifice and challenges, and offers tools and support for building a new life in New York. As suggested above, in these sites, faith in Our Lady of Guadalupe, undocumented immigration status, and Mexican nationality constitute primary modes of identification and offer a frame for making meaning out of personal experiences. These vectors are not accidental and to some degree are not even entirely organic, their potential strategically maximized by community leaders. Nonetheless, they are, frequently, compelling and empowering. Guadalupanism offers rich narrative, symbolic and performative potential; it is at once familiar and available to immigrants but resignified by migration to a new context. Indeed, Our Lady of Guadalupe often appears in immigrants' narratives from the very moment of their arrival. Thus it is fitting that we too, should begin there, after a brief discussion of my choice of terms.

Im/migrants: A Question of Terms

I use the term "immigrant" throughout this book in reference to the participants in my study. Anthropologist Nicholas De Genova argues for the use of the term "migrant" over "immigrant" "to retain a sense of the *movement*, intrinsic incompletion, and consequent irresolution of social processes of migration" (2005: 3). While "intrinsic incompletion and consequent irresolution" indeed were a marked component of the experiences of the people among whom I conducted my research, movement, notably, was not. The vast majority of people who participated in this study named their inability to travel to and from Mexico freely as the most obtrusive and limiting aspect of their undocumented status. An activist and director of Casa México in New York City, Jerry Domínguez, noted, "An undocumented person can buy a house, can buy a business. The undocumented person can get a driver's license legally, can sue the federal and city state government. An undocumented person has labor rights" (interview, June 24, 2003).⁶ He went on to explain that the only thing undocumented people cannot do is travel freely. While this is, obviously, an understatement, it is, in large part, the inability of undocumented immigrants to move freely that contributes not only to the production of an immobile and easily exploitable underclass within the United States but also to the truncation of some of the transnational social practices which, until recently, may have assuaged some of the more negative aspects of being considered an illegitimate denizen. As De Genova eloquently explains: "The legal production of 'illegality' provides an apparatus for sustaining Mexican migrants' vulnerability and tractability—as workers—whose labor-power, because it is deportable, becomes an eminently disposable commodity" (2005: 215). While some of the people included here have from time to time felt compelled to return to Mexico (the reason most frequently cited was to bury a parent), the trip back to the United States is so fraught with risk and expense that it represents a significant barrier to people considering themselves or me referring to them as "migrants." Because of current immigration laws, the vast majority of people I spoke with have never attempted such a risky journey, choosing instead to weather family crises at a distance or to bring their family members across the border to reunite and live together in the United States. This is one aspect that differentiates the population encompassed in this study from most studies of transnational migrants in other periods and places: rather than a population marked by diversity of immigration status and tenure in the United

States, this is a population composed almost entirely of recent undocumented immigrants.

Anthropologist Roger Rouse advocates the use of the neologism *im/migrant* in acknowledgment of how the term "immigrant" "suggests a process of unidirectional movement in which people reorient to their destination, [while migrant] suggests a process of movement back and forth in which they remain oriented to their place of origin," and that "matters have rarely been this simple" (Rouse 1995: 367). I agree with Rouse that neither term effectively acknowledges the complexity of most immigrants' experiences. Further, "migrant" carries an additional semantic load in its association with guest worker programs like the Bracero Accord and agricultural work, which continues to be a major industry for undocumented laborers in the United States, implying seasonality and a lack of rootedness.[7]

In a strictly legal sense, an "immigrant" is "a foreign national who has been granted the privilege of living and working permanently in the United States" (U.S. Citizenship and Immigration Services 2004), and all others—whether undocumented or student, tourist or work visa-holders, belong to the category of "non-immigrant," or are "illegal aliens." Most of the people with whom this research was conducted do not meet this definition of [legal] "immigrant." Further, many of them say they do not intend to live in the United States permanently, even if such status were made available to them. Nonetheless, most modes of legalization previously available have been eliminated and the border militarized. All of this makes circulation between the United States and undocumented immigrants' home countries extremely difficult and dangerous, and as such, many people who might otherwise have behaved like "migrants" say they have been forced into semi-permanent, albeit undocumented, settlement. Asociación Tepeyac employs the term *inmigrante* or immigrant, and I choose here to do the same, forcing us, as that organization does in its activist platform, to question the status, or lack thereof, of this permanent and yet disenfranchised population living within the United States.

In juridical terms, there are three main statuses which apply to immigrants: illegal alien, legal immigrant, and naturalized citizenship.[8] In vernacular understandings, however, categories are differently imagined. For many, the category "illegal" is objectionable because the U.S. economy depends upon the labor of foreign workers, without granting a sufficient number of work visas to them, and thus their "illegal" status is no fault of their own, but a failure of the state to recognize them as legitimate contributors to the economy and social life of the United States. Many immigrant advocates prefer the term "undocumented" as a less pejorative way of identifying those who lack documents, such as a visa, enabling them to live and work in the United States legally. Often immigrants who cross the border leave behind their identifying documents issued by the Mexican state, and are literally "undocumented," lacking any form of identification issued by a state agency on either side of the border. Nevertheless, "undocumented" is also commonly used to refer to those people who may hold a Mexican passport, birth certificate, electoral registration card, *matrícula consular* (the identification document issued by the consulates to Mexican nationals living abroad), or a state-issued driver's license but lack any document conferring them the ability to work and live in the United States legally. Other scholars and activists advocate using the term "unauthorized immigrants," referring to the fact that many enter the country without passing through a checkpoint, yet may have multiple identifying documents.

For Mexican participants in my study and in discourse within many Spanish-speaking immigrant communities and media, people who are undocumented or "illegal" are said to lack "papers," *faltar papeles,* and it is this lack which constitutes their persona non grata status vis-à-vis the U.S. government. Lacking papers is a way to describe someone who does not enjoy current legal status in the United States. As such, someone who has multiple identifying documents, such as the *matrícula consular* or a Mexican passport, is still said to lack papers or be undocumented. Conversely, those who have a visa, LPR status, or are citizens (naturalized or native-born) are said to have papers. While this is contradictory because technically a U.S.-born citizen has the right to never obtain or show any identity document demonstrating that status in his or her lifetime, and there is, as yet, no national identification card, the distinction is clear to immigrants in their discursive elaboration of the meaning of *having* versus *lacking* papers. While the specificities of which "papers" individuals have do sometimes emerge and take on importance, for the most part the immigrant community is imagined by its members to be composed of those with and those without papers.

As far as the U.S. government is concerned, obtaining papers is accomplished by qualifying for one or more set modes for gaining or adjusting status, and then doing so, advancing progressively through various stages, culminating in citizenship, after which point it is imagined one never again need engage the state as anything less than a fully enfranchised citizen. For immigrants, this process can be mysterious and arbitrary, frequently leading people to depend upon fraudulent legal "professionals" who imply that legal status can be obtained through deploying their qualified understanding of U.S. immigration law, and that anyone has a claim to legal status.[9] An "amnesty" such as the 1986 Immigration Reform and Control Act (IRCA) is imagined as a great equalizer, enabling those who have come to understand they have no other means to obtain legal status to qualify for it. Except under sweeping legislation like IRCA, immigrants who entered the United States without inspection or who have overstayed their visas are automatically barred from adjustment of status.[10] Because attitudes toward immigrants within the United States range from militant xenophobia (Chávez 2001, 2008) to welcoming embrace with the vagaries of the national economy, current assessments of "national security," and attitudes about the skin color, language, and religion of those who at any given moment are perceived to be knocking at the nation's door, the use of the term "amnesty" can sometimes imply political suicide for elected officials. As such, a wealth of euphemisms has developed, such that former President George W. Bush touted an "earned legalization" of foreign workers, while the Mexican government has rallied for "regularization" of the status of its citizens in the United States. Immigrants attempting to make sense of this semantic jockeying listen for indications that a given proposal or negotiation might enable them to obtain "papers" and that there will not be prohibitive strings attached, such as a truncated path to citizenship.

In their activism, los comités guadalupanos and Asociación Tepeyac insist that the most important factor affecting the lives of the majority of Mexicans in New York City is their undocumented migratory status, and this is the reason I must revise prevailing theories about transnationalism and cultural citizenship to apply them to the case at hand. Dominant scholarly understandings of transnationalism are premised on the ability of immigrants to construct a "circuit" (Rouse 1991) compressing the physical distance that separates "home" and "host" locales and enabling immigrants to imagine that they live simultaneously in both (see Basch, Schiller, and Szanton-Blanc 1994; Glick Schiller, Basch, and Szanton-Blanc 1992; Gupta and Ferguson 1992; Kearney 1991, 1995). Robert Smith, author of *Mexican New York*, illustrates such a circuit, showing that through technology, such as the telephone, Internet, and videos, immigrants from the town of Ticuani, Puebla can experience a simultaneity, even if delayed. Although they may not be fully enfranchised political actors in either location, in the in-between space created by their transnational practices, he argues they are often able to accumulate greater prestige, social capital, and power than they might ever have enjoyed in Mexico (2005). Achieving this status is dependent in Smith's study upon the ability of immigrants to circulate freely, and while his informants might stand on a Brooklyn street corner and conduct the negotiations that will bring potable water to one or another's grandmother back in Ticuani, sufficient numbers must also be able to travel—sometimes in the space of a weekend—to deliver the capital, ensure its proper distribution, and supervise the hometown association's projects. Further, a great deal of the particular kind of transnationalism he describes in his book—which shapes gender roles, social networks, and intergenerational dynamics—is dependent upon the ability of families to travel to the annual *fiesta* in Ticuani, or at other intervals of the year.

In the intervening decade between the initial research contributing to the evolution of the notion of transnational circuits, including Smith's, and my own research, the population of Mexicans in New York changed. Indeed, since 1965, Mexican immigration has been progressively restricted in what De Genova calls "an active process of inclusion through illegalization" (2005: 234). While there have always been undocumented immigrants, now they are the overwhelming majority, and their ability to construct a transnational circuit involving physical circulation between home and host countries has been limited. While some U.S.-born children do spend summers in their parents' hometowns, families usually cannot travel together. Further, recent immigrants are more diverse, not composed predominantly, as in the past, by male heads of household or unmarried males who migrate to provide for their families back in Mexico. Now, more immigrants marry in the United States, and increasingly have extended families here, and more women are migrating as part of a family unit and alone. As such, the costs and risks associated with traveling to Mexico and crossing the border again or not being able to return at all are less tolerable. As De Genova writes, "'illegality' is the product of U.S. immigration law" (2005: 234). The changes in immigration law and the demographics of the migrant community mean not only that most immigrants are not "legal" but, without sweeping immigration reform, will never be able to become legal.

3

Los Comités Guadalupanos and Asociación Tepeyac

Their Formation and Context

Oh Danny Boy, the pipes, the pipes are calling
From glen to glen, and down the mountainside.
The summer's gone, and all the flowers are dying.
'Tis you, 'tis you must go and I must bide.
　　　　　　　　—Frederick Weatherly, "Danny Boy," 1910

México lindo y querido,
si muero lejos de ti,
que digan que estoy dormido
y que me traigan aquí.
　　　　　　　　—Chucho Monge, "Mexico Lindo," circa 1950[1]

On December 11, 2007, Asociación Tepeyac convoked all of its present and past members to attend *las mañanitas*,[2] an evening launch of the Guadalupan feast day celebration, which for the first time in history would be held at Saint Patrick's Cathedral on Fifth Avenue. While one or a pair of masses at the Cathedral on the Virgin's feast day, December 12, had become an annual tradition, Tepeyac had long worked to celebrate the Virgin with all of the pomp that they associate with the celebration in Mexico. Launching the feast with las mañanitas on December 11 became an important measure of the Mexican community having "arrived," able to command the New York City Archdiocese's attention and resources. Before television news cameras and reporters, tourists and diocesan representatives, Joel Magallán, Tepeyac's executive director, asked those who had gathered to join in celebrating the ten-year anniversary of the organization's founding. The event, which was described in Mexican newspapers the following day as having been "just like" las mañanitas at the Basilica of Guadalupe in Mexico, featured popular musicians and a prestigious mariachi ensemble, and was emceed by a known Mexican newscaster. Starting on the eleventh and continuing late into the evening on the twelfth, Saint Patrick's Cathedral hosted multiple masses, the arrival of a torch from the Basilica accompanied by thousands of white uniformed runners, mariachis, flower- and image-bearing devotees alone and in family groups, "Aztec" dancers, and dozens of comités guadalupanos, each with their own banner. On the evening of the eleventh, tourists visiting the cathedral might have been surprised to hear a Spanish-language service which included a Guadalajara-based "Irish-Mexican" folk singer performing "Danny Boy" in English or honoring a man named O'Dwyer, the president of Tepeyac's Board of Directors. The performance of "Danny Boy" was followed by a rousing rendition of what has been called the unofficial national anthem of Mexicans, particularly those who find themselves far from home, "México Lindo." It was sung by the grandson of Jorge Negrete, who wore typical *charro* regalia.

While both songs are nostalgic laments for those who have migrated and whose performance is an important part of assertion of national identity by Irish and Mexican expatriates, it is unlikely both have been sung in the same place in such quick succession. Many of the hundreds of Mexicans gathered in the cathedral may also have been surprised by the connections asserted throughout the service between Mexicans and the Irish, but this public performance of affinities makes perfect sense if we follow the history of the arrival of Mexicans in New York City and their embrace by the Catholic Church. While the claims by some media and organizers that the celebration had been carried off "just like" in the Basilica of Guadalupe in Mexico may seem hyperbolic if we attempt to compare the celebration in New York with the one held each year in the "original" site, if we interpret the celebration as a powerful indicator that Mexicans had achieved an unprecedented stature and legitimacy within the archdiocese, the bravado is warranted. It is in that context that the Irish are inseparable from the story of Mexicans in New York's Catholic Church. The founding of los comités guadalupanos and Asociación Tepeyac cannot be separated from the institutional context of the "immigrant church" in New York City. In that story, which could, alternatively be told as one of ethnic succession (Light 1981), fictive coethnicity (R. Smith 2002), Latino ethnogenesis (Mittleberg and Waters 1992), panethnicity (Ricourt 2003), of urban

Catholic history, or of migration, here I will focus on it as one small story which has its beginnings in the nineteenth century, but comes to its most dramatic point in Bronx parishes in the 1990s.

In this chapter, I will briefly describe that history and then trace the formation of the comités and the Asociación. This book could have been structured around the intertwined and yet contrasting stories of the two parishes introduced in this chapter. Instead, I focus on three kinds of activities that both parishes engage in not only for the ways they illustrate different modes of mobilization and institutional contexts, but also for the way they illuminate the experiences of Mexican immigrants in New York City more generally.

The Catholic Church often has often been called "the immigrant church," both because it entered U.S. social life as a minority denomination and because it was the principal site for reception and assimilation of Irish, as well as Polish, French, German, Italian, and other immigrants from the mid-nineteenth century forward (Gleason 1987: 39; also Milliken 1994). The Church projected itself as a haven for the preservation among first-generation immigrants of language, faith, and culture, which were understood to interpenetrate each other so thoroughly that they were impossible to separate (Gleason 1987: 42). To give up language was feared, among German Catholic leaders in particular, as a way that immigrants might abandon their religion: language was seen to serve faith. Instead of simply attending their neighborhood church, Germans, Poles, or Italians would attend a parish named after their own patron saint and tended, in many cases, by a priest from their community of origin. While mass would continue to be celebrated in Latin until after Vatican II, priests tended their parishioners' other needs, including hymns, sermons, and sacraments, in their native language (Badillo 2006: 79). Within the same neighborhoods, different immigrant groups attended different churches.

It is practically conventional wisdom that with modernization, traditional religious practices fade in importance. In Bellah's classic formulation of the role of faith in the United States, civil religion takes the place of "old world" religious affiliations, providing an "open and flexible pattern of membership," "a favorable environment for an individual to work out problems," and the promotion of "voluntaristic, pluralistic democracy" all suited to American civil society (Bellah 1970: 43, 72). In this formulation, immigrants, as they assimilate to American social life, will leave behind old-world traditions as they are subjected to the modernizing, individualizing trends of U.S. modernity and its civil religion. In its original, Rousseauian formulation, civil religion lends legitimacy to the state, which became essential with the republican separation of church and state in modern democracies (León 2005: 54). Civil religion is a kind of social glue contributing to consensus, even normative sociality among immigrants. In this view, immigrants become participants in the public sphere by the same measure they shed the trappings of old world customs and beliefs. National parishes are then seen as a "way-station" (Davies 1995), which, if allowed to exist indefinitely, could result in the segregation of minority parishioners and failure to assimilate (Dolan 1985; Milliken 1994). This was the fear that led Francis Spellman (Archbishop of New York 1939–1967, named Cardinal in 1946) to favor an "integrated" parish as early as 1940, fearing that the reinforcement of ethnic identity in national parishes could go to the extreme of retarding assimilation (Badillo 2006: 80). But, for much of the first half of the century, and indeed in some ways to the present, places of worship have been viewed as prime sites for immigrants to learn how to be "American." Herberg (1960) points out that to a degree, religion (albeit only some kinds of religion) was exempted from the pressures on immigrants to shed their past identities in favor of new, generically "American" identities:

> Of the immigrant who came to this country it was expected that . . . he would give up virtually everything he had brought with him from "the old country"—his language, his nationality, his manner of life—and would adopt the ways of his new home. Within broad limits, however his becoming an American did not involve his abandoning the old religion in favor of some native American substitute. Quite the contrary, not only was he expected to retain his old religion . . . but . . . it was largely in and through religion that he, or rather his children and grandchildren found an identifiable place in American life. (Herberg 1960: 27–28)

Civil religion corresponds in some ways with the integration of immigrants via the "melting pot" in classical theories of assimilation. Just as the melting pot presumably takes in immigrants with all of their "Old Country" ways, habits, and beliefs, and makes them "American," civil religion rubs the idiosyncratic edges off of lived religion, using innovative, U.S.-forged theology to turn Jews and Christians from all over the world into God-fearing "Americans."[3] This is what scholars of Latino religions Anthony Stevens-Arroyo and Ana María Díaz-Stevens call the

"Americanizing prejudice" of the Church toward devotional practices not viewed as sufficiently "mainstream" or "American" (1998: 59). So, for example, we see Jewish groups adopting more congregationalist patterns and also splintering into a proliferation of smaller, personalistic branches in the United States, influenced in part by the majority religious group, Protestants (Seltzer 2008; also see Warner and Wittner 1999 on the emphasis toward congregations). The national parish model, even as it honored immigrants' faith practices and language, sought to integrate and assimilate them as quickly as possible, viewing the retention of ethnic attributes as a failure to assimilate.

By the time of the great Puerto Rican migration to New York City from 1946 to 1964, the national parishes that had received prior generations of Italian, German, and Irish immigrants had been supplanted by a focus on ethnicity by the Catholic Church, as a result of the largest effort ever within the archdiocese to serve a particular cultural group (Gleason 1987; Glazer and Moynihan 1963; McGreevy 1996). The arrival of so many immigrants, many of them from rural areas who were nominally Catholic but had little experience with the Church as an institution, was called "a state of emergency" by Cardinal Spellman (Vidal and Dolan 1994: 75). In response, radical philosopher and priest Ivan Illich opened a center in Ponce, Puerto Rico for training diocesan priests. Not only were priests trained in the Spanish language and educated in the political and social history of the island, but Illich advocated a cultural immersion of sorts, compelling seminarians to hitchhike from town to town, depend on locals' hospitality, eat only as the poor did, and participate in celebrations of popular religiosity (Díaz-Stevens 1993a). These are the priests who came to serve in 130 parishes throughout the New York City diocese, instituting Spanish-language masses and more culturally sensitive celebrations of popular religion (Vidal and Dolan 1994: 103). In this period, rather than tend to Puerto Ricans within the old model of the National Parish, the Archdiocese opted for a language-based pastoralism, in which, in addition to the regular English-language mass, pastors gave a second, or more, masses in Spanish.[4] This "church within a church" enabled the "matriarchal core" (Díaz-Stevens 1993b) of the church to develop, with female lay leadership of parish groups and the cursillo movement. With time, and with the growing diversity of Spanish-speaking Catholics in New York City in the ensuing four decades, some of these same priests advocated an integrated Hispanic mass, shorn of culturally specific expressions of popular religiosity.[5]

However, there is no evidence that such a homogenization of faith practices, much less secularization among immigrants, has occurred (Leonard et al. 2005: 1). Immigrants may be at least as, if not more, religious in the United States than in their places of origin. Instead of shedding their cultural specificity, in places of worship, immigrants frequently learn as much about being certain kinds of ethnic Americans as they do about being "American." In the national parishes of the twentieth century, we see the creation of broader Catholic nationalisms than might have existed prior to migration: Italians, for example, forged a group who previously had identified as Neapolitans, Sicilians, and so on: "The 'Italian' of Italian American is as a creation of life in the cities not a reference to some essential ethnic or historical identity" (Dolan 1994: 78; Orsi 1992; Orsi 1999: 57; Tomasi 1970, 1975). Similarly, in the contemporary period, the move by the Church to subsume many national devotions and saint cults into a generic Marianism oriented always back toward Jesus has largely been a losing battle in which immigrant groups persist in invoking their particular devotions. Nonetheless, certain devotional practices, such as devotion to Our Lady of Guadalupe among Mexicans, become associated with a national group and are given precedence over the fervent devotion among migrants from a particular town to a local patron saint.

People who did not participate in the church as an institution may find, in the United States, that it becomes the center of their civic, social, and religious lives. These changes have begun to be amply documented by the many recent studies on immigrant religiosity (including Alba et al. 2009; Ebaugh and Chafetz 2000; Hondagneu-Sotelo 2007; Kniss and Numrich 2007; Warner and Wittner 1999; Zolberg and Casanova 2002). While the ethnographic data are prolific, social theory is still emergent as to what the vibrance of religious commitments among immigrants implies in our globalized, "post-secular," "post-modern" age. Further, an argument can be made that in spite of the U.S. Catholic Church's long commitment of pastoralism to immigrants, a more formal "Christian 'theology of migration'" is still in formation (Campese 2007: 175).

However, in spite of a lag in social theory and theology on the centrality of religious participation for many immigrants, there is a tremendous amount of creative work happening in immigrant communities in churches and faith-based organizations which demonstrates their centrality for many immigrants, some of whom described being surprised themselves by the depth of their involvement in a church-based social organizations. As one interviewee, Rosa, told me, "here it is different":

Aquí es diferente. Aquí vinimos y sufrimos. Así que aún más le pedimos a la Virgen, que nos haga fuerte para poder resistir todo. No hay quién no le pida a la Virgen. Aquí, por lo que sufre uno, la valoramos, rezamos más y vamos más a misa.

[Here it is different. Here, we come, and we suffer, so we ask even more of the Virgin, so she can make us strong, to tolerate everything. There's no person who doesn't name the Virgin. Here, for what one goes through, we value her, and look to her, pray more, and attend mass more often.] (Interview, November 8, 2000)

Scholar of religion Peter Beyer sees religion as a means by which collective identities are formed and made to act in political ways: "Religion, in other words, like the political system, is a social sphere that manifests both the socio-cultural, political and the global-universal" (1994: 67). Further, especially since Vatican II, there is an explicit basis for believers to assert that in church one can find not only salvation but emancipation: "There is a potential in religious tradition to move believers away from the sterility of reification and toward the dynamism of liberation" (Stevens-Arroyo and Díaz Stevens 1998: 51). Looking specifically at the experience of immigrants and minorities in the United States, Timothy Smith sees clergy performing an explicit role in the "marrying of ethnicity to religion on clearly 'modern' terms" (1978: 1167). He argues, for example, that the United Farm Workers in California built a labor movement not on shared Chicano ethnic identity but Catholic religiosity (1173). He sees migration as a "theologizing experience," moving social actors not only to turn to their traditions for answers to existential questions, but to modify those traditions and beliefs in the face of new questions and crises (1175). The individual experience of immigration, which Smith describes as "a remarkably solitary one," is "enlarged" in the religious community, and thus immigrant congregations are "not transplants of traditional institutions, but communities of commitment, and therefore arenas of change" (1178). Smith argues:

the acts of uprooting, migration, resettlement and community-building became for the participants a theologizing experience, not the secularizing process that some historians have pictured . . . the folk theology and religious piety that flourished in immigrant churches from the beginnings of American settlement were not merely traditional, but progressive.

Belief and devotion were powerful impulses to accommodation and innovation; and both helped legitimate the behavior, the perceptions, and
the structures of association that sustained the process of change. (1181)

Clearly, religion, whether bound to ethnicity or not, is a crucial vari-
able in immigrant forms of social organization, the formation of interest groups and political mobilizations. Smith is optimistic, even ecstatic,
about the potential of "ethnic religiosity" for the nation's purported project of integrative pluralism: "The ethnic springs of modern American religiosity have given the national culture not a backwater of static dogmas
and rituals but a many-channeled stream of conviction that mankind
must become one people" (1978: 1183). Smith provocatively draws connections here between immigrant religiosity in all its diversity (and not just
the synthesized Judeo-Christian/civil religion variety that was previously
imagined to come out of the melting pot), and a modern American creed
premised on unity and harmony in diversity, and thus lays the ground-
work for a model of citizenship emergent within such visions. In subsequent chapters, I describe how particular kinds of devotional practices
and political engagements among Mexican immigrants in New York serve
not only to connect participants to their past through idioms of national
identity, but to an imagined future premised on particular kinds of practiced citizenship.

Emergent in these contexts is the notion of religion as a zone for con-
testation by ethnic minorities in the United States. Observing U.S. society,
Tocqueville and Weber both remarked on the religious nature of American associational life (Rudolph and Piscatori 1997) and the high degree
of religious participation in the voluntary, private sphere (Beyer 1994). In
contemporary U.S. society, debates over issues like race, politics, art, privacy, and so on, tend to be articulated within and by "communities of
moral commitment," "distinct from yet integrated within their involvement in neighborhood, city or region" (Hunter 1991: 32). Herberg's observation that it is precisely as members of a religious tradition that immigrants can insert themselves into U.S. civic life can be seen to be no less
true of the twenty-first century than it was of the twentieth.

Religion can be a means by which collective identities are formed and
made to act in political ways. It makes sense then that religion would provide powerful idioms for activism and that the church would become a
key space for the Civil Rights Movement, Puerto Rican assertions of rights
in New York City in the 1960s, César Chávez's United Farm Workers, the

Chicano Rights Movement in the Southwest, and now, recent undocumented Mexican immigrants' mobilizations for rights in New York City.

How did such mobilizations by Mexicans in New York churches begin? Were they, as some assume, products of social networks and interconnections among Mexican migrant communities across the United States, the comités guadalupanos an extension of Catholic social organizing in California, Texas, Chicago, and other places? Or are the comités guadalupanos a transplant of a form of social organization found in Mexico and carried by migrants to their place of destination? Indeed, in small towns in la Mixteca, the mayordomía system and collective landholding with the ejido (at least until the 1990s) continue to be important forms of organizing social life, and confraternal organizations could, with their centuries of history (Brentano 1870; Driessen 1984; Flynn 1989; Moreno Navarro 1985, 1997), be considered a deep structure deployed by rural Mexicans even while living in New York City. Or, were the comités guadalupanos a new kind of social organization, formed *sui generis* in the context of Mexicans' recent migration to the United States? The answer is a combination of all of these.

Many pastors of churches with active comités guadalupanos tell similar stories when describing their realization that Mexicans had arrived to their parish. Father Skelly of Saint Cecilia parish in East Harlem recounted that in 1995, a small group of Mexican parishioners requested that he open the church before dawn in order for them to celebrate Las Mañanitas on Guadalupe's feast day. He was surprised, but acquiesced, anticipating that the event would be sparsely attended. He was even more shocked, however, when hundreds of people filled the pews of the church that December 12. The following year, some of the same parishioners requested that an image of Our Lady of Guadalupe be placed in the church. In spite of protestations from Puerto Rican congregants that it unfairly elevated the object of devotion of one ethnic group, he agreed, and soon, furtive devotees left daily offerings of flowers at the small image's feet. In the ensuing years, the image of Guadalupe migrated forward, ever closer to the altar. Eventually, the coordination of these devotional practices prompted the formation of a committee to accomplish the tasks associated with planning what frequently amounts to an increasingly complex array of devotional practices. In addition to Las Mañanitas, many parishes celebrate December 12 with a special evening mass, pray the *novena* for nine days preceding the feast, hold a mass for Saint Juan Diego on December 10,[6] a vigil the night of the eleventh (sometimes lasting until midnight), and hold a party featuring a dramatic reenactment of the apparition, folkloric dances, a talent show, food, and a *sonidero*.[7] While many parishes began only by organizing the Las Mañanitas the morning of the twelfth, the coordination of such a celebration requires a great deal of social capital, money, social networks, and organizational skills. The efforts to honor Our Lady of Guadalupe in a suitable fashion on her feast day are what prompted the formation of a comité guadalupano in many parishes. I now turn to the two comités guadalupanos in which I conducted extended ethnographic field research to describe the very different processes by which they were formed and the different role they play in their members' lives.

Saint John Parish's Comité Guadalupano

Father John Kenny, pastor of Saint John Church in Mott Haven, began to notice Mexicans arriving to his parish around 1990. They were not yet a constant presence at mass, nor were they becoming involved in the church's organization, but he began to find flowers left at the feet of the image of the Virgin of Guadalupe and noticed that on the twelfth of December, Mexicans turned out en masse. Inside the sanctuary, the church had "always" displayed a framed painting of the Virgin of Guadalupe, the ubiquitous reproduction of the image as it appears in the Basilica at Tepeyac. Many churches that were among the first to celebrate the twelfth of December and form Guadalupan groups in the early 1990s housed an image of *la guadalupana* that long preceded the arrival of Mexicans to the neighborhood.[8] It seems no accident that people were drawn to these churches, often choosing to travel to them rather than attend their local parish where the same visual signifiers of welcome were not present.

Doña Rosario Martínez de Magaña, a pious and devout Catholic and guadalupana, founded Saint John Parish's *grupo guadalupano* in the late 1980s with *visitas de la virgen*, in which a small group of women carried a statue of the Virgin from home to home, praying the rosary. The families privileged to host the Virgin gave donations for the annual feast day celebration. As Saint John Parish developed its reputation as welcoming of Mexicans and their religiosity, not only the December 12 festivities became bigger, involving as many as a thousand people in Las Mañanitas, but more *paisanos*, compatriots, began to attend mass. Doña Rosario instituted a weekly meeting of the grupo guadalupano, at first dedicated only to prayer and spiritual formation. When her daughter, María Lucía Magaña, came to the United States, she became involved at her mother's

Image of the Virgin of
Guadalupe, outside Saint
John Parish, Mott Haven,
Bronx, New York

invitation, attending the weekly meetings with members of about ten
other families.

Doña Rosario's husband had been coming to the United States for
years as an agricultural worker during the Bracero guest-worker program. The Magaña family history is an illustration of the ways workers
and their families flexibly adapt to the flows of capital. Originally from
Oaxaca state, they first moved to rural Guerrero and later Mexico City,
where their children were born. When regional migration proved to be
an insufficient strategy for economic survival, Don Leonardo began his
sojourns in the United States. When the Bracero program ended, due to a
chance acquaintance with a paisano who had settled in the New York area
and spoke favorably of the availability of work there, Don Leonardo decided to try his luck, and settled in the Mott Haven section of the Bronx.
He was followed shortly thereafter by his wife, Doña Rosario, who left
their children in the care of her parents in Mexico City. In the Bronx, she
worked as a seamstress, earning less than $200 a week for 10 hours work

per day. She sent home as much money as she could, but her now adult children were struggling to make ends meet. As they were able, they sent for their children one by one, in an effort to increase the total earnings of their binational household, reunite the family, and offer their children greater opportunity. After they were eligible to adjust their status with the "amnesty" (Immigration Reform and Control Act, IRCA) of 1986, Doña Rosario and Don Leonardo began to sponsor their children's legalization under the family unification provisions of the law. In the intervening years, the entire family gained naturalized citizenship, and many of the grandchildren were born in the United States.

From that formative period to the present, leadership of the comité guadalupano at Saint John Parish has been overwhelmingly dominated by Doña Rosario and her daughters. While several men have played important and long-standing roles in the group, membership is dominated by female kin. In all the time I have spent at Saint John Parish, I have only seen Doña Rosario's husband, Leonardo, a handful of times, and each time he seemed to be only a passive participant in the December 12 feast day and other masses. I have never met Doña Rosario's four sons, and while I have seen María Lucía's husband accompany her frequently to mass and special events, he does not attend the meetings of the comité. Instead, Rosario and María Lucía are the de jure and de facto leaders, respectively, of the group, and two of María Lucía's sisters are among the most reliable attendees and active participants in the group. This female-dominated structure extends beyond the Magaña family. Francisca, Julieta, María Santos, Laura, María José, Olivia, Eva, Tania, and a handful of other women attend the Wednesday night meetings most every week, constituting the core membership of the group and providing most of the labor—unpacking the weekly *compra*,[9] cooking and decorating the church for December 12 and other parties and events, attending meetings and protests, and so on. While mothers bring along their infants, older children are often left home with husbands.

I asked one participant, María Santos, how her husband felt about her coming. They are an extraordinarily close and affectionate couple. She ran away from her family to join and eventually marry Raúl Santos in the United States, and when he is not working, they tend to do everything together. He is particularly fearful of being discovered as undocumented, and they generally avoid any situations which might put them in contact with government agencies or representatives—declining even to visit relatives in New Jersey because he is fearful they will be unable to buy a train ticket without revealing their lack of fluency in English, and by extension, their undocumented status. Even though they live less than a block away from the church, I wondered whether Raúl had ever objected to María attending the meetings or accompanied her. She said he knew that she got a lot out of it—that it was a chance for her to *desahogarse*, to express her feelings or "vent" with others, and that it put her mind at peace to attend. While he preferred to relax at home, he always encouraged her to go, even when she sometimes returned late in the evening.

Laura likewise said when she attends meetings, her husband enjoys the opportunity to watch television in peace, and that her kids also seem to enjoy a break from her. She said sometimes she feels lazy and would rather stay home watching the *novelas* on television, but that her husband tells her to go to the meeting, because it will make her feel better. Francisca sometimes arrives slightly harried, explaining that she cannot leave home before preparing the evening meal, but her husband also encourages her to attend. María Lucía Magaña's husband is home with their four children most weeknights; he seems to do most evening meal preparation, childcare, and homework assistance in her absence. Maria Lucia works as "social justice minister" of Saint John Parish after completing her full-time shift at a local hospital. She seems to require minimal sleep, often telling me to call her as late as midnight.

A few couples attend the meeting together and their participation seems to be joint—they either attend together or not at all. Rosaura and Julio always attend together. Josefina and Juan attend with their two young children. The one time Josefina came without Juan, it was an exception that illustrated the rule. During the introductions, she took the opportunity to explain that Juan did not want to attend anymore, and began crying. As it turned out, they were in the midst of a conflict with her mother-in-law, who had been attending the group for many years, and until the problem was resolved, he did not wish to expose himself to negative looks from his mother or her friends. Manuel and Felipe attended the weekly meetings for several months with their friend Edson, all three from Guatemala.[10] When Manuel's wife Carolina and Felipe's wife Marta migrated, arriving to the Bronx together, along with Edson's younger brother Martín, they began to attend as a group. The other men who participate are either unmarried or unaccompanied in the United States by their spouses, including a divorced 60-year-old Colombian man, Mario, a father and son who recently migrated from Nayarit, Mexico, and the Guatemalan men who attended together until their wives arrived. These men actively participate, but do not have formal leadership roles. This contrasts—we will see shortly—with Our Lady of the Rosary Parish.

María Lucía Magaña's participation in the group began simply by attending the prayer group with her mother, but shortly thereafter she took on a leadership role. She said she was overwhelmed by the injustice and poor living conditions of her compatriots in the neighborhood. She lived with her parents across the street from the parish when she first arrived, and was shocked by the littered streets, prostitution, crime, and rampant labor and housing exploitation. With her, the grupo guadalupano took on its dual character. As María Lucía says at half past eight each Wednesday night, by way of transition, "La reunión tiene dos partes: la parte espiritual y la parte social" [the meeting has two parts: the spiritual and the social]. She was not engaged in activism in Mexico, but describes her process of awakening to the social problems facing her community and developing the willingness and ability to act as a process driven solely by the feeling of horror and injustice at the predicament of Mexicans in New York.

While María Lucía's own awakening to social injustice was certainly organic, the formation of the social justice agenda of the grupo guadalupano was not. Saint John belongs to South Bronx Churches, an ecumenical coalition put together by the Industrial Areas Foundation (IAF), a network founded by Saul Alinsky in Chicago in 1940 that today comprises affiliates across the country. IAF develops "organizations whose primary purpose is power—the ability to act—and whose chief product is social change" (2008). Some Alinsky-inspired networks, like PICO National Network, which links faith-based organizations in networks designed to engage individuals to seek solutions to urban problems, seem impressively capable of empowering participants. Wood effectively describes such an empowering environment in an Oakland, California, PICO-affiliated church group (2002). While the links between South Bronx Churches, IAF, Alinsky-style community organizing, and Saint John Parish are not frequently discussed, María Lucía did tell me in an extended interview that she attended a ten-day intensive leadership training institute in Texas in conjunction with her role as social justice minister. She also occasionally mentioned such Alinsky-oriented terms as "one to one."[11] Her training in this style of organizing was reflected in her practice as "social justice minister" at Saint John Parish, but compared to some other comités guadalupanos, little social change is actually effected here in the specifically Guadalupan idiom that is seen in the other settings we focus upon in this book.

In Saint John Parish, guadalupanismo, undocumented status, and Mexican nationality form the basis for the group's existence, but while these vectors contribute to cohesion in Our Lady of the Rosary Parish, here their role is very different. While people might gather in the room as Mexicans, undocumented immigrants, and guadalupanos, they are assumed to want to surpass these markers in the interest of self-improvement and transformation. At Saint John's comité, becoming a citizen is cast as being enfranchised in a system in which religious faith and national identity can recede to the background, no longer necessary for the production of claims for rights and dignity—and this is constructed as the ultimate goal. Those who enjoy such status are elevated to the position of "experts," from whom the rest are expected to learn. As a native-born U.S. citizen who speaks fluent Spanish, I was a cultural broker, but more, a model in my own person of what the members of this group were assumed by its leader to aspire to become, and yet—as detailed above—barred from the possibility of becoming. When I spoke, a hush fell over the room and my words were given exaggerated importance. Occasional observations I made to María Lucía privately were often reiterated in the context of the group: "Alyshia says . . . " These rhetorical moves by María Lucía seemed designed by her to attempt to recast my opinions and words in terms acceptable to her while at the same time lend her own statements some of my cultural capital. While I was far more comfortable with my role at Our Lady of the Rosary, at Saint John I was disturbed by the situation in which I found myself and used every request for my opinion as an opportunity to defer to the collective knowledge and opinion of the group, although I realized this was not possible. Construction of collective knowledge was not often permitted here, only the transmission of "expert" knowledge, from which those who were being cast as categorically inferior, the non-citizens, were expected to benefit.

The executive director of Asociación Tepeyac, Joel Magallán, regularly complained to me that Saint John Parish does not adhere to the association's guidelines for comités, in particular the requirement that regular elections be held for officers who will lead the group, represent the group in the governing body of the association, and serve as liaisons between the parish and Tepeyac. He deprecatingly refers to Saint John as a "prayer group," not a real comité. He also recently told me that part of what makes Saint John "different" from other comités guadalupanos is its link to the IAF network, and thus, in his view, it is an outlier in the landscape of comités guadalupanos.

María Lucía responds to the charge that the group is undemocratic by saying that they do have regular elections to elect the *directiva,* the officers of the group, of which she frequently mentioned she was not a member.[12] When there is a conflict or an uncomfortable topic arises, she demurs, saying it is a matter for the directiva to decide, even though she runs the meetings and I never actually saw the directiva meet, plan to meet, or make a decision without her.[13] Rosaura and Julio, elected officers of the co-mité and very active members of the Asociación independent of their affil-iation with Saint John, struggled to take on a formal leadership role in the comité and to open channels with Tepeyac, but often failed. For the fore-seeable future, the Magaña family does not seem likely to pass the baton of leadership to others. Before we turn to the second parish-based comité guadalupano in which I focused my research, Our Lady of the Rosary, it is important to describe the clerical presence in los comités guadalupanos.

Along with an image of the Virgin of Guadalupe, the parishes where Guadalupan confraternities were formed early on and have persisted also seem to share—at least at the time of their formation—a sympathetic, Spanish-speaking priest. All of the priests who joined in Tepeyac's origi-nal steering committee, *Grupo Timón* (described below), to develop an archdiocese-level response to the pastoral and social needs of the grow-ing Mexican community in New York City, also happen to be children of Irish immigrants. Father Kenny became pastor at Saint John Church in 1979, but was baptized at its font seven decades ago. He grew up in this neighborhood, one of a passel of children of first-generation Irish immi-grants. He is the only one of his family still living in Mott Haven; even his twin brother moved to pastoral Maine.

Given Asociación Tepeyac's quite explicitly socially activist agenda, the way it situates the theology of the Virgin of Guadalupe within a lib-erationist discourse, and its willingness to challenge political authority to promote the human rights of the undocumented, I imagined when I began this project that the clergy involved in the Asociación's formation might be Jesuits, probably Latin American, and trained in Liberation The-ology's mandate of the preferential option for the poor. Instead, I discov-ered that the priests who are actively supportive of parish-based comités guadalupanos, did not emerge from the same order; none of them were Jesuits, none were Latin American, and none would confess to being a liberation theologian. Father Kenny is a Diocesan priest, meaning he was trained in the seminary corresponding to New York City's Archdiocese in order to serve a parish within the same. Unlike an Order which might

Mexican couple emerges onto the street outside of Saint John Church after being married

send its members around the world, diocesan seminarians are drawn from the local area and their loyalty is to the surrounding community. They are "jacks of all trades": they do not have the luxury of engaging in a single mission, such as service, meditation, or pedagogy, like many of the orders. They are influenced certainly by the ideological stance of the cardinal serving during their seminary training and their own individual political and social formation, but they are not trained within a particular philosophical tradition. On the contrary, whenever I asked Father Kenny an abstract question about the relationship between politics and religion, for example, or the theological justification for aiding undocumented immigrants, a look of utter boredom came over his face. Usually, he answered with the statement, "I do what my parishioners need me to do."

During Cardinal Spellman's tenure, Father Kenny traveled to Puerto Rico as a seminarian, and speaks a fluid, if Bronx-accented Spanish. When he began to see an influx of large numbers of Mexican parishioners at Saint John's, he began taking his "vacations" in Mexico, often in Puebla state, volunteering to serve in rural parishes, or sometimes vacationing in the conventional sense, visiting scenic Playa del Carmen in Quintana Roo state or Acapulco. When parishioners ask Father Kenny if he likes *misiotes*, *mole*, and other Mixteca delicacies, he is able to give a connoisseur's answer, and often he is personally acquainted with the parish priests of his congregants' home communities in rural Puebla state. It was his personal connections and petition that led to a group of Mexican nuns being placed in Saint John Parish when he decided he needed help serving the particular cultural and pastoral needs of the Mexicans in his parish. Whenever the pastor is mentioned in conversation with a parishioner, inevitably a wave of affection washes over the person's face. Whenever I had my camera in the church, I received multiple requests from people who wanted me to take their picture with Father Kenny. People often recounted how amazed they were at his ability to notice, in a mass attended by a thousand people, those families who had not come for a few weeks, or even a year, and make a special stop at their pew before mass, still dressed in sweatpants, turtleneck, and hiking boots—never a clerical collar—to greet them before donning his robes. Following mass, he has a small line of people waiting for a moment with him to request a blessing or counsel. The celebration of Father Kenny's birthday is even larger than the festivities surrounding the parish's patron saint each year.

In 2002, Saint John Parish was on a list compiled by the Cardinal, Edward Egan, of potential closings, due to its need for more than $1 million worth of renovations simply to restore it to structural soundness and the archdiocesan perception that it and another nearby parish could consolidate. Throughout a winter in which netting was prayerfully placed under particularly unstable sections of plaster ceiling and buckets littered the pews to capture rain water, Father Kenny called on benefactors in a web from Maine to California. Due almost entirely to his charisma and personal network, nearly $1 million was raised and the church was saved (even while Father Kenny told me that he was on Egan's "black list" for publicly protesting the Cardinal's closure of churches). When I asked María Santos about the first time she came to Saint John, she told me:

> Cuando nosotros fuimos fue el día de la Virgen de Guadalupe, llegamos antes de misa y el Padre salió y nos saludó a todos como si nos conociera, a mí esposo le habló bien, le dijo, "¿qué haces muchacho ahí?" Le empezó a hablar y luego le dice que si nosotros los mexicanos nos decíamos primos y le saludó y le dijo que si le ayudaba a tocar las campanas. . . . El trataba así a la gente y saludó a todos, preguntó cómo estaban, a mí me habló, me saludó, sin conocernos, porque era la primera vez que íbamos, ese día de la Virgen y dice: "¿Cómo están, bien?," dice, "qué bien que vinieron a misa juntos, qué bien que llegaron temprano," ahí nos estaba

platicando y de ahí se iba a tocar las campanas, "ahorita regreso," nos dijo
el padre. Por eso le digo como que se siente uno ahí bien, no sé si en
otras iglesias se da porque no he ido a ninguna otra. . . . [Al padre] lo
encuentras por la calle y te platica.

[When we went it was the day of the Virgin of Guadalupe, and we arrived
to mass early. The Father came out and greeted all of us as if he knew
us. He spoke nicely to my husband, he said, "What are you doing there,
young man?" He started to talk to him and then he asked if we Mexicans
call each other "*primo*," cousin, and [my husband] said yes, and then he
asked if he would help him to ring the bells . . . That's how he treated
people, he greeted everyone, asked how they were. He spoke to me, he
greeted me, without knowing us, since it was the first time we'd gone,
that day, the Virgin's day. He said, "How are you? Good. It's good that
you came together, it's good that you came early"; that's how he chatted
with us, and then he went to ring the bells, saying "I'll be right back."
That's why I say that one feels good there, I don't know if it's the same
in other churches, I haven't gone to any others, but if he sees you in the
street, he will talk to you.][14] (Interview with María Santos, June 2003)

Father Kenny was a regular presence at the comité guadalpano's meetings
in 2000. He usually was there for the initial prayer and blessing, greeting everyone collectively, and usually individually as well, and then at the
end of the day's business, blessing them and sending them on their way.
When he invited me to have a typical Poblano dinner with him in the rectory in the spring of 2003, I asked him why he did not seem to come to
the meetings of the comité guadalupano as often anymore. I knew he had
been sick, that he was also trying to restrict his activities (he was then 65
years old) and insist on personal time to practice tai chi and swim, and I
did not want to imply that he should do more. He said that he found that
parish groups functioned better the less he intervened. He regretted that
when he entered the room, he changed the dynamic: people deferred to
his opinion and sought his approval for everything, while the less he got
involved the more leadership seemed to develop and be exercised independently of him. In fact, when he did attend, when asked for an opinion
or guidance, he often made people laugh by replying, "Boca cerrada, no
entran moscas" [flies can't enter a closed mouth]. As we will see, this benevolent and cheerful but hands-off approach differed from the relationship the Comité of Our Lady of Rosary parish had with its pastor.

Our Lady of the Rosary Parish Guadalupan Committee

Upon approaching Our Lady of the Rosary Parish, the first thing a visitor is likely to notice is a shrine with an image of the Virgin of Guadalupe in a dedicated area just outside the rectory (previously described in the Introduction). A small statue, encased in glass, she is surrounded by silk and fresh flowers, plaster, and iron in the decorative grillwork of the fence that surrounds her. I did not notice on first glance, but Father Byrne later drew my attention to the small tombstone at her feet, embedded in the gravel, which is dedicated to "the unborn child."[15] The church was freshly whitewashed, and this combination—of whitewashed plaster and a street-side shrine—made me think of rural churches in Latin America, in contrast to Saint John's gothic stone and marble.

Our Lady of the Rosary Parish was founded in 1852, a half-century earlier than Saint John Church, by clergy of Fordham University, a Jesuit University. While it has received many generations of immigrants from many countries, the centrality of immigrants to its projection of a parish identity is less than at Saint John. Especially since the departure of its beloved pastor, Father Byrne, in 2002, there seems to be more emphasis within this church relative to other churches on forging a generic Catholic identity, devoid of vernacular religiosities. This runs contrary to the redoubled efforts of the parish's comité guadalupano to forge a unique Mexican identity, which lead to significant tensions, as we will see in chapter 5.

In his two decades at Our Lady of the Rosary Parish, Father Byrne witnessed a transformation in the neighborhood. Although when I met him his six-foot frame was doubled over at the waist with arthritis and he would, in 2002, be overcome by years of accumulated exhaustion and pressed into an extended convalescence, Father Byrne was not yet 60 years old. He entered the diocesan seminary just as Father Kenny finished it, and they remained friends. Also like Father Kenny, he is second-generation Irish and a Bronx native, raised near the intersection of Tremont and the Grand Concourse. The University Heights section of the Bronx experienced a heavy influx of Italian immigrants early in the last century. New York's former mayor, Rudolph Giuliani, son of Italian immigrants, was baptized at the church that corresponds to the neighborhood north of Fordham Road, just east of Grand Concourse, where many Mexicans I interviewed live. Father Byrne said the neighborhood changed in the 1960s or '70s with the construction of Co-op City and the flight of "the white, ignorant minority." An influx of African Americans and Puerto

Ricans was followed in the 1980s by Dominicans. Mexicans began moving into this neighborhood only in 1996–97.

This area continues to be home to immigrants, but not in high proportions relative to many other neighborhoods in the city. Further, the church draws people from a broad swath of territory, not simply the immediate area surrounding it. Unlike Saint John Parish, where the vast majority of the comité's members live within a stone's throw of the church, most Mexican parishioners at Our Lady of the Rosary Parish travel there from other neighborhoods, all over the northern part of the Bronx, near and far. The Mexican population in the Census tract that corresponds directly to the parish is only 207, or 4.2 percent of the population. In contrast, the population of Census Tract 237.02, northwest of Our Lady of the Rosary and where many of the Mexican members of Our Lady of the Rosary's comité reside, is twice that, or 8.3 percent Mexican. If we consider *el Barrio Italiano*, Mexican residents' name for the Bronx's little Italy, with Arthur Avenue at its heart, the number of Mexicans rises to 13.65 percent of the total population. Although there are several parishes in the area I just described, many members of the comité told me they passed them by on the way to Our Lady of the Rosary Parish. This area is far more heavily residential than the South Bronx, and with the vast green expanse of Bronx Park flanking its eastern boundary, it feels less industrial, congested, and polluted. While all of the Bronx was impacted by the economic and social crises of the 1970s and '80s, this area, with its diverse and bustling shopping district, was not as deeply affected as the South Bronx and has rebounded in grand fashion in recent years.

In 1992, a woman in Our Lady of Rosary Parish requested a mass for the Virgin of Guadalupe on her feast day, but, according to Father Byrne, this preceded any significant Mexican presence in the parish. Five years later, following the formation of Asociación Tepeyac, the comité was founded with the initiative of the Asociación, which identified Our Lady of Rosary and its pastor as being very welcoming, offering space for meetings and activities, and sufficiently close to where many Mexicans lived for them to participate actively. This formation is categorically different from that of Saint John Parish with its very local membership and agenda. Their activism, while similarly focused on education, housing, labor, safety, and health, is closely aligned with Tepeyac's agenda, but is broader in scope than Saint John's—occurring on a citywide and even national level.

Father Byrne remarked that the comité guadalupano was the only group in his parish organizing along ethnic lines, and that he felt that there was a tendency by Mexicans to become so involved in the comité that they failed to participate actively in parish-wide initiatives and activities or to take on leadership roles in the parish. The formation of the comité and its membership was strategically managed by Tepeyac and local Mexican leaders looking for a site in the northern Bronx in which to mobilize large numbers of Mexicans. The comité, perhaps necessarily, exhibits less investment in and loyalty to the parish itself—a fact that would become quite evident with Father Byrne's failing health and retirement.

Like Father Kenny, Father Byrne, in conversation, would often signal similarities he perceived among the culture, work ethic, and religiosity of Mexican immigrants to the Irish with whom he grew up. With their perceived piety, large families, working-class values, and low social status vis-à-vis other recent immigrant groups, clergy and others in New York often compare Irish immigrants of a century ago and Mexicans today. In hushed tones, it is even said that they are considered to be the Catholic Church's best hope for the future in terms of their numbers, birth rate, and loyalty to the church. It is thus no accident, perhaps, that members of Grupo Timón and like-minded priests including Father Byrne share so many characteristics in common with one another.

When Father Byrne was a seminarian and was told he would be sent to Puerto Rico for language training and socialization into the particular culture and religiosity of the island, he balked. A nonconformist, he did not want to be sent off to the same place all of the other seminarians were sent, so, he said, he tried to imagine something that would be completely different and requested placement in Chile. Arriving in the last days of the Salvador Allende administration and witness to the military coup of 1973, Father Byrne clearly draws his political sensibilities from that complicated time. He was inspired by the human rights activism in the face of grave danger of church organizations like the *Vicaría de la Solidaridad* and his residence in one of the more revolutionary *barrios populares*, which had been a base of popular support for Allende and became a site for focused resistance to and repression by the military forces of *junta* leader General Augusto Pinochet. In spite of this highly politicized seminary experience, even Father Byrne is not openly a proponent of Liberation Theology. Like Father Kenny, his pastoral style was one of matter-of-fact advocacy, affection, and indulgence.

While he would have preferred Mexican parishioners to be more involved in the parish, he viewed his role as similar to Father Kenny's: "I let them do what they want to do. Self-functioning is what you want." He knew some other groups in the parish resented the placement of an image of the Virgin of Guadalupe outside the rectory and complained that the comité guadalupano took advantage of the parish as a meeting space without contributing. He rejected this, acknowledging the group's significant contributions of labor, time, and money to the reparation of the church and their cultural contributions to the life of the parish. He told me with a mischievous wink that he even went so far as to prevent other groups from learning unsavory details about the comité which might have fueled their claims, such as the fact that one time they organized a dance which ended with a knife fight between rival youth gangs.

The first time I attended a meeting of the comité guadalupano of Our Lady of the Rosary Parish, I was overwhelmed by the contrasts between it and the comité of Saint John Parish. What follows are my unedited field notes of my first impressions from that night in the fall of 2000:

I was shown to the rectory and it became clear how different this group is—by the end of the night, I couldn't imagine how it could be more different from Saint John's in every sense. Omar Fuentes sat at a table, and chairs were arranged in a circle. Only ten or so people were there at 8:00 p.m. The directiva slowly took seats at the table, Omar, who identified himself as *Poblano*, from Puebla, Eduardo (who I met before), Eduardo's wife Guadalupe, Pablo Fuentes (a relative of Omar?) and Emiliano. Alberto rushed around making coffee. The women who were there sat and chatted, and even Guadalupe, the only woman on the directiva, said nothing throughout the meeting. There is a very, very different gender makeup to this group! I realized, in contrast, that Saint John's really has very few men who attend regularly—and those who do are older men, and a small handful in their late 20s/30s who seem to accompany their wives or come alone. Here, there were more men than women, lots of young men—even a considerable contingent of teenagers with kind of rebellious-looking haircuts and baggy jeans, and men accompanied by other men. There also seemed to be a lot of camaraderie between the men. In the considerable time before the meeting finally started at 8:40, men were speaking to each other, shaking hands, circulating actively around the room, while women, also amiable, seemed less mobile and less involved in talking with people outside the group they came in with (with one notable exception, a woman who was cracking jokes and loudly talking with men, women, and children on all sides). A group of four little boys, in a funny imitation of the male networking happening, excused themselves from the kids' free-for-all in the hall and quietly sat in a row of chairs throughout most of the meeting, attentive to all that was happening. Many of the men had cell phones, some wore shiny large gold crucifixes, and many wore cowboy boots and pressed western-ish shirts . . .

That night, the performance of gender roles and relations most impressed me: the way women came in and took seats around the circle, in kin groups, and did not interact much with people outside of that narrow and spatially manifested relationality, while men changed seats continuously and during any break in the meeting, moved to the center, rings clinking in handshakes and embraces, cell phones ringing, voices in loud camaraderie, to conduct what was clearly an equally important agenda of business. Soon, though, I learned about the specific interrelations that contributed to this dynamic. Here, many members of the comité hailed from the same region in Mexico, and still more had become embedded in complex webs of *compadrazgo*[16] after migrating.

To give only one, perhaps particularly vivid example, I will illustrate the interconnectedness of one group within the comité. Ana, Mirna, Rocío, and Manuela Araya are four sisters from a small town in the area of Atlixco, in Puebla state. In their hometown, Ana and Rocío liked to participate in folkloric dance, and had heard of Rubén, a well-known director and choreographer of this dance style in the area. After the sisters moved to the United States in the early to mid-1990s, one by one following their father, Ana was introduced to Rubén at a party. Although she was impressed by his dance credentials, she found him to be overbearing and arrogant and did not appreciate that his reputation as a choreographer preceded him. Nevertheless, Cupid's arrow did her in, as she tells it. They eventually wound up falling in love, marrying, and had their third child in 2003. Rubén, formerly employed at the World Trade Center (WTC), sought aid at Asociación Tepeyac after September 11, 2001, when he found himself unemployed. He worked as a volunteer on Tepeyac's WTC aid project and other projects, and soon was hired to direct the Asociación's cultural programs, including its annual arts festival. He also directs the *ballet folklórico* of Our Lady of the Rosary Church, and it wins nearly every competition in which it competes, inspiring awe and envy throughout the city's network of Mexican folkloric dance groups. Mirna is married to Alberto, who in 2002–2003 was the president of the comité guadalupano of Our Lady of the Rosary Parish. Rocío is the principal dancer of the ballet, and has begun to direct another troupe among children. While Rocío's husband does not attend the meetings of the comité, his wife's deep involvement and his relationship as *concuño*[17] of Rubén and Alberto ensure that he is present at most of the comité's events and can be seen with Alberto outside the church with their children, and usually Rubén and Ana's three children as well, while their wives participate in dance rehearsal. The Araya sisters might on the surface appear comparable to the Magaña women of Saint John Parish. Although Rocío was one of the *capitanes* of the torch run for 2002, and the sisters do express their opinions occasionally in the context of the meetings and certainly they do so at home, they do not hold leadership positions in the comité. It is the men who as concuños, connected by marriage to the sisters, have come to represent one of the core nodes of leadership in the comité. Further, it is notable that when they migrated, none of the sisters were married or knew their future spouses, and the sister who has the least public role and the least visible ties to leadership in the comité is, not coincidentally, the unmarried youngest sister, Manuela.

Here, formal leadership of the group regularly changes hands with democratic elections of the officers every two years. Nevertheless, the pattern by which a leadership role is developed and power accumulated shows parallels with the mayordomía structures, which are the traditional political and religious governing structures in many of the rural Mixteca towns from which members of this group hail. In that structure, while women do a great deal of the labor, both physical and social, it is men who are the formal authority figures, the office holders in the cargo system. In that system, young men begin to volunteer their services and eventually work their way up the hierarchy through increasing contributions of labor and capital as well as successful accumulation of *confianza*, roughly translated as trustworthiness. In 2000, Alberto, although already married to Mirna and father of a young son, appeared to me to be a youth without status in the structure of the comité—he made coffee, accompanied the ballet, and did other small tasks. Nevertheless, he was always present and contributing to whatever task was at hand, and in this way, in the three subsequent years, he accumulated the necessary social capital and authority to become president of the comité. While in a rural mayordomía, such accumulation of status can take a lifetime (Chance 1985), in the rarefied diasporic environment of the comité, the process can apparently be accelerated. Further, former leaders, like Don Omar, president of the comité in 2000, do not pass out of the sphere of influence, but like *mayordomos* who have already served in rural Mexican towns, by 2002 he came to fill an elite role as elder, adviser, counselor, and often final arbitrator of the comité. As former regional leader of the Asociación, Omar now enjoys a lifetime position on Tepeyac's *consejo de honor*, honorary council, advising the entire network of comités guadalupanos in the city.

The comité guadalupano of Our Lady of the Rosary Parish subscribes to the discourse that "we are all undocumented," and that is the organizational strategy underlying its activities. Even though the statement is not literally true of every member, those for whom it does not explicitly apply do not say as much, and are in fact more likely to identify themselves as undocumented for strategic organizational purposes. The group also assumes other commonalities as a basis for participation, similar to the vectors of identity named earlier: Mexican nationality, devotion to the Virgin of Guadalupe, and willingness to work for the benefit of the community.

As a result of this cohesiveness in group identity and definition of the terms of community formation in this site, the comité guadalupano at Our Lady of the Rosary has produced an extraordinary degree of internal trust, as evidenced in the following two examples—first regarding the way the group responds to internal conflict, and second, some of the concrete products of the group's cohesion. In August 2003, there were tensions within the comité of Our Lady of the Rosary Parish because one of its members, Miguel, had begun his own misión guadalupana, taking an image of the Virgin of Guadalupe from home to home, in prayer. Fundraising is one important aspect of la misión guadalupana; the collection box which accompanies the Virgin is emptied each week and deposited into a savings account for the annual feast day on December 12. Nonetheless, there was no implication that this conflict about a duplicate misión was entirely about money or that the wayward member of the comité had been improperly collecting funds. Rather, his actions were depicted in the ensuing discussion—in which the man was not present—as an insult to the comité, its organizational efforts, and its leaders. While there was a great deal of anger toward this person, which was expressed in the meeting as well as privately in conversations I had with comité members, the course of action chosen by the group was extraordinarily nonconfrontational. It was decided that there was no use chasing or berating this wayward member: "como a un borreguito, hay que esperar que se amanse otra vez" [like a sheep, we have to wait for him to become docile again]. They mandated that he would be treated with respect and brotherly affection and thus brought back into the fold, without openly confronting him for his undermining actions. And in fact, in the next Sunday's mass, the man was dressed in the same clothing the members of the comité designate for the masses in which they take a leadership role—white pressed shirt, black pants, and a medallion of Guadalupe— and I saw several members of the comité warmly embracing him. This quite threatening schism was resolved with an internalization of the tensions and an effort to affectionately redirect a transgressor inward, back to the fold.

Second, the cohesion achieved in this parish is perhaps best demonstrated with a satellite group that has emerged, involving—comité members insist—virtually all of the same people, but meeting outside of the parish. The *caja de ahorro*, as its members refer to it, or community chest, was formed in 2003, and like the comités guadalupanos, it represents an important shift in migrant activities from attention to "home," characterized by remittances and longing, to attention to the host locale, with investment in a future in the United States.[18] The members of this group say they formed it after they realized that as individuals they cannot get ahead of the daily struggle for subsistence without legal residency, credit, and the ability to save more, but that as a group they can save quickly, become a corporation, and invest on a large scale, even while their immigration status remains unchanged. The group meets weekly and each member contributes $25 to the collective coffer. The group plans to buy an apartment building, which they will renovate themselves using the skills and tools they have acquired working in construction, and rent to their members and other paisanos in a close circle of friends and family. This investment will provide economic gain as an investment but also enable them an escape from predatory landlords, high rents, and living environments where they fear for their children's health and safety. Even while conflicts about money and its expenditure seemed at one point or another to plague every family and organization I encountered in the course of my research, this group, which involves the circulation and group management of many thousands of dollars, was a remarkable example of the extraordinary trust afforded by the confianza shared by its members and like the comité is premised on the same foundation of national identity, guadalupanismo, and shared migratory status.[19]

The communitarian discourse of trust and cooperation developed in Our Lady of the Rosary, building on Tepeyac's premise that "we are all undocumented," is so powerful as to subsume the sometimes very vivid contradictions of it posed by individual circumstances. Before beginning our discussion of Asociación Tepeyac's formation, I illustrate one example of this at Our Lady of the Rosary Parish. Marco, described sweeping in the opening of this book, is a ubiquitous presence at Our Lady of the Rosary Parish, attending every meeting of the comité guadalupano, as well as meetings of other groups, and he was often simply "around" when I was at the parish. He seems to enjoy privileged access; I frequently heard the church secretary ask him to open rooms with her keys, or take care of this or that problem around the parish. In spite of this privileged role, I also had the sense in each encounter with him that he had secrets to keep. Awkwardly tall, lanky, younger than most men in the comité, and wearing punk rock t-shirts, he was alternately open with me and guarded. One morning, we sat at the kitchen table in the rectory basement, surrounded by the smell and accoutrements of the many cats who lived there. Within a few moments, some of Marco's struggles were revealed to me. A father of three, he had left his family in Toluca, a suburban satellite of Mexico City, a few years earlier. He managed to support his family, who accompanied him here, for a couple of years, working in construction. Then, afraid of the negative influences that surrounded them in this neighborhood, he sent his wife and children back to live with his in-laws. However, since they left, he has been unable to send them even a cent. He is now dependent on the sympathy of various compadres who allow him to sleep on their couches for a night or two. He said coming to the United States had been "a very bad investment": "Ha sido una inversión muy mala porque no he hecho nada yo de dinero aquí, me he endrogado mucho y cuando uno abre los ojos dice, 'no, esto no es felicidad.'" [It's been a very bad investment because I haven't made any money here, I've fallen into a lot of debt and then one opens one's eyes and says, 'no, this is not happiness.'] [20]

Marco is, perhaps, the most powerful counterexample imaginable of the discourse of communitarian cooperation and upward arc of prosperity and rights posited at Our Lady of the Rosary Parish and illustrated so vividly by the caja de ahorro. He is, in his own blunt terms, a failure, and possibly an embarrassment for the extremely proud community that surrounds him. Nevertheless, he is, at the same time, one of the comité's most eloquent spokespeople, reproducing the group's prevailing discourse, even while it directly and painfully contradicts almost every reality faced in his own life:

Entonces una de las bases es llegar a eso, ser una comunidad unida, sin distinción de nadie y crecer juntos, así como nos vimos en la pobreza, juntos crecer en la riqueza. Entonces pienso que esa es una meta bien importante, llegar a eso con todos los mexicanos. Pues es una triste realidad que me pongo yo en mi lugar, que así como yo me sentía sólo y me pude haber hundido en las drogas pues hay mucha gente, y es una realidad cierta, pues, en mi paso me he encontrado gente que se han tirado a los vicios, en el alcoholismo, en las drogas, en el sexo. Eso pues no es bueno, para una buena imágen del mexicano es bueno crecer juntos y parejos.

[So one of the basic things is to arrive at [the goal], to be a united community, without any distinctions. To grow together, and just as we live together in poverty, to grow together in wealth. Well, I think it's a very important goal, to arrive at this with every Mexican. It's a sad reality when I look at my own position, just as I felt alone and I could have sunk into drugs, there are many people, and it's the truth, that in passing I have found people who've fallen into vice: alcoholism, drugs, sex. That is not good. For a good image of Mexicans we have to grow together and at the same pace.]

While this might read as a narrative of redemption through faith, in the next moment, Marco described his continuing struggle with debt, drugs, and other problems which prevent him from providing for his family. Nevertheless, throughout our conversation, and in many other informal circumstances, I witnessed Marco effortlessly reproduce the narrative of communitarianism, solidarity, economic success, national pride, and guadalupanismo that prevails in this comité, with no hint of irony on his part. At Our Lady of Rosary Parish, the development of this narrative is so complete that it is reproduced even in spite of contradictions in individual circumstances. In this way, this comité manages to retain its members even as they go through spots of trouble. In contrast, at Saint John, people who experience difficulties often stop attending meetings of the comité guadalupano, wary of criticism and gossip, but also of putting a stain on the overall arc of upward improvement that has been traced for its members. At Asociación Tepeyac, the same vectors of identity—Guadalupanism, Mexican nationality, and undocumented status—have been deployed in similar ways since the organization's foundation, but in a different context and by different social actors. We now turn to the formation of that organization.

Asociación Tepeyac de New York

Asociación Tepeyac is an umbrella organization which, during the time of my research, was comprised of forty comités guadalupanos based in parishes in the five boroughs of New York City. Staff and volunteers frequently insisted to me that *la Asociación* was nothing more than its member comités, saying that they set the agenda, take leadership roles in advancing its projects, and their members are its main constituency. The organization was founded, by a steering committee called Grupo Timón, in 1997 by a handful of priests concerned about the needs of the Mexican parishioners they had watched rapidly fill their pews. The group included Father Kenny of Saint John Parish. The group approached the diocese to call for a specific pastoral initiative directed at the particular needs of Mexicans in the Archdiocese of New York and the Brooklyn Diocese. Father Kenny said the initial intention was for a pastoral organization that could serve as a home for Mexican Catholics in New York City, to protect and to serve them: "faith would be the floor, the walls were protection against raids and violence, and the roof would be the church" (interview, October 11, 2000). Father Skelly, pastor of Saint Cecilia Parish and another member of Grupo Timón, remarked that while in the 1970s it was challenging to "fight the system" for his parishioners' rights with corrupt landlords and abusive employers, at that time his parish was made up mostly of African American and Puerto Rican U.S. citizens who needed services. He said the great difference now is that without documents, recent immigrants are much more vulnerable to exploitation. He said advocates like himself are in a bind when they know that their work might lead to their parishioners being evicted, or in the worst case, deported, since without legal status, undocumented immigrants have little leverage to demand humane treatment.

While the Committee for Hispanic Affairs is concerned with Latinos in general in the archdiocese, there are many smaller pastoral campaigns directed at subgroups within the larger Catholic population. In collaboration with the Jesuit Conference of Mexico, the Committee for Hispanic Affairs arranged to bring Jesuit brother Joel Magallán Reyes[21] to New York from Mexico to conduct a survey of Mexicans in the diocese and establish a pastoral agency to serve them.

Joel Magallán hails from Zacatecas, one of the states located in Central Mexico with a long history of migration. Zacatecas reared agricultural workers in the Bracero program and several generations of laborers who

Banner of Asociación Tepeyac, 2000

have found themselves throughout the Southwestern United States and Chicago. Thus, it is one of the states in which migration has long been a way of life, dollars are nothing new, and where the luster and myth of *el norte* has long since worn off. Joel completed his studies as a seminarian in the Jesuit College of Mexico, and after fulfilling many other roles, worked as an organizer in the Pilsen district, a largely Mexican area of Chicago, before being sent to New York City by the Jesuit Conference.

Hermano Joel arrived in New York City at the behest of the archdiocese in 1996. He traveled throughout the city, talking with members of existing comités guadalupanos, like the one at Saint John Parish, as well as community leaders, deli workers, flower vendors, parish priests, and others. He often would sleep on the couches of those he interviewed. He ate at their tables, savoring the flavors of home with them, so hard to achieve with the still notable lack of suppliers of Mexican products. The same families gave him the clothes he wore, including the ubiquitous black down jacket he continued to wear every winter day during the period of my research. This period of reconnaissance was perceived differently by different sectors of the Mexican population. The Magaña family remembers this as the beginning of the end of their privileged position as the first comité guadalupano in the city. At the time, there was a discussion between the members of Grupo Timón and Joel Magallán about locating a new city-wide Guadalupan organization at St. John Parish. This plan was eventually abandoned. María Lucía still complains that Joel never recognized their efforts to organize Mexican religiosity and advocate for their paisanos long before there were other groups doing the same. He simply arrived and took over, they say, without respect for the years of sacrifices they had made to bring the Mexican community together, such as it was. Others speak fondly of Joel in this period, his humility and tirelessness, and regret that when they call the offices of Tepeyac it is no longer Joel who answers, and that he no longer comes round to baptisms or to eat a meal at their kitchen tables. Joel himself, remarking on a since aborted decision to leave the position of Executive Director of Tepeyac, commented that he wished he had more time *para poder convivir*, to spend time with those families who were so hospitable to him when he arrived in the city. Spending his days on the phone or in meetings with consular representatives, foundation executives, and members of the press had sapped him of his joy for community work.

Joel worked with the New York Archdiocese to establish a pastoral office, then called *El Centro Guadalupano*, from which Asociación Tepeyac was born. In the beginning, the organization worked to coordinate the comités guadalupanos into a single network through promotion of devotional activities dedicated to Our Lady of Guadalupe, cultural events such as arts festivals, sports (a 5K run on Cinco de Mayo and a soccer league), and through Urgent Affairs, it addressed emergency situations: family members seeking information on a relative who had not arrived after crossing the border, transporting a deceased relative to Mexico for burial, advocating for tenants in danger of eviction or workers who had not been paid.

In multiple interviews during 2000–2003, Joel insisted that the comités guadalupanos were an organic social form, "natural" to Mexican immigrants because of the parallels they shared with the mayordomía structure in their hometowns. Only in 2008, after being assured that this book's release would occur after his planned departure as executive director of Tepeyac, did he admit to me (and agreed I could write) that the comités structure had more complex roots. He confessed that although he never felt comfortable admitting it given the "politics" of the New York Archdiocese, in fact, he drew his inspiration for the structure of the comités from Liberation Theology's Christian ecclesiastical base communities (*comunidades eclesiales de base,* or CEBs*),* in which people come together to explore, discuss, and plan strategies for transforming the structural conditions of their own oppression. In the CEBs, scripture is discussed through the lens of God's preferential option for the poor, Gustavo Gutierrez's liberationist interpretation of the Bible, which emerged following Vatican II. When CEBs became associated with revolutionary social movements in Latin America in the 1970s and early 1980s, Liberation Theology and many of its precepts became associated by some with "red priests" and Cold War hemispheric politics. While I was convinced by Father Kenny and Father Byrne that the correlations I eagerly sought to draw between some aspects of their pastoralism and the comités guadalupanos in their parishes and Liberation Theology were a misinterpretation, their unwillingness to even entertain a discussion of the interconnections is surely a sign of the political climate of the archdiocese. As a Mexico-trained Jesuit lay brother, Magallán was able to draw on Catholic social teaching and his own experiences with rural Mexican CEBs and the mayordomía system to build a very effective organizational template for the comités which was implicitly liberationist and also sufficiently "organic" for its members, who were as likely as the parish priests to shy away from anything "political." Nonetheless, as strategic as Joel's intervention was, each comité is unique and built upon preexisting social relations in the parish. Before choosing Saint John and Our Lady of the Rosary parishes for our field research, I surveyed many comités guadalupanos and found that no two are alike. While some are run by the parish priest as prayer groups, others function almost entirely outside of the church structure to coordinate social events and activism with little devotional content. The two I chose not only were among the most vital but offered the greatest contrast in terms of their loyalty to and embeddedness in Asociación Tepeyac's agenda.

The mission of Asociación Tepeyac de New York during the period of my research was the following:

> *Asociación Tepeyac* is a non-profit 501(c)3 network of 40 community based organizations, whose mission is twofold to promote the social welfare and human rights of Latino immigrants, specifically the undocumented in New York City. The Association Tepeyac is also dedicated to inform, organize, and educate Mexican immigrants and their families about rights, resources, and processes to develop leaders, organizations, and communities, to build a great Mexican community, integrated to all races and cultures in New York [*sic*]. (Asociación Tepeyac de New York 2004)

As with many grassroots organizations, there is a mythos attached to the early formational period of the organization. Having spent years observing Asociación Tepeyac, I see this nostalgia as being part as well of the perhaps inevitable shift that has occurred by which the organization has gone from being a movement, a collection of spontaneously mobilized local groups, into a nonprofit agency, forced to adapt to the expectations of funders, comply with regulations governing nonprofit organizations and seeking to rationalize, systematize, and make more efficient their capacity to attend to the needs of their constituency who are cast now as clients, not simply as members. Joel and the community leaders who helped him form the organization in the early stages often talk of the period when they had only a pair of five-gallon paint buckets to sit on, no computer, and one faulty telephone line.

By 2000, the Asociación had distanced itself substantively from the archdiocese. While it continued to receive some funding from it, and the five-story townhouse it occupies was a convent belonging to the Church, New York's biggest landowner, Tepeyac works to maintain its independence. In recent years, diocesan funding has further declined and Tepeyac has been funded largely by private foundations, as well as the city, which funds particular services such as after-school programs the organization runs. Estela Morales was present from this early stage. When I met her, she was often billed at speaking engagements and protests as the spokesperson for Tepeyac, and in that period she was a more visible and vocal presence even than Joel, ubiquitous in Spanish-language print and television media. When I asked her about the relationship between the organization and the archdiocese, she told me dismissively that it was demographics and convenience that caused Tepeyac to emerge from the archdiocese, but that it would not take much for the organization to seek other allies. She said that priests who had watched their churches become empty now find that the vibrant, youthful, and prolific Mexican community represents their future, and as such that Mexicans wield more power than they know. She described some of the ways that Mexican parishioners had begun to realize their strength. She told me of a parish in Staten Island where the priest relegated the Guadalupan feast day celebration to a tiny basement chapel. The Mexican parishioners countered that they expected 500 people to turn out. When the priest did not agree to reaccommodate them, they responded that there might be another church in the neighborhood, even if it was Evangelical, Episcopalian, "whatever," that would give them the space they needed, but that they would not go there just for December 12, they would stay there, and perhaps the priest who had been unwelcoming of them would come to miss the $500 or $1000 they brought to the collection plate each week.

Morales is another interesting personage among immigrant organizers in New York. She is not from the region most immigrants in New York are from, the Mixteca, nor from one of the historic sending states like Zacatecas; she is from even closer to the mouth of the wolf—as one aphorism describes it—the northeastern border state of Nuevo León. Eldest daughter of a single, working-class mother, she grew up in a poor neighborhood in a border town, in fact in the Red Light district, with the border never far from her consciousness, and most people she knew criss-crossed it regularly in their daily lives. I was surprised after becoming acquainted with this straight-talking, even militant activist that as she grew up her greatest dream was to become a prostitute. She recounts how she spent her childhood days imitating the struts, gestures, and cat-calls of some of the sex workers in her neighborhood, and fabricating mini-skirts for herself from their discarded remnants. In fact, she credits her skill at public speaking to the eloquence and forthrightness with which these women not only defended their rights but attracted their customers. Estela had worked in a youth group in her Brooklyn parish for eight years before coming to work full time for Tepeyac. And while the demands of her personal life and her job were often relentless, until she finally left New York a few years ago to live close to her family in Houston, she seemed never to tire of her work.

In spite of the deliberateness with which Joel came to New York to organize the existing comités guadalupanos, Asociación Tepeyac emerged in an improvised fashion, growing in fits and starts as demand, personnel, and funding allowed. Much of its organizational philosophy is easily traced to Joel, who is eloquent and inspiring in his formulation of a movement, founded on guadalupanismo and human rights. In speaking with any staff member or volunteer who has been with the organization for a significant amount of time, this discourse is dominant and consistent. In fact, as much as I tried to scratch the surface, assuming there must be some members of the organization operating with alternative agendas, rationales, or even a dose of cynicism—I found a remarkable coherence of mission and message at all levels of the organization.

Nonetheless, there was a disjuncture between this mission and message and the everyday nuts-and-bolts approach used to achieve them. I learned this in part by personal experience. While I always left conversations with Joel inspired to begin whatever volunteer task had been sketched out for me, I was then often immediately confronted with a complete lack of the materials and information necessary to actually do so. In my interactions with different departments, I learned that there was often an utter lack of awareness of procedures and roles played by other members of the staff, even when such information would have greatly facilitated their own work. Once, I arrived at the setting for an event only to learn that it had been canceled because of rain. Feeling frustrated that I had not received notification of this by e-mail or phone, I was surprised to see some staff members arrive shortly after I did: they also did not know the event had been canceled.

A large part of the lack of awareness from one department to another has to do with how the staff is recruited and organized and the periodic changing of the guard by much of the personnel. Most of the labor of the Asociación is accomplished by interns who spend six months in fulfillment of the Mexican government's social service requirement for graduating from university. Normally, social service must be completed within the Republic of Mexico and it is usually a 12-month commitment. Through personal connections, Joel has negotiated an arrangement with ITESO (Instituto Tecnológico de Estudios Superiores del Occidente), a Jesuit university in Guadalajara, Jalisco. Within this arrangement, six to ten students in their last year of university come to New York to fulfill their social service requirement at Asociación Tepeyac, serving the Mexican migrant community. While completing social service in six rather than twelve months and in New York City might seem irresistible to students at ITESO, those who arrive at the doorstep of the West Fourteenth Street offices of Asociación Tepeyac are soon stripped of any illusions they may have had of a glamorous life in the Big Apple. The student interns work as many as 20 hours a day, for no pay, and rarely even leave the building. I asked one intern what she thought of the city three months into her sojourn here and she replied that she had not seen much, although she proudly added that one Sunday afternoon she had been able to visit the Metropolitan Museum of Art. Nonetheless, the interns seem, without exception, to view their experience here as life-altering and express no regret about their decision to come and about the work they accomplish.

One Friday afternoon, a couple of days after Christmas, I arrived at Tepeyac. The offices were closed to the public, but I had come to make photocopies of the clippings files. I entered the building and unwrapped my scarf, and as usual, within seconds, I was greeted by a toothy, slobbery pit bull named Morris who bounded down the stairs, leaping off the last step to crash into me, more or less at eye level, and tried to get me to play. Morris has scars, wears no collar, and while he appears in the annual staff portrait as "chief of security," he often makes first-time visitors to the offices momentarily regret their decision to open the front door. But before long he can usually be found frolicking on the floor with toddlers or occupying a chair at the conference table. Morris's owner has blue hair, several piercings, and blasts Mexico City–based punk rock and ska behind the closed door of his office. On this day, when there was no one around to be put off by it, music penetrated the building and as one group of late teen/early twenty-somethings fooled around with the intercom cracking jokes to each other from the far reaches of the building, another tried printing out some new designs on t-shirts. Someone pleaded for assistance as the rice for the daily staff lunch burned and the smell of smoke wafted up the stairs. On first glance, this might seem more like a frat house than the largest and most prestigious Mexican migrant organization in New York City, but indeed it is in this environment that a great deal of work gets done for undocumented immigrants.

It seemed obvious to me that if in an organization founded as a network of parish-based devotional groups by and for Mexican immigrants who in their majority are undocumented, without secondary education, and from poor and indigenous communities in Mexico, and most of the labor is being accomplished by middle and upper-class Mexican university students who enjoy student visas, that tensions and possibly resentment must inevitably surface. When I asked the interns about this, they tended to be surprised at the question, as though it had not crossed their minds. They usually responded that although they often received befuddled questions from Tepeyac clients about why anyone would work so hard for no money, they felt that the intensity of their labor and the fact that they had a small taste of the immigrant experience by having little cash and limited English skills helped bring them close to the organization's constituency. When I asked members of Tepeyac what they felt about the revolving door of ITESO interns, they were grateful that they were contributing so many labor hours, at no cost, to the organization, and often described a process by which the interns came to understand *la problemática* faced by their compatriots in New York and to be compassionate toward them. Trust, *confianza*, and rapport were established by individuals in personal interactions with Tepeyac's members and clientele. For example, after September 11, 2001, the interns who had only just arrived for their semester in the city found themselves suddenly thrust into a situation much larger than themselves. While two took the first plane back to Mexico, the half dozen who remained worked even longer days than is normally demanded of ITESO interns and were plunged into the confusing morass of advocacy for the unnamed and overlooked victims of the World Trade Center in a still emergent web of service providers.

One intern was assigned to accompany Josefa, a woman who was found wandering from hospital to hospital in lower Manhattan. Five months pregnant, she left her hamlet in la Mixteca, crossed the border with a *coyote*, a trafficker in human beings, and traveled to New York to search for her husband, who had not contacted her after the disaster. Lacking any proof that her husband had worked in the twin towers or even that he existed, she was ineligible for federal relief programs. Tepeyac took as sufficient proof the fact that Josefa had left her five elder children and undertaken such grave personal risk to search for him, and assigned an intern to assist her in identifying what assistance she was eligible for, securing prenatal care and a place to live, and deciding what to do next. While the cultural and class divide in the Mexican context between Josefa and the intern was vast, and simply being in the United States was not going to alter that, the fact that someone would be willing to spend their days in the frustrating task of searching for a man who had left no traces of his life or death brought Josefa and the ITESO intern into a close relationship which persists to the present.

The events of September 11 forever altered Asociación Tepeyac's role, mission, and reach (Gálvez 2009). While in the immediate aftermath of the tragic events of that day it did occur to many observers that there could be countless invisible victims of the tragedy, undocumented workers, who would not appear on payrolls and other official kinds of checklists by which people were slowly accounted for, it was Tepeyac that not only immediately noticed this possibility but began to coordinate relief efforts for this special sector of victims and their families, hailing from a dozen or more countries. All told, Tepeyac provided services for 113 missing people and 857 dislocated workers, most of whom were not eligible for any federal assistance. The first stage of the program involved visiting hospitals, compiling lists, speaking to consuls (not just Mexican) and relatives abroad to determine who was missing. Later phases involved counseling, financial support, and long-term efforts to aid displaced workers and survivors in compensating for the loss of a job or a provider, with language, literacy, and computer courses. One beneficiary was Josefa, who now has a road-side stand where she sells food and refreshments on the

Josefa's new home, near Atlixco, Puebla, Mexico, 2002

main highway transecting la Mixteca, enabling her to support her children in her husband's absence.

The aid of nearly three dozen foundations enabled Tepeyac to do this work, and at the same time transformed the organization. While previously the staff was a skeleton crew who accomplished things with volunteers and relied entirely upon participation by los comités guadalupanos, two dozen staff members were retained to sustain the day-to-day services offered by the Asociación, and the comités became more engaged in long-term planning, cultural and religious events, protests, and so on. As a result, Tepeyac began to offer a wide variety of services administered by professionals, including *Proyecto Chamba*, a labor advocacy program; English as a Second Language, Spanish literacy and computer classes; psychological counseling; urgent affairs, which involves such topics as advocacy with health care providers, assistance to bereaved families in repatriating the remains of a deceased loved one to Mexico (see Lahiri 2003), or aiding in the search for a missing person; and advice and grant-seeking support for small business owners.

The transformation from a collection of grassroots organizations that emerged with a faith-based human rights platform into a formal nonprofit organization and service provider caused not a few growing pains. The stark contrast between the ITESO volunteers and the constituency of Tepeyac was only magnified by the hiring of a small army of paid workers to carry out the day-to-day administration of services. The staff was composed of people who arrived by several routes. There are those who are Mexican nationals and trained professionals who offer their services to the organization; several of those in this category are former ITESO interns who completed their degree in Guadalajara and have returned to work in the United States indefinitely. There are also staff members who emerged from the comités and either came with the skills necessary to do their jobs, or worked their way up, first as volunteers, gaining training and experience, and came to occupy important paid positions in the organization. Rubén, Our Lady of the Rosary's choreographer, is an example of someone in this category, who was a beneficiary of the WTC relief program, then became one of the organization's most visible spokespeople, a coordinator of the torch run and the massive cultural events program. Very few members of the staff are U.S.-born or -raised children of Mexican immigrants. This can be expected to change as the second generation and a larger middle class emerge, enabling more young people to entertain the notion of careers in the nonprofit sector. Finally, there are a few members of the staff who are not Mexican, and often see their roles as activist and professional, rather than based on nationalism or guadalupanism.

Some members and clients of the organization complain that not only is it impossible to get Joel on the phone these days, but that when they go to the office they are likely to be tended to by someone who is not Mexican, perhaps even a *gringo*. While the hiring of Mexicans appears to be the ideal, the actual composition of the staff reflects the difficulty of finding Mexicans willing and able to fill all positions. Even the fact that three-quarters of the survivors served by the WTC program were not Mexican (although two-thirds of the dislocated workers served were Mexican) is alienating to some of the core membership who see Tepeyac as a Mexican organization.

The Asociación has devised several means to address this perceived disjuncture between the organization and its base. First, ITESO's unpaid interns are now "adopted" by and live with families of comités guadalupanos in each of the five boroughs. This enables the interns to gain a clearer understanding of the work and role of the comités, to become better acquainted with the city and its neighborhoods, and most importantly, to learn about the lives of their paisanos who are undocumented immigrants and develop closer bonds with them. Second is the formation of various *comisiones de trabajo*, work commissions, which are dedicated to specific tasks and projects, such as cultural events, labor advocacy, media, and so on. The comités are asked to provide representatives to serve on these commissions and ideally, the staff becomes the hired help serving to realize the projects envisioned and coordinated by the commissions. Third, each comité is being encouraged to file for its own 501(c)3 non-profit status under federal law, with which they will be able to seek grants and administer funds independently of Tepeyac and of the parishes that house them. Tepeyac seeks to serve as facilitator of this process, but envisions that each comité will have its own sovereignty as an organization. Each of these initiatives was very new when I completed my residency as a researcher at Tepeyac, and I am unable to comment on their results, but I found their implementation to be a creative response to the alienation experienced by some members of the comités from the organization they constitute.

Since the time of my core research, Asociación Tepeyac has begun to downsize again. Much of the funding that supported the organization's rapid expansion following September 11, 2001 could not be retained in the long term, and many of the staff have been laid off. The organization has had to focus more attention on services for "at-risk youth," a category for which the city funds intervention, while the organization's mission to serve undocumented immigrants has become practically unfundable. The organization's ability to continue to fulfill its original mission is in question. In a poignant example of such change, Rubén, whose salary could no longer be conjured up each month from funding sources, is now waiting tables in Lower Manhattan again.

In the following three chapters, we will focus upon particular activities engaged in by the comités guadalupanos and Asociación Tepeyac to examine how they engage participants and transform the way participants think of themselves, as members of a community, as rights holders, as human beings.

4

Our Lady of Guadalupe
The Image and Its Circulation

Why Guadalupe?

According to Guadalupan hagiography, in 1531, the Virgin of Guadalupe appeared to an Indian convert, Juan Diego, as he crossed the Cerro de Tepeyac, to attend to his ill uncle. She asked him to communicate to the authorities, especially Bishop Juan de Zumárraga, to build a shrine in her honor on that peak. Juan Diego demurred, saying he could not neglect his uncle, and that the ecclesiastical authorities would not pay attention to him, a lowly Indian. She insisted, using Nahuatl terms of affection, and he agreed he would make an attempt to communicate her message. He attempted to gain an audience with the bishop but was refused. This went on for three days, and finally, after asking for some sign to give the bishop as evidence, she filled his *tilma*, cloak, with roses. When he again went before the bishop and opened the tilma, spilling Castilian roses onto the floor, the Virgin's image was imprinted on the cloak, leaving no doubt as to the provenance of his message.[1] In this story, on the hill at Tepeyac, it has been said that Mexico was born.

In Asociación Tepeyac, which takes its name from that hill, the legend is recounted frequently and with quite explicit objectives. Estela Morales, staff person, told me, "The apparition of the Virgin appeared at a very crucial moment, when there was a lot of oppression for the indigenous people. Her apparition changed the indigenous people's status to the category of human being" (interview, November 12, 2000). She meant this quite literally, noting that the timing of the apparition can be read as a divine final word on the topic of indigenous people's humanity, ability to become Christian, and even the purity of their faith. It is also figurative. Joel Magallán explains that the image displayed in the Basilica of Guadalupe, which is said to be the original imprint of the Virgin's image, was

Statue of Our Lady of Guadalupe
for sale on Fourteenth Street,
photograph by Eileen O'Connor

not understood by the Spanish but contained codes comprehensible to
the indigenous people, who on the hill of Tepeyac had traditionally worshipped the Mexica mother goddess, Tonantzin (see also Burkhart 2001;
Castillo y Piña 1945; Elizondo 1981; Guerrero 1984; Rodríguez 1994). While
her queenliness was later crudely represented by a crown that someone
painted onto the fabric, Joel told me her noble status as daughter of a king
or god was self-evident in the rings she wears and the colors, green and
pink, of her robes. She is said to be an advocation of the Immaculate Conception of the Virgin Mary, bearing the baby Jesus in her womb, not holding him (like the Guadalupe statue associated with the devotion in Spain).
This, he said, was also obvious to the Nahuas, as she wears a black ribbon
around her waist, a pre-Columbian indication of a pregnant woman's need
for special consideration. The flowers so crucial to the apparition story
were also associated with Tonantzin and fertility in general,[2] and the offering of flowers continues to be one of the most common and important
of popular devotional practices associated with Guadalupe. The beams of

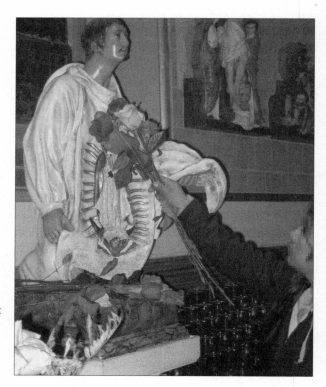

Woman holds
flowers as an
offering before Saint
Juan Diego in Saint
Bernard Parish,
2005, photograph
by Eileen O'Connor

light that radiate around her were, according to Joel, unmistakable signs that she is the mother of light and life, and the sliver of moon on which she stands (which could, for the Spanish, be read as a sign of the defeat of the crescent of Islam), signaled in Mesoamerica the constant struggle—and codependence—between the moon and the sun. In a moment when everything had been taken from the indigenous people—culture, religion, life, gods, language—she was a sign of hope that life would go on, explicitly conveyed in culturally specific syntax (interview, November 13, 2000; see also Elizondo 1981).

Marian and other miraculous apparitions have long been associated with times of political or social strife. Katz holds that the Virgin Mary

> is a cultural figure in that she enters the intricacies of a culture, becomes part of its web of meanings, limitations, structures, and possibilities. She contributes to making and sustaining culture, and reinventing it, at the

same time that she herself is made and sustained by culture, in dynamic exchanges with her devout. (2001: 8)

In Mexico, the Virgin of Guadalupe is the premier symbol of the nation (Castillo 1996; Johnson 1980; LaFaye 1993; Poole 1995; Wolf 1958). She is at the root of the first assertions of Mexican sovereignty, when Miguel Hidalgo, responsible for the *Grito de Dolores,* called for revolution against the Spanish in 1810, carrying her image on banners and shouting "¡Viva la Virgen y Muerte a los Gachupines! [Long live the Virgin and death to the Spaniards]"[3] (Castillo y Piña 1945: 104). In 1821, Agustín Iturbide declared himself Emperor of the Imperial Order of Guadalupe in front of her basilica at Tepeyac (Johnson 1980: 195). Likewise, Emiliano Zapata was a devout guadalupano, who carried her banner and ensured she was named *generalísima,* supreme general, of the revolutionary forces in 1911. Her shrine outside of Mexico City today receives between 12 and 20 million visitors per year. Her devotees have also transported their devotion with them along paths of migration.

Accounts as early as Bernal Díaz's *The Conquest of New Spain* refer to indigenous devotion to Our Lady of Guadalupe at a site called Tepeaquilla or Tepeyacac (1963: 363) and others mention indigenous belief in the miraculous powers of the water running near her shrine and the pre-Columbian worship on the site of an earth goddess called Tonantzín. Yet, it was not until 1648 that an account of the apparition was published, Miguel Sánchez's *Imágen de la Virgen María, Madre de Dios de Guadalupe,* and in 1649, Luis Lasso de la Vega's *Huei tlamahuicoltica* (commonly *Nican Mopohua)* (Sousa, Poole, and Lockhart 1998). While scholars may continue to struggle to prove or disprove the apparition story, the veracity of the apparition account is irrelevant to my purposes (and not only mine if the canonization of Juan Diego, the first indigenous saint, by Pope John Paul II in July 2002 in spite of any evidence that he ever lived is any indication, or for that matter Pope Pius XXII's declaration in 1946 of Guadalupe as Patroness of the Americas [see also John Paul II's *Ecclesia in America* 1999]). One of the Vatican's requirements for acknowledgment of the cult was demonstration of a continuous tradition of devotion dating to the original apparitions; "In the Catholic Church special care should be taken that we hold to what is believed everywhere, always, by everyone" (Vincent of Lérins, fifth century, cited in Poole 1995: 138). Florencia, author of *Polestar of America,* and lobbyist for the Virgin's cause in Rome, argued that tradition was its own motive of credibility: "It needs no more support than that of itself" (ibid.).[4] Indeed, if the depth and ubiquity of devotion to the Virgin of Guadalupe among Mexicans through to the present day is any measure (Anzaldúa 1987; Brading 2001; Castillo 1996; Paz 1985; Poole 1995; Wolf 1958), her cause indeed needs no more support than that of itself. Stevens-Arroyo and Díaz-Stevens go so far as to suggest that it is "precisely because the historical origins are less than convincing, a devotion as powerful as that of Our Lady of Guadalupe among the Mexican peoples is all the more religiously significant. The creativity of the religious imagination of the people has made something greater than a history without belief could have provided" (1998: 56). In this sense, the Virgin's power is not measured in the veracity of the claims surrounding her apparition but in the strength of her devotees' faith in her. As a Mexico City taxi driver reportedly said when told that an abbot's investigation had uncovered no historical evidence that Juan Diego had existed: "The Virgin of Guadalupe is the patron saint of all America; everyone believes in her, and it doesn't make any difference what the abbot may say; nothing will cause believers to lose their faith. I hope that God will forgive him, because the people won't" (quoted in Poole 2005: 5).

Nevertheless, while devotional tracts recount the apparition resulting in the conversion of 10,000 Indian souls (or as many as 8 million according to some accounts), for two centuries following Sánchez's work, devotion to Guadalupe was a *criollo* phenomenon, emerging at the precise moment when the new world-born sons of Peninsular Spaniards sought discourses of legitimacy and collective identity for their nascent campaign for independence from the colonial regime (Poole 1995: 2; see Alonso 2004; Klor De Alva 1995; Sommer 1991). Not until the mid-eighteenth century was the apparition of Guadalupe cast as particularly favoring the indigenous Mexicans, and she only became a symbol of indigenous resistance in the nineteenth and twentieth centuries.

Given that *La Guadalupana* was a moral referent for the conquest of the Americas, it is ironic that the Virgin of Guadalupe would come to be identified as protectoress of the weak, the poor, and the indigenous, and opposed to la Virgen de Los Remedios, patroness of the gachupines in the early Republican period (see Turner and Turner 1978). As Kurtz argues, in the Conquest, "symbols were mechanisms by which the contestants expressed power relationships" (1982: 203). In spite of this, the continued resonance of the Virgin of Guadalupe as a symbol is attributable to her role as arbiter of indigenous and other subaltern people's humanity. Or, as Elizondo writes of contemporary devotion, "in living communion with the *Virgencita*, the present is projected into the future" (1981: 71).

The fact that the apparition accounts date it to 1531, just a decade after the end of the violent conquest of New Spain by the Spanish, is a key point and is a powerful indication of a shift in the Iberian project away from domination by the sword to colonization and evangelization by the cross. Even though the millenarian motivations of the Spanish conquest of the "New World" were ever-present from its start, by 1531, these had been, perhaps, separated enough from the violence of initial contact to lend credence to more humanistic interpretations of the evangelical project.

In the early years of the conquest and colonization of the Americas, there was a great deal of debate regarding the category of person to which indigenous people rightly belonged. This was a debate with profound implications. If indigenous people were not human, meaning they did not have souls, the argument went, the Spanish could enslave, murder, and exploit them without moral qualms. On the other hand, if they had souls, the Christian invaders had the moral obligation to shepherd them into the Church and were limited in the ways in which they could exploit them. This debate was particularly fierce with respect to the *encomienda*, the organization of indigenous residence for maximal exploitation of labor. Complaints about the cruelty and inhumane treatment associated with this slavery-like institution emerged from Erasmian Christian-humanist circles and were especially well-articulated by Fray Antonio de Montesinos in the early sixteenth century, as well as Bartolomé de las Casas, "Protector of the Indians," who engaged in a series of debates with Juan Ginés de Sepúlveda on the topic (Ricard 1966). Related to these discussions was a debate as to whether Indians were apostates or infidels. If they were infidels, having never heard the word of God, the evangelical project was a feasible, well-guided effort to bring these innocents into the fold. Las Casas' argument held that indigenous people were innocents, with souls, inadvertently clearing the way for the heightened importation of African slaves, who were viewed as apostates. However, there were some who held that Saint Thomas the Apostle had preached in the New World,[5] and that thus the indigenous people were not innocents but apostates, having heard the word of God centuries before and rejected it, making them no better in the Iberian Christian moral order than Moors or Jews.

In addition to determining the morality of slavery and the encomienda, the eligibility of indigenous people to prosecution by the Inquisition, as well as the feasibility of evangelization projects, the debates about the category of person to which indigenous people were assigned would provide the subtext to the development of the cult of the Virgin of Guadalupe in New Spain and is relevant to the contemporary mobilizations of Mexican immigrants in the United States under the Guadalupan masthead.

In an interview in November 2000, Estela Morales, spokesperson for Asociación Tepeyac, explained to me that the Virgin of Guadalupe has always been where the poor are, on the side of those who struggle for rights and dignity, whether in the conquest period when indigenous people were persecuted in their own land and driven from their homes, in the War for Independence, when she was taken as a symbol by Miguel de Hidalgo in the Grito de Dolores, in the Revolution, or accompanying Mexican and Mexican American migrant farm workers in California, led by devout guadalupano César Chávez. It is only logical that she would follow her children further into *el norte*, to advocate for them as immigrants in New York City.

Indeed, according to some analysts, the association of Our Lady of Guadalupe with social justice is not a product of anything historic in the formation of her devotion in Mexico, but her strategic revindication by United States-based social movements such as the United Farm Workers mobilized by Chávez, and Chicano theologians of liberation. This alignment of Guadalupe by activists and theologians with the poor and oppressed is dated to the decades following the Second Vatican Council (1967) and its articulation of the church's preferential option for the poor (Badillo 2006; León 1997, 2005; Stevens-Arroyo and Díaz Stevens 1998). Through a feedback effect, some of the theological innovations of Guadalupan devotion among Mexicans in the United States have, according to this line of reasoning, influenced guadalupanismo in Mexico. Indeed, in Mexico, the truncation of public Catholicism after the Mexican Revolution, and the 1917 Constitution's official secularization of public life and termination of the Church's public role, "public Catholicism" according to Palacios' compelling argument, became a contradiction in terms (2007). Further, Mexico's deeply conservative theological orientation, which does not engage in the development of strategies to address the structural issues of social injustice (Palacios 2007: 19), contributes to a relative paucity of social justice–oriented pastoralism and theology. Indeed, some participants in my research said that in Mexico they associated Guadalupanism with "church ladies" (*las viejitas que van a misa*), not the progressive social activism with which they found it associated in many Catholic parishes in

New York City. In contrast, the U.S. Catholic Church since the late 1960s has been called by some "revolutionary," taking to heart Vatican II's preferential option for the poor and siding with immigrant and refugee movements (Gleason 1987). While I never found priests or lay members of New York churches or Tepeyac members referencing liberation theologians like Andrés Guerrero or Virgilio Elizondo,[6] there is no doubt that Chicano Liberation Theology has permeated much Catholic social justice work and Hispanic ministry in the United States, and to an increasing degree, Mexico.

Nonetheless, although the PRI officially separated the church and politics for much of the twentieth century, Guadalupan devotion in Mexico had already been sufficiently formed for the accretion of her power in all realms—including worldly realms of human structural relations—to continue unabated. In my research, I found that it was precisely the outsider status of the Virgin, her incorruptible status above the mean realm of politics, that enabled her to be seen by devotees as an advocate, too powerful to be co-opted or exploited by any party or politician. In "Hidalgo: History as Social Drama," Victor Turner makes the argument that religious symbols have always been associated with political action in Mexican history, referencing the "crusade aspects" of the nineteenth-century Independence movement, headed by secular cleric Hidalgo, in which "Castilians became Moors," in other words, the illegitimate invaders to be ousted by the legitimate heirs of the land (1974: 105). In Turner's classic formulation, the symbols that gain the greatest weight in social life are those that are already there: "when a major public dramatic process gets under way, people consciously, preconsciously, or unconsciously take on roles which carry with them, if not precisely recorded scripts, deeply engraved tendencies to act and speak in suprapersonal or 'representative ways'" (1974: 123; see Leach 1976). Likewise, Geertz famously wrote, "sacred symbols effect a mutual correspondence between a group's ethos and worldview . . . by serving as 'models of'" and 'models for' reality," or what he calls a process of "confrontation and mutual confirmation" (1973: 90–93). This is what Stevens-Arroyo and Díaz-Stevens, drawing on the work of María Jesus Buxó i Rey, call "the religious imagination," a dynamic process of bringing symbols to bear on the construction of religious meaning in new contexts, including linking experiences to "cognitive and emotional strategies for survival in a changing world" (1998: 55). Thus, even more than if she had been an accessible symbol, seized upon and batted about through the conflictive and authoritarian regime of the PRI, Our Lady of Guadalupe, by her official elimination from the political realm, accrued greater power and valence as a symbol above and beyond the political realm, becoming available to but not easily co-opted by social movements. In this book, we can follow the story of one way the social justice–oriented U.S. Catholic pastoralism and the Guadalupanism of Mexican migrants have come together in New York City parishes at the start of the twenty-first century.

Activities organized by Asociación Tepeyac are premised on the notion that Our Lady of Guadalupe is the advocate of her children, that she will follow, protect, and defend her children wherever they may find themselves. This is simple enough and perhaps not unlike any other saintly protector. However, there are two important discursive moves made in the articulation of this protection. First, in this Guadalupan drama, Mexican immigrants in the United States are cast in the role of Juan Diego. Not an average devotee, Juan Diego, like many recipients of miraculous apparitions, is a lowly neophyte, unschooled in Christian doctrine. When Guadalupe appears to him, speaking in his native language, she descends from her highest throne in heaven to the lowest stratum of humanity. Her willingness to do so provides further evidence of her holiness: while mortals are captive to their own hierarchies and prejudices, she is able to discern true faith in a rough package. What is more, she takes on his features—not only language, but her clothing and her dark skin color are taken as proof of her affinity for the poorest and most humble. In spite of her queenliness, she resembles the Indians. At the same time that her assumption of Juan Diego's traits proves her miraculousness, it also corroborates Juan Diego's humanity. For those who doubted that Indians and neophytes could be true Christians, true children of God, she provides a definitive answer. The doubters here are the authorities: Bishop Zumárraga, and by extension all of his peninsular brethren who need a miraculous sign—Castilian roses in January—to recognize the truth. For Asociación Tepeyac to cast contemporary Mexican immigrants in New York City in the role of Diego is to reconfirm their humanity. Second, it is to imply that the authorities—U.S. immigration authorities, lawmakers, and others—are doubters, people who have not yet seen the truth or need help in recognizing it.

When this theologically infused drama is overlaid on the contemporary secular terrain of immigration law and border enforcement, it quite effectively renders juridical notions of sovereignty petty and moot. When immigration laws and border enforcement dehumanize people who are the children of God, it is the law, lawmakers, and law enforcement who are acting in defiance of God's will, and a change to such entities is the only morally appropriate response. Rather than a co-optation of the Virgin's image to a political cause, the assertion of Guadalupe's support of the struggle for the rights of immigrants is logical, even overdetermined. To question or fail to recognize that she, naturally, supports the struggle of her devotees for rights and dignity would be to question her. Now, I turn my attention to the link between images and devotion before examining the circulation of Guadalupan images by Mexican immigrants in New York.

Images and Devotion

The Council of Trent, convened 1545–63, affirmed the presence of Christ in the bread and wine of the Eucharist in its thirteenth session. In decrees from its twenty-fifth session, the Council affirmed the practice of venerating saints but reined in the production and worship of images of saints, mandating that images only be displayed after a Bishop's approval and that the faithful should never forget that in praying before an image they were venerating the saint, not the image of him or her (see P. Brown 1981; García Ayluardo 1994; Webster 1998). These moves are, in a sense, contradictory: on the one hand affirming that mundane, worldly objects could be infused not only with the power of, but the very presence of Christ, while on the other hand asserting that other elements of faith, such as saints' images, were empty of the divine, and merely mnemonic aids for prayer, managed and corroborated by clergy. Given that the Council of Trent was the Catholic Church's response to the Protestant Reformation, the effort to assert the Church's uniqueness proactively while reining in the excesses so vociferously condemned by Martin Luther makes sense (Bossy 1970). However, these kinds of contradictions have never been resolved and have continued to mark distinctions between orthodoxy and religion as it is practiced to the present day. When images of Our Lady of Guadalupe and Saint Juan Diego were carried in 2002 from the Basilica over land to New York City in Asociación Tepeyac's Antorcha Guadalupana (see chapter 6), all along the journey, the faithful maneuvered their way to the images to kiss them and touch their fingers against them. The images, having come from the Basilica at Tepeyac, were not simply representative of the Virgin; they were, in very important ways, infused with her. The devotees' efforts to have some of Our Lady of Guadalupe's essence rub off on their lips or fingers are testament to the power of their faith. Goizueta writes, "This notion of reality . . . distinguishes Mexican-American popular Catholicism from post-Enlightenment views that establish a clear separation between a symbol, or sign, and what the symbol 'points to,' or signifies" (2002: 125). This statement could be viewed as overly essentialist in reference to the present and as an example of the kind of orientalism of colonial evangelizers that contributed to tremendous amounts of violence against natives viewed as overly "idolatry"-prone in the Americas. Nevertheless, there is an equally pronounced post-Enlightenment Eurocentrism to the assumption that a right balance between the sacred and the secular is a signal of civilization and modernity.

Emile Durkheim's predictions of disenchantment aside,[7] we must view the ability of Our Lady of Guadalupe not only to manifest herself tangibly in devotees' lives but to cross borders and accompany them into the United States as a profoundly significant fact. The sober belief that the Virgin is to be found wherever those who believe in her may be is not only a vestige of pre-Reformation popular Catholicism, it is a continuation of a five-centuries tradition, and an artifact of globalization. Another traveling virgin, worshipped among Bolivians of Quillacollo, bears the name Our Lady of Urqupiña, which means "she is already on the hill" in Quechua. Thus, when she travels, locally or transnationally, she arrives in advance of those who might be credited with having "brought" her there:

> Being in time and space, not as a worldly traveler or even a migrant, but through religious procession and multiplication, Mary, blessed by God's grace which she passes on to her fellow humans, leads the pilgrims home. She leads them to her home, where she receives them individually to hear their pleas and to grant them—miraculously, if somewhat predictably. (Reu 2008)

Likewise, other advocations of Mary have tremendous powers of self-replication to both be delivered by but also to precede the arrival of their devotees in new settings. When those new settings are to be found increasingly further afield due to transnational migration, we see a coming together of the forces of globalization with the forces of Marianism (Gálvez and Luque 2008; Hiraj 2008). Our Lady of Guadalupe's image then, as ubiquitous as it may be, is never without meaning and her meaning is not static, but rather dynamic: greater with a provenance traceable to the Basilica or a blessing from the bishop on the Virgin's feast day, lesser with mass produced candles, stickers, t-shirts, and *estampas* that have not been blessed or sanctified.

In the rest of this chapter, we will examine the tremendous power the image of Our Lady of Guadalupe has for the Mexican immigrants in New York City who are devoted to her, exceeding even the power she had in their lives prior to migration. We trace that power in the various ways in which Our Lady of Guadalupe is made present in devotees' lives, accompanies the transformations they experience, and is an ally in the particular struggles they face as immigrants. In addition to examining the way Guadalupe is said to accompany her faithful across the border, we look at the ways that she draws them to the comités guadalupanos and lends meaning to the group's activities. Then, we closely analyze the procession of her image in la misión guadalupana performed by comités guadalupanos and the ways that procession offers us a glimpse of what performed citizenship looks like.

Migration as a Conversion Experience

Our Lady of Guadalupe takes on new meanings and power in her travels at the same time that her devotees also are transformed on their journeys. Can migration—the literal experience of leaving one's home, crossing the border, and arriving to live and work in a new place—be likened to a conversion experience? How do religious practices and beliefs intersect with migration processes in the ways immigrants arrive to and make their lives in a new setting? In the migration process, immigrants' relationship to Guadalupe is transformed along with their identity. For many immigrants who are undocumented (the majority of Mexicans in New York City), the journey itself is a harrowing one.

Since the 1990s, the border has become increasingly militarized. No longer is the journey a sprint—a quick, surreptitious bolt over a fence or swim across the Rio Grande (Río Bravo)—but rather it is a marathon, testing immigrants' physical and emotional endurance. Forced by increased surveillance of the urban sections of the border to cross the Sonora Desert at the most dangerous and inhospitable stretches of the U.S.-Mexico border, immigrants rely on the expertise of *polleros* or *coyotes*, smugglers, to whom they or family members have paid as much as $4,000 to escort them *al otro lado,* to the other side. In 2006–07 alone, 437 immigrants died of exposure, dehydration, and violence in attempts to cross the border (M. León 2008). Women frequently experience sexual abuse during their journey, often at the hands of the very smugglers to whom their family members have entrusted their safe passage. Immigrants are routinely robbed, beaten, or experience extortion by coyotes and fall prey to petty thieves, drug traffickers, and corrupt law enforcement officers. During their journey, and even after crossing the border, they know they may be swept up by border patrol, or by one of the vigilante bands of Arizona ranchers, so-called Minutemen and others, who have taken immigration law into their own hands with roundups of immigrants using rifles, night vision technology, and even unmanned spy planes. Even those who make it often struggle with their decision, having left behind children, a spouse, or ailing parents and knowing that with immigration law as it is, any return visit will require another risky and costly border crossing in order to get back to the United States.

While the river crossing has a certain metaphorical grace, hearkening comparisons with baptism and rebirth consistent with theories of assimilation, the desert crossing is more effectively compared with the story of the Israelites' escape from Egypt in Exodus and its frequent themes of slavery, deception, and violence. Like them, many Mexican immigrants feel they face an impossible situation of hardship in their home communities and that the alternative, even while it involves personal risk and unknown dangers, is preferable and offers the hope that perhaps they will find freedom and establish a new home. Freedom is often described as the possibility to *superarse*, literally to overcome or better onself: be financially independent, contribute to the family, perhaps study, and, above all, ensure that one's children have better life chances. Aside from the "usual" difficulties faced by immigrants who must adjust to a new language, new cultures and ways of life, and face exploitation and discrimination in the workplace, housing, schools, and healthcare, immigrants who come on foot across the Mexican border literally brave death in order to arrive here. Even the deaths of hundreds of immigrants along the border each year, such as the tragic demise of 19 Mexican and Central American immigrants who suffocated in a tractor-trailer on a Texas highway in early May 2003, has not deterred the daily flow of people willing to risk their lives for an opportunity to make a living. While immigrants never go so far as to liken New York, or the United States in general, to a "promised land," they argue that here one's work is compensated with a living wage, jobs are available, their children's education is free, and they often comment that there is less corruption and structural inequality than in their home country.

Carolina came to a meeting of the comité guadalupano at Saint John Parish in early April 2003. She prayed fervently and audibly during the opening prayer. When asked to introduce herself, she told the story of her arrival the day before in New York. She had set out from her village in Guatemala over two weeks before, traveling the length of Mexico stowed in the hidden compartment of a car. Periodically, someone would check on her or hand her false Mexican identity documents which she used when she and the other immigrants being guided by the same smuggling network crossed into Mexico and were passed off to a new coyote. She crossed the U.S.-Mexico border still hidden in the vehicle's compartment. She said she prayed, during the two-week journey over land, to the Virgin of Guadalupe. When she told me her story again later, she paused below an image of *la Guadalupana* in Saint John Church to point to her and tell me emphatically, "Es a ella, a ella le rezaba y fue ella que me trajo hasta aquí" [It is to her, to her I prayed and she delivered me here safely].

To be Guadalupan *in Mexico* is, arguably, an unmarked religious identity. Guadalupanism is so central a part of Mexican Catholicism as to merit little mention in contemporary scholarship except when coupled with other, more remarkable circumstances (such as apparitions on microwave oven plates or subway tiles). However, the experience of migration, if analyzed as a rite of passage or conversion experience, qualitatively changes the relationship between the Virgin of Guadalupe and her faithful. Upon coming to the United States, Guadalupan devotion among Mexican immigrants can be intensified and even resignified, in two main ways. First, the very experience of migrating can be understood as a rite of passage and a conversion experience; second, for many Mexicans, devotion functions differently in their new environment than it did in their place of origin.

Border-Crossing as a Rite of Passage

For many Mexican immigrants, migration has come to constitute a rite of passage. In much of la Mixteca, it is understood that when a teenager finishes the equivalent of eighth grade, he or she will leave for el norte. This journey, in which youths are drawn into networks and traditions larger than themselves and asked to sacrifice their own comfort, safety, and home for the sake of the greater good—their family's well-being and perhaps the lure of adventure, dollars, and independence—and in exchange are granted bona fide adult status, is a classic rite of passage. In Turner's reading of Van Gennep's rites of passage, there are three phases:

separation, margin (limen), and *aggregation* (Turner 1969: 94). During the liminal period,

> the characteristics of the ritual subject (the 'passenger') are ambiguous, he passes through a cultural realm that has few or none of the attributes of the past or coming state . . . Liminal entities are neither here nor there; they are betwixt and between the positions assigned and arrayed by law, custom, convention and ceremonial. Thus liminality is frequently likened to death, to being in the womb, to invisibility, to darkness, to bisexuality, to the wilderness, to an eclipse of the sun or moon. Liminal entities . . . may be represented as possessing nothing. They may be disguised as monsters, wear only a strip of clothing, or even go naked to demonstrate that as liminal beings they have no status, property, insignia, secular clothing indicating rank or role. . . . It is as though they are being reduced or ground down to a uniform condition to be fashioned anew and endowed with additional powers to enable them to cope with their new station in life. (Turner 1969: 94)

De Genova critiques the use of the rite of passage model in describing migration for its teleological assumptions, arguing it fits too neatly within "hegemonic liberal nationalist mythologies of assimilation," charting the transformation of sojourner "migrants" into immigrant "settlers" (2005: 87). I sympathize with this critique, but find fault not with the metaphor of transformation but with the assumption that the transformation migrants undergo is in direct service to the assimilationist project, and that migrants cease to be what they were to become: "legitimate immigrants who can who can rightfully imagine themselves into the imagined community of the 'American' nation" (De Genova 2005: 88). To acknowledge that migrants undergo life-altering transformations is not to assume that this transformation makes them more palatable to the nation-state as citizens or that their transformation entails an erasure of what they were before. I would also argue that the rite of passage metaphor is especially applicable to religious identity in the sense that while migrants do not leave behind their religious selves, neither do they carry them across the border intact. As Orsi writes, "The identities of migrants and immigrants constructed and disclosed in religious ritual were not recapitulations of who they were in the places they left, however, or were never only this. Urban religions have offered occasions for new possibilities of selfhood to be crafted, discovered, assayed and represented" (1999: 56).

Indeed, border crossing is an experience that transforms its practitioners. While migrants are out of touch with their families, on their journey, "neither here nor there, betwixt and between" (Turner 1969: 94), they are transformed. In describing his border crossing, Roberto told me about how he arrived to Nogales, Mexico, in only a few hours on a public bus from his hometown in Querétaro state. He waited for nightfall in a cheap boarding house. There, at the appointed time, he met up with a coyote who escorted him and a dozen others to a lonely spot in the desert, pointed North, and told them that someone would be on the U.S. side to pick them up along the road near dawn, but that over the next several hours they had to go 10 or 12 miles on foot, and steer clear of the highway. Carrying nothing but the clothes on his back and a plastic jug of water, he set out and before long, it was as though he was all alone. The other people with him might as soon have kept him company as stolen the pair of hundred dollar bills he had hidden in his pants. "Possessing nothing," having "no status, property insignia or secular clothing indicating rank or role": Turner might have been describing Roberto and a thousand others like him who undertake the Sonoran crossing every day.

The decision to undertake the journey to the United States, which immigrants know could result in death, is a profound one, and as is to be expected, it is in such moments that we might expect to see faith, especially in figures of protection, either shattered or bolstered, but rarely stay the same. Just as the crystallization of Jewish cultural identity is rooted in the story of Exodus, for Mexican immigrants, the border crossing becomes the marker of a specific individual and collective identity. As a "theologizing experience," migration moves social actors not only to turn to their traditions for answers to existential questions, but to make their traditions answer for new problems and questions (T. Smith 1978).

María Santos told me a particularly harrowing tale of extortion and rape at the hands of the coyote her boyfriend Raúl (now her husband) had hired to deliver her from her home in Puebla state to the Bronx. Making the story even more poignant was the fact that the coyote was supposed to be *de confianza*, trustworthy, because he was Raúl's sister's boyfriend. She told me that her border-crossing experience made her look on the Virgin of Guadalupe as a personal defender. She told me that during her journey, the liminal period in which she was out of touch with her family and Raúl, she found herself locked by the coyote overnight in a seedy border town motel room with Raúl's sister. That night, a woman telephoned Raúl in the middle of the night, and without identifying herself reassured him,

"No te preocupes, ellas están bien" [Don't worry, they are fine]. To this day, no one can explain the mysterious telephone call, since only María had a telephone number for Raúl, and while María seemed slightly chagrined to relate such a metaphysical story, she was clearly reassured by the notion of someone looking out for her. It may seem cruelly ironic that the woman on the phone was reassuring Raúl at the same moment that María and his sister definitively were *not* fine, but in fact were in a tremendous amount of danger. Yet for María recounting the story a few years hence, the Virgin was not a protectoress in the sense that she prevented harm, but rather a source of solace that helped María make sense of the horrors she had faced and understand that she would make it through and survive.

These processes create cohorts: those who went through the same rite of passage at the same time are inextricably bound to one another, even if they never see each other again. These offer powerful alternatives to the alienating and disillusioning experience many of them have of learning that as "illegal" immigrants they are likely to be exploited and treated as less than human. Turner notes that having gone through the same rite of passage, "among themselves, neophytes tend to develop an intense comradeship and egalitarianism. Secular distinctions of rank and status disappear or are homogenized" (Turner 1969). This experience produces *communitas*, bonds that are "undifferentiated, egalitarian, direct, extant, non-rational, existential" (Turner and Turner 1978: 250). I would not go so far as to say that Mexican immigrants are able, through involvement in los comités guadalupanos, to forget the internal differences of class, legal status, gender, and ethnic difference which cause strife and conflict within their community. However, I would argue that the notion of communitas is useful for understanding the ways that guadalupanismo, in conjunction with Mexican national identity and assumed undocumented immigrant status, are turned into a vector of commonality enabling mobilization in the comités and the creation of communities. Those who migrate from different states in Mexico, who might never have crossed paths in their home country, recognize each other as paisanos in the United States. Those who have crossed may never speak about what they experienced, but share a bond with others who have shared the same journey. I have observed immigrants ask each other "¿Cruzaste en el desierto?" [Did you cross in the desert?]" or "¿Viniste de mojado?" [Did you come as a 'wetback'?] Affirmative answers are frequently greeted with a weighty nod of the head: no follow-up questions are required. Likewise, immigrants who did not cross the border in this way and sons and daughters of immigrants frequently report that stories of their family members' crossing are not readily shared with them, but kept secret, unspoken.

Guadalupanismo can link together Mexicans (and a few non-Mexicans) into religious communities of practice as well. In this way, national identity, migration status, and the experience of migration, as well as devotion to Guadalupe, reinforce one another and produce the conditions for the formation of immigrant communities among people who did not previously know one another or consider themselves to share much in common.

Members of los comités guadalupanos often recounted to me the process of becoming involved in a parish following their arrival, and the ways this caused them to reevaluate their opinions of the church and the role of religious practice in their lives. Religion itself as a mode of community formation is novel for many immigrants. In Mexico, where religious diversity historically has been minimal,[8] the church is neither the prime site for popular devotional practices nor for social and political activities. For the church in the United States to present itself as a site for devotion, social interaction, and political activism is astonishing for many immigrants.

Moreover, immigrants often come to see religious affiliation as an important adaptation for life in the United States. They learn that the church is one of the few accessible sites of social organization, even while so many other zones in the public sector remained closed to them. Many people say that in Mexico, they attended church for baptisms and weddings, but little more. They remark that clergy there tend to be aloof, disconnected, "no se sientan contigo a conversar" [They don't sit down with you to talk]. In fact, many of the rural municipalities in la Mixteca do not have a resident parish priest.[9] Religiosity tends to be home-based. In many parts of Mexico, wakes, celebrations of the Day of the Dead, and altars for prayer and offerings are part of intimate family life and occur in the home, or in the case of the Day of the Dead, in the area of the cemetery where the family's dead is buried (see Norget 2006). Several people told me, in reference to their religious identity in Mexico, that they felt more comfortable calling themselves *guadalupanos* than *católicos*, either because of negative experiences with the clergy and the church in Mexico, or a lack of meaningful interaction with them. Upon arriving in New York City, however, Mexican immigrants often learn quickly that guadalupanismo offers a means to connect with their conationals, incorporate themselves into established social organizations, and access a discourse of rights and personhood. I discuss this modality of mobilization in detail in later sections.

Because of the trauma of the migration experience as well as the shift in meaning by which the Virgin of Guadalupe goes from being everyone's patroness (in Mexico) to being a special advocate for a specific group (Mexicans in the United States), the meaning attributed to the Virgin and her relationship to her devoted is radically transformed, and transforming. The relationship to La Guadalupana becomes a personal one that is at the same time capable of generating a collective identity among others who have experienced a similar transformation (see Matovina 2005; Matovina and Riebe-Estrella 2002; Rodríguez 1994).[10]

I turn now to look closely at one particular way in which los comités guadalupanos reach out to new immigrants, and others who are not folded into los comités guadalupanos, at the same time that they trace the bounds of their nascent communities, through la misión guadalupana. La misión guadalupana is one of the original roles of many Guadalupan Committees. This refers to the practice of circulating an image of the Virgin of Guadalupe from home to home within the community.

La Misión in the Parishes

Alberto: Nosotros tenemos una misión guadalupana. Llevamos a la virgen con su mensaje. Cada ocho días, por todo el año.

Doña Lisette: Anda por aquí en Jerome Avenue. Ha estado yendo poca gente y ojalá que ahora asistan más.

Otro señor: Eso es lo que nos ha reunido a todos que estamos aquí—

Lisette: En la misión, no vamos bien. Son pocas personas, y esperamos a veces hasta las 9:00, y no llegan. Muy pocas personas, ni diez personas; no lo veo bien. Por nuestra madrecita, porque ella nos abrió el camino, todo lo que tenemos hoy es por ella. Y creo que el día que tengamos todo, nos vamos a olvidar de todo. Sin nosotros, ella no puede caminar.

Alberto: Es grande el bulto y tiene sus floreros, y se necesitan como ocho personas, para que no se quede sola.

Otro señor: No es mucho, a cambio de todo lo que nos está dando.

Don Omar: Una propuesta. Si formemos los grupos, pero ustedes, la mesa directiva tiene que hacerlo, uno de ustedes, cada vez.

Alberto: Ya eso estamos haciendo.

Don Omar: Como dirigentes tienen que llevar la información a la gente. De la propuesta de amnistía, de las cuentas bancarias, et cetera. Aunque la gente no venga aquí, que estén enterados.

Pónganme a mí, a ver quién va conmigo, quién me apoya? Don Roberto, me ayuda?

Roberto: ¿Cómo no?

Don Omar: Muy bien.

[Alberto (president of the comité guadalupano of Our Lady of the Rosary parish): Here we have a misión guadalupana. We carry the virgin with her message, every eight days, all year long.

Doña Lisette: She's around here, on Jerome Avenue. Not many people are coming [to la misión] and I hope people start to come more.

A man: That's what's brought us all together here . . .

Doña Lisette: The misión is not doing well. There are few people [who participate] and we wait sometimes until 9:00, and people don't arrive. Very few people, not even ten people, it's not working. For our little mother, because she opened the path for us, everything we have today is because of her. And I'm afraid the day we have it all, we're going to forget her completely. Without us, she can't walk.

Alberto: She has her stand, her vases, and her box, and she needs at least eight people, so that she is not alone.

Another man: That's not a lot, compared to all she does for us.

Don Omar [founder of the comité]: I have a proposal. What if we form groups, but you, the board have to do it, one of you has to participate each time . . .

Alberto: We're doing that.

Don Omar: As board members, you have to take the information to the people. The amnesty bill, the information about bank accounts, etc. Even if people don't come to the comité, they need to be informed.

Put me down. Let's see, who will come with me? Who supports me? Don Roberto, will you help me?

Don Roberto: Of course.

Don Omar: Very good.] (Comité Guadalupano, Our Lady of the Rosary Parish, September 8, 2003)

In this excerpt of dialogue, Doña Lisette reports on the relatively small number of people who have been coming out to carry the Virgin each

Saturday and remarks that it is not much to ask in exchange for all that she has given those gathered here. She appeals to the devotees' affection for *nuestra madrecita* [our little mother]. Don Omar follows by proposing a rationalization of the misión, asking the directiva to take turns leading the group in procession each week. He also demonstrates both his personal charisma and the techniques of leadership he gathered over years of involvement with Tepeyac and as one of the founders of the Comité Guadalupano of Our Lady of the Rosary Parish by following his remarks with a call to action: "Who will come with me? Who supports me?" He names one of the members of the group who he surely considers an ally, knowing he will not say "no," and expecting that when Don Roberto agrees to come on board, others will follow.

Don Omar also notes here the importance of the misión in defining Our Lady of the Rosary's community. "Community" is not an easy term to define or delimit; rather, the work of defining "us," for the purposes of mobilization or distribution of resources, is one of the key organizational tasks of the committees and it is accomplished largely in the misión. It is a space in which devotion to Our Lady of Guadalupe is articulated as an obligation and a gesture of gratitude, as well as an effective means of mobilizing and recruiting other Mexican immigrants.

I was privy to a discussion one late January night in 2003 in the Bronx that made this clear to me. The January meeting of the Guadalupan Committee at Our Lady of the Rosary Parish had hardly begun when a few members began to discuss the current location of the Virgin. I was only half-paying attention, waiting for what I still imagined to be the real work of the committee to start. But ethnography has a way of reminding us that what we expect to find and what is there and important for us to notice are often two very different things.

One man said, "el propósito del comité es traer a la gente por medio de la Virgen" [the purpose of the committee is for people to be brought in through the Virgin]. As the conversation continued, I noted the following comments:

> Doña Lissette said: La Virgen nos ha dado mucho y ahora que ya nos puso muchas cosas, vamos a dejar que ande sola? Siempre necesita de dos hombres por lo menos para levantar a la Virgen. [The Virgin has given us so much and now that she has given us many things, we're going to leave her to walk alone? She always needs at least two men to carry her.]

Someone else prefaced his comment with: Todo lo que tenemos es por nuestra madrecita. [Everything we have is because of our little mother].
Another person said: "Mucha gente ni sabe, ni se preocupa si la Virgen salió.
No, a la mejor hay que dejar la misión. [Many people don't even know,
don't bother to know whether the Virgin went out. No, maybe we'll have
to give up la misión.]

It was a frequent rhetorical practice in this group for members to deliver ultimatums: perhaps we should dissolve the committee, perhaps we
can't celebrate the Virgin's feast day, perhaps we should give up la misión,
as a means to inspire action and commitment on the part of the members. Further, the bonds among the comités members were always rhe-
torically reiterated by the use of "comadre" or "compadre" at the start of
any comment: "Comadrita, yo me refería a que la gente llega tarde, se dice
que a las 7:30, y después se sale a las 9:30, y ya a las 12:30 estamos recien
regresando" [My dear comadre, I was referring to the fact that people arrive late. We say 7:30 and then we don't go out until 9:30, and it's 12:30
a.m. by the time we're getting back].[11]

Apparently, sometime before Christmas, the Virgin went to the home
of one of the committee members who does not live nearby. It was not
clear at the time how far "far" is, but people's comments constructed this
man's home as being outside of what would be considered parish bounds
and the jurisdiction of the comité as it had thus far been imagined.

The issue of parish bounds is far from circumscribed. In early modern
Europe, urban parish bounds were the main and perhaps only relevant
definitions of community. Secular, government, and social lines were
imagined as either redundant or secondary to parish lines. In colonial
Latin America, parishes came to more explicitly signify social and ethnic lines, as well as space and population in more generic terms. Parishes
of Peninsular Spaniards, of "Indians," of free blacks, among others, were
seen as a means of promoting evangelization, containing and controlling
different population groups and constraining intermixture, and revolt of
subalterns (Abercrombie 1996, 1998).

In the United States, as discussed above, urban parishes were drawn
along convenient geographical lines until the mass immigration of Euro-
peans at the turn of the twentieth century led to the innovation of "national parishes." With their supplantation by Spanish-language masses,
no longer was cultural specificity to be celebrated as it had been with the

national parishes, but conflated. All Latin Americans were asked to worship a single Mary, not their local advocation of the Virgin, and with emphasis on universal Catholic feasts was meant to eliminate the particular, culturally specific celebrations parishioners might have preferred.

The arrival of Mexicans in New York City and their reception by the church can be interpreted to represent a reversal of these trends: an unofficial return to a national parish model. One testament of this is the consolidation of Our Lady of Guadalupe parish on Fourteenth Street with Saint Bernard Parish. Our Lady of Guadalupe was, in reality, a chapel, never intended as a full-service parish. But the persistent presence of Mexicans at mass each Sunday, even as the sanctuary's few pews could not accommodate them, led the diocese in 2003 to turn the much larger Saint Bernard Parish, two blocks to the west, into Our Lady of Guadalupe at Saint Bernard, and to make efforts to welcome Mexican worshippers as members of the parish (Wakin 2003). Badillo argues that Mexicans are presenting the case for a new model of pastoralism to Latino immigrants demonstrated by their impact on New York City's Catholic landscape (2006: 176). Even while the diocese and many priests emphasize a generic Marianism, because of the unevenness of Mexican residential settlement in the city and the informal ways that parishes friendly to them attract ever larger numbers of Mexican parishioners, in effect, a number of "Mexican parishes" have emerged around New York City. As described in the preceding chapter, the process usually begins when a few Mexican parishioners make a request to sing Las Mañanitas at dawn on December 12, or perhaps construct altars for the Day of the Dead. The response they receive to such requests can determine whether or not the parish will attract an influx of Mexican parishioners. Instead of going to the local parish that corresponds to their address, people I interviewed said they attend the parish they believe best fulfills their religious and social needs, which often means the parish with an established comité guadalupano, an image of Guadalupe within the church, perhaps a shrine outside at which flowers can be left at all hours, and a priest who is understanding of their needs. Thus, they challenge notions of locality and map a new kind of devotional community.

As such, that January night at Our Lady of the Rosary Parish, Guadalupan Committee members discussed whether the Virgin should continue on in the distant neighborhood in which she found herself and where several other families had requested she come for a visit, or return to what was considered her home neighborhood. Many of those involved in the discussion do not live within walking distance of the parish, choosing to worship here, perhaps, because of the vitality of the comité guadalupano, among other reasons. This fact is not incidental, but rather is central to the work accomplished by the performative resignification of space in the misión guadalupana.

One man said that the Virgin should come home and that she needed to be escorted by the appropriate quorum of people, especially men, who could carry her and her accoutrements in a manner befitting her status. Someone suggested that "we" are the only ones who can properly care for the Virgin, referring to those who regularly attend these meetings. Another man, the president of the committee, said the Virgin knows why she does what she does and a woman interjected that perhaps she wanted to continue on in that neighborhood because she had work to do there, to bring those families into the fold of the church and the committee. At issue in this discussion was who the relevant and operational "we" was, whether all Mexicans, all Guadalupanos, all parishioners of Our Lady of the Rosary Church, or only those members of the committee present at the meeting. The discussion also addressed whether it was the business of the Committee or the Virgin's wish to expand that "we" to include potential members of "us" whose only barrier to participation was not being already involved in the committee and living in a distant neighborhood. Eventually, the committee did allow the circulation of the Virgin to trace a new boundary that night, to draw the line around "us" a bit larger, allowing her to stay on for three more weeks among those people who had already requested she visit, before she would be brought "home."

In September 2003, the comité of Our Lady of the Rosary Church again discussed the misión and its purpose. While deciding how to organize teams with a sufficient quorum of men to take turns carrying the Virgin each week, members of the comité, including one of its founders and the regional *dirigente* for the North Bronx, Don Omar Fuentes, told the office holders that one of their number must always accompany the misión, because they were the ones best able to bring news and information to the families that hosted the Virgin. These families, Don Omar said, are isolated, they do not know their rights, they are not members of the comité or the Asociación, and the misión is the only way to inform them and recruit them.

At Saint John Parish, *visitas de la Virgen* were the start of the grupo guadalupano in the late 1980s, in which a small group of women carried a statue of the Virgin from home to home, praying the rosary, a misión guadalupana.[12] The families privileged to host the Virgin gave donations for the annual feast day celebration. This practice is one of the earliest and most enduring practices of many comités guadalupanos. As Saint John Parish developed its reputation of being welcoming of Mexicans and their religiosity, not only the December 12 festivities became bigger, but more paisanos began to attend mass. It was after this that Doña Rosario instituted the weekly meeting of the grupo guadalupano, at first dedicated only to prayer and spiritual formation.

The increase in migrant flows to the Bronx has aided Doña Rosario and her daughters' recruiting efforts; it seems there is always someone new to the parish and new to New York, at each meeting of the co-mité. One night in June 2003, two friends, Edson and Manuel, introduced their younger brother and wife, respectively, who had just the day before arrived to New York.[13] Their journey from Guatemala had taken 20 days. Edson and Manuel described how the two were going to seek work, but their first stop was to the comité guadalupano. They prayerfully gave thanks to the Virgin for their safe arrival, but also attended closely to the evening's discussion of social issues related to immigrants.

Along with Doña Rosario's visitas de la virgen, images of Our Lady of Guadalupe served as beacons to potential members of the church who hail from Mexico.

> Laura: Sí, respetan mucho a la Virgen los mexicanos, si ven a la Virgen, há-gase cuenta que ahí hacen un parón, a la Virgencita que pusieron ahí, pasa un mexicano y se persigna, se voltea, otra gente se pasa no'más derecho.
> Alyshia: Se puede ver quiénes son los mexicanos.
> Laura: Un mexicano pasa, la ve, se detiene, la ve, se persigna, pasan los niños chiquititos y le dicen a la mamá . . . . "allí está mamá Lupita."

> [Laura: Yes, Mexicans respect the Virgin a lot. You'll notice, that there, they stop, in front of the little Virgin they put there. If a Mexican goes by, he crosses himself and he turns, and other people just pass right by.
> Alyshia: You can tell who is Mexican.
> Laura: A Mexican goes by, he sees her, and he stops, he crosses himself. The little children pass, and they say to their mother . . . "there's Mama Lupita."][14]

The lintel near the image of Our Lady of Guadalupe at Saint John Parish

Roberto and his wife, Anjélica, told me they came to Our Lady of the Rosary Church because they passed by and saw an image of the Virgin of Guadalupe outside. Everyone who passed by, they said, crossed themselves, and they knew that there were fellow Mexicans in the neighborhood because they saw offerings of fresh flowers at her feet. Like a beacon, she called to them and let them know that here, they would be welcome, and here they would find others who knew them.

In the rectory of Saint John Church, in December 2002, Sisters Luz and Gertrudis[15] recruited an army of helpers to shellac, frame, and hang an immense image of the Virgin of Guadalupe they had imported from Mexico and were preparing to hang outside the church to replace the faded and weather-worn image that had been there for years. The nuns, who had been stationed at Saint John Parish for three years, said of the image of the Virgin of Guadalupe that was placed outside the parish in the late 1990s that she was a beacon, that with her there, even the amount of chewing gum discarded on that particular segment of the sidewalk decreased. Along the lintel of the door on that side of the church reads the text from the *Nican Mopohua*, the Nahuatl account of the apparition of the Virgin, published in 1649 by Luis Lasso de la Vega: "Yo soy tu madre/ estás bajo mi sombra/ que ya nada te apene/ ni te dé amarguras" [I am your mother/ you are in my grace/ may nothing trouble you/ nor fill you with bitterness] (Sousa, Poole and Lockhart 1998).

Thus, just as the image of the Virgin of Guadalupe serves as a beacon, attracting immigrants to those parishes where Mexicans have established a presence, the misión is the means by which comités guadalupanos recruit people to their cause. She reassures those people still isolated from the rest of the "community" that this group is composed of people of faith who are paisanos, and that they are neither seeking to proselytize nor to solicit. As such, not only is the misión the key means by which the comité establishes its territory, it is also the main way it recruits new members.

A common feature of narratives told by participants in these organizations is the reluctance they initially overcame upon joining the comité. If we assume that there is something routine or expected about the participation of Mexican Catholics in diasporic devotional organizations dedicated to Our Lady of Guadalupe, we miss the multiple efforts that were frequently made by the current members of these organizations to resist joining. The stories people told me about their process of deciding to participate in these organizations revolved around a few common themes. Some people said that they had never belonged to a church or lay organization, that in Mexico they viewed their religious practice as a private, domestic affair. While frequently this home-based religiosity was punctuated by enthusiastic participation in national fiestas like the Guadalupan Feast Day and Los Días de los Muertos, they deliberately participated in such activities on their own terms: sitting in the back of the church during mass, arriving late and leaving early, or avoiding the church altogether. Many people I interviewed told me they were not regular churchgoers in Mexico. Rather, they attended when there was a celebration: baptism, wedding, *quinceaños*, feast day, or Christmas Eve, or they visited the church to pray, leave flowers for the Virgin and perhaps make a private *promesa*, requesting the Virgin's intervention during an illness or other calamitous circumstance in exchange for some specified demonstration of faith. Some associated churches and lay organizations with fundamentalist fervor and social conservatism, unfeeling priests and judgmental parishioners. The bloody legacy of the Cristero War in some of the regions from which Mexicans in New York originate further taints lay devotional organizations with collective memories and fears of fanaticism. Others joined lay organizations in Mexico such as youth groups that ran in torch runs in the month preceding Guadalupe's feast day but viewed the church itself as their grandmothers' territory, not the place for young people. Thus, when invited to participate in a comité guadalupano in New York City, many people initially demurred, expecting to see *"unas viejitas que van a misa,"* old ladies who go to mass.

When I asked whether her participation in the church since she has been in New York is different from when she was in Mexico, Laura told me:

No sé, no me llamaba la atención, porque yo en México no estaba tan acercada a la iglesia. No, la verdad, no, pero no sé, como que empecé a venir y a venir y me empezó a gustar, y ahora no quiero ir a otra iglesia. No sé, aquí es muy importante que uno se involucre en la iglesia, porque aquí te enteras de muchas cosas de tu comunidad que encerrada en tu casa no te enteras.

[I don't know, it never really appealed to me. In Mexico, I wasn't that involved in the church. The truth is no, I started to come, and I began to like it, and now, I don't want to go to any other church. I don't know, here it seems very important that one become involved in the church, you learn a lot of things about your community that you wouldn't learn just being closed up in the house. (Interview, August 6, 2003)]

Similarly, María Santos said,

Bueno en México no, la verdad es que no participé, no así, como aquí que dan pláticas. . . . pero aquí es bonito, porque en la misa el Padre habla, no sé como que, allá como que el Padre sí está cerca de uno pero no tanto, y aquí el Padre, por ejemplo, habla bien, luego como que platica, va y viene, cuando da la misa, va y viene, anda platicando con la gente, hay mas voluntad con todos, nos hace estar más en confianza, es bonito.

[Well, in Mexico, no, the truth is I didn't participate, not like now. Here they give talks and it's very nice. In the mass, the Father talks and I don't know, there, it's as though the priest gets close to people, but not like here. Here the Father speaks well, as though he was just conversing, he goes up and down the aisles during the mass, up and down, and talks with the people. There's more good will with everyone, he makes us feel comfortable; it's really nice. (Interview, June 17, 2003)]

Others told me that while they may have been relatively active in church and religious organizations in Mexico, they came to the United States to work and that joining a church or participating in religious activities quite simply was not on their agenda. Many people told me that they work six days a week and that they needed their one day of rest to relax, do laundry, or spend time with their family, and for some, dedicating time on their day off to attending mass or a religious meeting or activity was simply not appealing.

The members of los comités guadalupanos frequently insist that their main purpose is to pay homage to their mother, Our Lady of Guadalupe, who has, they often repeat, done so much for them. The political activist work of the comités is folded into this purpose: a means of redeeming the Virgin's children from exploitation and oppression, always in her name. I never observed that the comités concealed the political content of their work; however, I frequently saw that the members of the comités struggled with what they perceived as the difficulty of recruiting new members on an explicitly activist platform. If joining a religious organization is negatively viewed by some recent migrants, political organizations can be the object of even greater stigma. Not only do many people view political organizations (especially parties and unions) in Mexico as corrupt and in some cases complicit with creating the social and economic conditions that led them to emigrate, but they often sense that in their new context, as undocumented immigrants, to be associated with organized labor or political parties is to invite trouble from their employers, or worse, attract the attention of law enforcement authorities. Recent migrants in particular prefer to *evitar broncas*, stay out of trouble, and avoid unwanted attention. For this reason, comité leaders frequently remarked that if they simply knocked on people's doors and began talking about amnesty, they would have little luck. In an interview, Alberto, the president of the comité, told me that with the image of the Virgin, the group's members can go door to door, taking information and inviting people to participate; that she is the only way that people will open the door and hear them out. In this way, the misión, while one of the least spectacular activities of the comités guadalupanos, is justifiably referred to by some members of these groups as their most important.

Mapping Faith and Claiming Rights

Let me tell you, when it's cold and dark and we have a long way to go, all I want to do is put the Virgin in the back of my Durango and drive her to the next house, but you can't do that. No one wants you to do that. You have to walk her there. And sometimes funny things happen. One time we were in a neighborhood far from here, and we ran into another misión. They were coming this way, and we were going that way, they had their Virgin on her pedestal, and we had ours, and it was like *"Pasen Ustedes," "No, no, pasen Ustedes primero," "No, insisto, Ustedes"* And that's how we went around each other.

(Interview with Rubén, November 2002)[16]

Michel de Certeau wrote that walking is an enunciation—that with their footsteps, pedestrians overlay the objectivist and arbitrary maps of architects and city planners with poetry, with their own meanings: "the walker transforms each spatial signifier into something else" (de Certeau 1984: 98). In this way, not only does a *"migrational,* a metaphorical city" slip into "the clear text of the planned and readable city," but these practices can constitute resistance to a hegemonically imposed order: "walking affirms, suspects, tries out, transgresses, respects, etc., the trajectories that it 'speaks'" (99). It can only be assumed that if an individual can enunciate new meanings, resignifying the arbitrary places and their uses rationally imposed on the landscape, that collective circulation through space represents an even more powerful resignification with broader-reaching and more lasting ramifications. Orsi describes this with reference to what he calls "urban religious topographies": "city people have appropriated public spaces for themselves and transformed them into venues for shaping, displaying and celebrating their inherited and emergent ways of life and understandings of the world. They have remapped the city, superimposing their own coordinates of meaning on official cartographies" (1999: 47).

The particularly strong political and meaning-making potential of procession is described eloquently by Pnina Werbner in her discussion of Muslim Pakistani immigrants and their processions in Great Britain (Werbner 1996). She writes that "the *conquest* of space, its inscription with a new moral and cultural surface [is] an act of human empowerment" (309). Similar to de Certeau's discussion of walking as an enunciation, she writes, "this marching . . . must be grasped as a performative act, an act of *metonymic* empowerment which inscribes and reinscribes space with sanctity" (emphasis in original, 311). The empowerment Werbner refers to is cast in the terms of cultural citizenship, "the moral right of communities to be 'in' this new environment" (311), and echoes the staged acquisition of rights through "a broad range of activities of everyday life" posited by Flores and Benmayor in their work *Latino Cultural Citizenship*, "through which Latinos and other groups claim space in society and *eventually* claim rights" (emphasis added, 1997: 15). Indeed, Werbner casts the religious processions of British Muslims as a preliminary assertion, which, in time, may *evolve* into what Werbner posits as real resistance to their subordinate and disenfranchised status: "once people have marched openly in a place, they have crossed an ontological barrier . . . Once they have organized a peaceful procession, they know they are capable of organizing a peaceful protest. Such processions can thus be seen as precursors to more overt (democratic) political protest" (332).

Certainly, procession is "an act of *metonymic* empowerment, which inscribes and reinscribes space with sanctity" (Werbner 1996: 311). However, I contest the way Werbner characterizes the assertion of rights as a graduated evolution from devotion into politics. While la misión guadalupana is not understood to be a protest and is profoundly local, tracing participants' notion of their home community step by laborious step, it is a *political* practice which both intends and accomplishes a resignification of space and of the actors who participate in it. Similarly, the placement of an image of Our Lady of Guadalupe in the church's public space is a metonymic claim over territory with political implications (see Gonzalez 1997). The same is true of the *Viacrucis* described in chapter 5, which is more overtly political and translocal, and the torch run discussed in chapter 6, which is transnational and openly contests U.S. immigration laws. Politics, in its most basic sense, is the process through which services and benefits (including space) are allocated among competing sectors of society (W. Lloyd Warner [1941] quoted in Padilla 1985: 64). But of course services and benefits are distributed according to socially constructed categories of merit and status. As such, as Wood succinctly states it: "politics is profoundly a cultural enterprise . . . [it is] about creating meanings" (2002: 153). When the very presence of undocumented immigrants in the United States is "illegal," it is arguable that none of their actions are simply protopolitical. Further, the metonymic cannot be seen as a proxy for the prepolitical, but is rather deeply political. When we zero in on those actions in which immigrants participate self-consciously and publicly as a community of faith and of immigrants with a very concrete goal: the acquisition of greater rights and dignity *as* immigrants, we cannot see this as anything less than politics. Daniel Ramírez eloquently wrote, "politics is the art of the possible" (2007: 186). While utopian, this is exactly the kind of politics engaged in by participants in the misión guadalupana. Although they are not making strategic or empowered claims over space, nor are they able to assert their rights in the official sphere of civil society, these guadalupanos are nonetheless imagining themselves into being as citizens. As symbolic as this is, it is nevertheless profoundly real.

Unfortunately, much writing on social organizations and civic activism privileges the exercise and acquisition of democratic skills in the formal political realm. Access to such realms and such skills, in our unequal society, is distributed "predominantly to those better off . . . with negative implications for democratic voice and equality" (Wood 2002: 130). In this model, truly participatory and egalitarian democracy requires that all citizens be on equal footing to express their needs and opinions, make claims, and engage the state and fellow citizens. As such, involvement in the workplace, voluntary organizations, and religious congregations are cast as "pre-political settings" in which citizens may—or may not—acquire the skills necessary for participatory democracy. Building on this, networks of faith-based community organizations like PICO see religious congregations as a prime site for "teaching democratic skills equally," building on a font of already shared meanings and discourses of fellowship (Wood 2002: 130). Palacios describes Oakland's Saint Anthony Parish in which Mexican immigrants "learned the civic process by doing the civic process . . . They learned to be citizens together: seeing each other as peers and becoming involved with each other's opinions, values and commitments" (2007: 112). As inspiring as this is, there is an implicit dichotomization here between participants in their roles as religious actors and as citizens. While the dispositions required of a person who is deeply involved in a congregation are seen to facilitate the development of democratic skills acquisition, such dispositions are still viewed as prepolitical or protopolitical. In these settings, immigrants rehearse for the day when they can make their voices heard in more impactful ways. In this way, we are continuing to allow the nation-state to be the final arbiter of belonging: investing citizenship with all of the privileges, *and option of exclusion*, that serve the project of securing the borders and capping the number of beneficiaries of the state's largesse. As citizenship has become more stringently defined bureaucratically, this kind of social analysis fuels its definition in the symbolic realm as well, as a hyper-privileged sphere of participation only by some: whether defined as those holding legitimate, juridical membership in the citizenry, or those sufficiently schooled in democratic skills. Instead, and I will elaborate on this further in the remaining chapters of this book, I view the mapping of sacred space by comités guadalupanos as a political act with implications for definitions of citizenship in the here and now, not simply a rehearsal for a future enfranchised condition.

When members of Our Lady of the Rosary's comité guadalupano travel through the streets of the Bronx, to the home of someone who has been hosting the Virgin of Guadalupe for the past week, to escort the sacred image to the home of the next host family, their steps trace a pathway that derives meaning from their passage. Space—a Mexican and Gua-dalupan space—is, to use de Certeau's words, "actuated by the ensemble of movements deployed within it" (1984: 117). If, as Ana Alonso argues, "hegemonic strategies . . . concretiz[e] the imagined community of the nation by articulating spatial, bodily and temporal matrixes through the everyday routines, rituals and policies of the state system" (1994: 382), it is only fitting that an effective way for subaltern actors to contest these hegemonic strategies is through everyday rituals and routines. Alonso calls for increased anthropological attention to "how the organization and representation of space is implicated in ethnic formation and inequality, in state strategies of asymmetric incorporation and appropriation." She asks, "How do spatial practices become a focus of intense social strug-gles?" (1994: 394). In this project, my task is similar to De Genova's, who draws on Henri Lefebvre in his emphasis on the "production of Mexican Chicago as a conjunctural space with transformative repercussions in all directions" (2005: 99; also see Peña 2008); or as Davalos puts it, refer-ring to Chicago's Pilsen District Via Crucis, "While participants' physical bodies engage and experience domination, the Via Crucis has become a practice through which struggle is performed" (2002: 42). The power of people living, working, and engaging in symbolic activities in space that is purportedly off-limits to immigrants is significant. Referring to the same Via Crucis, Goizueta writes:

> Through these practices, then, Mexican Americans stake out a place for their religious faith in the public arena, thereby breaching another barrier established by the dominant culture. In the process, the religious values expressed subvert—at least for a time—the economic, productive, utili-tarian values associated with the public arena (for example, traffic stops,

businesses close). . . . Such processions thus transform public space, claiming it as cultural space within the larger dominant culture. (2002: 128)

Thus, the transformation of spaces and of participants is mutually constitutive, and always in a lopsided dialogue with the nation-state and its laws, which would deny them not only such a proprietary relationship to space, but also their own personal transformation into citizens. A problem here, however, is that processions are contingent and contextual. De Certeau effectively describes this quandary in reference to walking:

> Surveys of routes miss what *was*: the act itself of passing by. The operation of walking . . . allows us to grasp only a relic set in the nowhen of a surface projection. Itself visible, it has the effect of making invisible the operation that made it possible. These fixations constitute procedures for forgetting. The trace left behind is substituted for the practice. It exhibits the (voracious) property that the geographical system has of being able to transform action into legibility but in doing so it causes a way of being in the world to be forgotten. (1984: 97)

Implicit here is a theory of power. Public rituals serve to remember the originary events of the nation (Connerton 1989; Durkheim 1947 [1915]; Halbwachs 1992). For example, if we look at Corpus Christi, a universal feast eagerly promoted by Spanish clerical and administrative representatives in the colonies as an evangelical tool and a didactic one, it signified the triumphalist assertion not only of the Eucharist, the host transformed by transubstantiation (Rubin 1991), but also of its bearers, the European Christians. In 1651 in Mexico City, there was a terrible quarrel between the clerics and the viceroy about who should occupy the prime position just behind the monstrance bearing the host in the annual Corpus Christi procession. This is significant because the Crown favored its own viceregal administrators, reconfirming for anyone who might have forgotten, the colonial hierarchies the procession was meant to illustrate (Curcio Nagy 1994: 10; see Motolinía 1950). Further, the route of the procession itself was imagined, in Mexico City, as in Cuzco, Lima, and in many centers of colonial Latin America, to trace the bounds of civility, mapping as well as melding bureaucratic and ecclesiastical understandings of the city's territory, the specifically sacred space surrounding the Cathedral and the space sacralized by movement, the plazas and streets down which the host was carried (Abercrombie 1996; Dean 1999; Fernández Hervás 1992;

Sánchez Herrero 1974). As much as these impositions and retracings and their intents were clear in the minds of all of those present from the first moment a Castilian honed cornerstone was laid on top of the wall of an existing temple (Fraser 1990), procession, as a performance in space and time, has a unique power to enunciate meanings indelibly in the minds of participants and observers: "the single most important experiential feature of the genre . . . is its spatiotemporal dependence"; through the "activation" of the processional enactment, members of the audience experience its meanings "kinesthetically and mimetically as an integral part of their own transient reality" (Webster 1998: 59; see also Brown 1998; Eade and Sallnow 1991; García Ayluardo 1994).

Yet, the processional routes of a group of largely disenfranchised undocumented immigrants, whether local or transnational, are quite likely forgotten by all but the direct participants in them. While their reiteration, every week or every year, helps to more memorably trace them in space, it is arguable that they become invisible as quickly as they are performatively made visible. Nevertheless, the tracing of the paths serves to indelibly map the community, in this case the Mexican immigrant community—*los indocumentados* and *los guadalupanos*—in the minds of its members, linking them to each other in the hyperlocal space of the neighborhood as much as in the transnational space of their migration. Cumulatively these performances lend themselves to the production of an empowered immigrant community and a redefinition of citizenship, as I will continue to argue in the following chapters.

5

El Viacrucis del Inmigrante
and Other Public Processions

The Way of the Cross: Mexicanizando New York

Segunda Estación.
Jesús carga una cruz que no merece y sufre lo que no debía sufrir. No-sotros no merecemos emigrar, dejar nuestra tierra y nuestra gente, sin embargo, tenemos que trabajar para sostenernos y sostener a nuestra familia, por falta de posibilidades en nuestra propia tierra.

Second Station.
Jesus carries a cross he does not deserve and suffers what he need not suffer. We do not deserve to emigrate, to leave our land and our people, nonetheless, we have to work to support ourselves and support our family, for lack of possibilities in our own land.[1]

Each year on Good Friday, many Catholics around the world participate in a Viacrucis, an enactment of Christ's journey to Crucifixion. The above quotes are from *El Viacrucis del Inmigrante,* the Way of the Cross of the Immigrant, organized annually by Asociación Tepeyac.[2] In this procession, the traditional script describing Jesus Christ's path is overlaid with a new script, comparing his travails at each of the stations of the cross to the humiliations and injustices suffered by immigrants. While this innovation on an old practice might seem a key site for examining contemporary religious identities among Mexican immigrants in New York compared to traditional, parish-based processions, in fact it is through participation in multiple Viacrucis that many Mexican immigrants enact and negotiate their multiple religious affiliations and identifications, all based on faith but vastly different from one another.

Viacrucis del Inmigrante, Broadway, lower Manhattan, 2003

During Holy Week in 2003, I attended four distinct Viacrucis processions: one a week before Good Friday inside Saint John Parish linked with a teach-in about Chiapas; a second in the streets surrounding Our Lady of the Rosary Parish and organized by the parish's Legion of Mary; the third in the streets surrounding Saint John Parish; and finally, El Viacrucis del Inmigrante organized in lower Manhattan by Asociación Tepeyac. While attending the Viacrucis at two different local parishes might be considered redundant or evidence of divided loyalties, it is not uncommon for members of los comités guadalupanos to attend multiple processions during Holy Week. As a researcher, attending multiple processions allowed me to examine the ways that participants' affiliations overlap and are not only parish-based, but also encompass citywide networks of Mexican immigrants.

While performances of the Stations of the Cross are now so common as to be thought of as timeless and universal by some Catholics, they did not become common in Catholic parishes until the late seventeenth century. "Timelessness" is attributed to the practice by linking its origins to Mary, who is said to have daily visited the sites in Jerusalem associated with her son's suffering. Pilgrimages by worshippers to the sites on the path to Mount Calvary have been dated to a few centuries after Christ. In the Iberian world, they date to the fifteenth century, when *Cofradías de la Pasión* organized around the crucified Christ began to appear, and in Córdoba, the West's first Via Crucis was reputedly created by a pilgrim returned from Palestine (Mitchell 1990: 42). Artistic renderings of the stations are

Flyer for *El Viacrucis del Inmigrante*, April 9, 2004

usually composed of 14 sculptural tableaux or paintings depicting the Passion of Christ and are a common feature in churches. The Stations of the Cross may be performed inside a church, with participants circumambulating the nave and using the tableaux as mnemonic devices to meditate on Christ's suffering at each of the stops. The images of the Stations of the Cross which surround the interior walls of Saint John's Parish in the South Bronx date to the 1870s and are considered notable for their craftsmanship, carved by Bavarian artisans when the church was constructed, and recently restored. While pilgrimages may occur throughout the year, processions of the Passion of Christ in Holy Week are frequently imbued with the greatest significance. The number and description of the stations became fairly conventional in Europe in the sixteenth century due to efforts by devotional writers to assert orthodoxy in this popular rite, but there has never been a specific set of prayers associated with the stations. Instead, the ways that laypeople and clergy decide to meditate on each of the stations as well as the prayers they choose to utter are variably laid over the basic outline of the stations:

1. Christ condemned to death;
2. The cross is laid upon him;
3. His first fall;
4. He meets his Mother;
5. Simon of Cyrene is made to bear the cross;
6. Christ's face is wiped by Veronica;
7. His second fall;
8. He meets the women of Jerusalem;
9. His third fall;
10. He is stripped of his garments;
11. His crucifixion;
12. His death on the cross;
13. His body is taken down from the cross; and
14. Laid in the tomb. (New Advent Catholic Encyclopedia 2007)

While many Catholic parishes use one of a number of fairly similar texts associated with the Way of the Cross, and there are certainly a number of generic renditions of the procession, it is not unusual that clergy, lay groups, and artists innovate entirely new scripts. In fact, this is a highly valued effort; given that the purpose of the pilgrimage is for the devoted to appreciate the sacrifice that Christ made and the suffering he endured, new strategies for provoking ever more fervent compassion are warmly received. Like most areas of church-based ritual, it is in the areas of devotion that are not strictly regimented and orthodox that a pastor or congregation's political and social inclinations can be expressed. For example, media reports indicated that after the release of Mel Gibson's controversial film, *The Passion of the Christ*, many Catholics expressed interest in bloodier, more dramatic, and more "traditional" representations of the Passion. This heightened orthodoxy was viewed by some as a rejection of more "feel good" representations Christ's life, which some have characterized as a result, in part, of the interaction between Protestants and Catholics in twentieth-century United States. Alternatively, some clergy and parishes have long viewed the Way of the Cross as an opportunity to make Christ's life and suffering more comprehensible and applicable to the trials faced by his faithful today and to draw parallels between the circumstances of his death and the forces of violence and persecution which exist in contemporary life.

While 2003 was neither the first nor the last year that I attended multiple Viacrucis performances, I will closely analyze the processions I witnessed from that year for what is revealed not only by the variation in the scripts read, but the very different ways in which faith, community, and belonging were performed and negotiated in each. The ways participation is negotiated between these different events illustrate many of the ties as well as the tensions between and among the members of the comités, the larger association, as well as the comités' parishes. The ways that participants in the comités organize their participation and the negotiations that occur to mitigate the conflicts of scheduling and participation in each of these events reveals much about the alliances and the fissures that crosscut locality as well as group identity. In these conflicts, Mexican parishioners are sometimes asked to choose where their loyalties lie: with the multiethnic parish of which they are members, or with the larger Mexican community asserted by Asociación Tepeyac. I will describe several competing processions and the ways that some of the members of Our Lady of the Rosary and Saint John parishes negotiated their participation in them. Finally, I will examine El Viacrucis del Inmigrante, a procession with an explicitly activist character. Unlike the parish-based Viacrucis which seek to link multiethnic parishes into a single, locally defined community, El Viacrucis del Inmigrante involves Mexican immigrants in a procession targeted at insiders. The question raised by the Viacrucis del Inmigrante is not whether it succeeds in recruiting outsiders (non-Catholics, non-

Mexicans, non-immigrants) to the cause or in fulfilling the tenets of civil religion, which are discussed below, but whether it succeeds in making its members feel that they belong to a collective and whether within that collective lies the potential for cultural and religious expression as well as greater rights acquisition.

Viacrucis at Saint John Parish, April 9, 2003

I arrived at Saint John Parish in the evening for a performance of the Viacrucis. In the nine days preceding the most holy celebrations of the parish's calendar (Good Friday, Christmas, the Feast Day of Our Lady of Guadalupe), parishioners often gather in the evenings to pray a novena, a series of nightly recitations of the Rosary. For Holy Week, the prayers are accompanied by a procession inside the church around the Stations of the Cross, with descriptions of the Stations interspersed with recitations of the Ave Maria. The pastor only sometimes accompanies these events, and frequently the church's several lay groups (Legion of Mary, El Grupo Guadalupano, El Cursillo, among others) take turns organizing them. On this night, I was told that two performance artists, *Las Hermanas* Colorado, Mexican-born and Chicago-raised sisters Elvira and Hortencia Colorado of Coatlicue Theater Company, would be filming the Way of the Cross. They said that the footage from that night would be shown to a collective in Chiapas in an effort to create greater solidarity among dispersed Mexican peoples. Perhaps because it was being filmed, the leaders of the comité guadalupano decided to use a different script than had been used at the previous night's Viacrucis. Instead of a generic rendering of the stations, this script had been written several years earlier for use in a large outdoor Way of the Cross organized by South Bronx Churches, an alliance of neighborhood congregations put together by the Industrial Areas Foundation (IAF). The text made connections between the suffering of Christ and the problems that existed in the neighborhood. While many of the problems highlighted had not ceased to plague the neighborhood, the document is an artifact of a particular moment in the late 1980s and early 1990s, when the South Bronx was reeling from the crack and AIDS epidemics and still ravaged by the aftermath of the fires of the 1970s. Each of the Stations of the Cross focused on a particular social ill, including drug abuse, abortion, racism, and poverty. For example, the first station makes a connection between Christ being sentenced to death and abortion, and the second compares

Christ carrying the cross to the failure of landlords to provide services, "se nos niega la calefacción y otros servicios esenciales en los hogares" [we are denied heat and other essential services in our homes]. The third station, in which Christ falls for the first time, is linked to "el crimen y la violencia en la comunidad" [crime and violence in the community]. Each station included a statement to be read by the "leader" and a scriptural reading, and in the third station, Habbakuk's lament was read:

> How long, O Lord, must I call for help,
>> but you do not listen?
>> Or cry out to you, "Violence!"
>> but you do not save?
> Why do you make me look at injustice?
>> Why do you tolerate wrong?
>> Destruction and violence are before me;
>> there is strife, and conflict abounds.
> Therefore the law is paralyzed,
>> and justice never prevails.
>> The wicked hem in the righteous,
>> so that justice is perverted. (Habbakuk 1: 2–4)

The fourth station addressed division in families; the fifth, oppression of workers and unemployment ("Do not take advantage of a hired man who is poor and needy" Deut. 24: 14–15); the sixth, racism, prejudice, and discrimination while Veronica washes the face of Jesus; the seventh addressed child abuse; and the eighth, exploitation of women. The ninth station, when Jesus falls a third time, focused on drug and alcohol abuse, with the leader's script read as follows: "Hoy día el Cuerpo de Cristo sufre la aflicción del abuso de drogas y del alcoholismo. Jesús cae de nuevo cuando miembros de nuestras comunidades abusan de las drogas y del alcohol" [Today, the body of Christ is suffering from the affliction of drug abuse and alcoholism. Jesus falls again when members of our communities abuse drugs and alcohol]. In the tenth station, Jesus is stripped of his clothing, and the text referred to service cuts by the government: "Nuestras comunidades experimentan cada vez más los cortes injustos de los gastos del gobierno" [our communities experience increasing and unjust cuts in government spending]. This station was accompanied by the brutal "Rebuke of leaders and prophets":

> Listen, you leaders of Jacob,
>   you rulers of the house of Israel.
>   Should you not know justice,
> You who hate good and love evil;
>   who tear the skin from my people
>   and the flesh from their bones;
> Who eat my people's flesh,
>   strip off their skin
>   and break their bones in pieces;
>   who chop them up like meat for the pan,
>   like flesh for the pot? (Micah 3: 1–4)

The eleventh through fifteenth stations[3] referred to the arms race, poverty and hunger, disrespect to elders, homelessness, and finally, the struggle for dignity and justice was linked with the resurrection of Jesus: "Jesús no sólo sufre y muere en su pueblo hoy. También resucita en ellos. Resucita dondequiera que sigamos su ejemplo de morir cada día en servicio humilde y fiel" [Jesus doesn't just suffer and die in his people today. He also is resuscitated in them. He is resurrected wherever we follow his example of dying each day in his humble and faithful service].

While outdoor Viacrucis are highly dramatized and symbolic, indoor ones are often meditative and quiet, the hymns and recitation of the Ave María providing moving counterpoint to the quiet shuffling from station to station by a closely gathered group. If many public Viacrucis illustrate in dramatic tableaux vivant the Passion of Christ, church-based ones invite silent contemplation of Christ's fate through greater emphasis on the text and the still images carved in stone. I asked about the selection of the text for this evening's event. Doña Rosario Martínez de Magaña, founder of the grupo guadalupano, was present at the South Bronx event years before when this script was first used and provided the oral historical link to this evening's event. Since the evening was dedicated to understanding the problems of Chiapas, she said, it was a way to make connections between the pilgrimage and the problems this community faced. She located the script in her files, which she remembered from years before, because she believed its emphasis on social justice issues was a good match to the evening's focus on the problems of the people in Chiapas.

After the stations were complete, in a little over an hour, a few congregants left. It is considered inappropriate to interrupt the Viacrucis for anything but Mass or confession, so unlike many other rituals I observed, this procession was not marked by the coming and going of its participants. After the procession was over, the participants who remained and gathered in the front pews of the large church were mostly members of the grupo guadalupano. María Lucía explained that the Colorado sisters wished to film messages for the people of Chiapas. This was the culmination of a few weeks' activities in which the sisters showed a documentary about femicide on the U.S.-Mexico border and conducted various discussions during the "social" half of the meetings of the grupo guadalupano. While an assistant filmed with a large professional video camera, the Colorado sisters listened sympathetically as attendees took turns speaking.

Nothing specific was said that evening about Chiapas or the current political context there. It seemed from remarks made that most people viewed Chiapas as chronically troubled by extreme poverty, and there were also passing mentions of the Zapatista movement. Many of the specificities that were mentioned are not particular to the southern Mexican state: deaths on the border, violence by men toward women, poverty, corruption, and political violence. Rather than solidarity, the videotaped sentiments were of sympathy: "We're praying for you." Rather than evoking a sense of pan-Mexican solidarity, which is what I understood to have been imagined by the performance artists in their proposal to the church to conduct this event, the comments by attendees illustrated the vast difference perceived to exist between the people in the church that night and the state of Chiapas. Not only was the South Bronx not Mexico, it was not clear that Chiapas was Mexico either: it was evoked as though it were a distant, alien place and rather than pan-Mexicanness, the night reiterated distance and difference. Furthermore, the script of the Viacrucis addressed problems associated with the local "community" but which were not among the problems most frequently cited by members of the comité guadalupano. Together with the videotaped messages for the people of Chiapas, these activities served to illustrate what members of this group were not. The evening's agenda kept with the group's purpose, which was frequently stated by its organizers as dual: spiritual and social. However, the disconnect between the content and meaning of the evening's activities and the concerns at the forefront of the participants' minds meant the event did not achieve its goal of fostering deep solidarity with the local South Bronx community or with the imagined people of Chiapas. Rather than solidarity or the theme of humility and awe before suffering the Viacrucis is meant to evoke, it seemed to reassert that the members of the comité guadalupano are doing well for themselves, compared to South

Bronx residents a decade earlier as well as the distant people of Chiapas, and thus have much to be grateful for. This contrasts sharply with other Viacrucis processions I attended that week.

The Viacrucis I just described took place the week preceding Holy Week. That same week, los comités guadalupanos of both Our Lady of the Rosary and Saint John parishes were consumed by discussions of the logistics of their members' participation in both the main public procession of the Way of the Cross on Good Friday in each parish as well as El Viacrucis del Inmigrante organized by Asociación Tepeyac. The content of the discussions reveals much about the positioning of the two comités vis-à-vis their home parishes and the larger association. First, I will examine a discussion I observed at the meeting of Saint John's grupo guadalupano that week:

> María Lucía: Tenemos un anuncio, de la Viacrucis en Federal Plaza. Los representantes de la parroquia sí van.
> Julio: No se trata de anunciar solamente sino animar, ¿no? Nos toca a las once, como parroquia.
> María Lucía: Este Viacrucis es importante porque es para la amnistía, ¿no? Pero se nos hace difícil porque cada parroquia tiene que hacer su Viacrucis y la parroquia no puede quedar sin feligreses. Personalmente, me siento mal que no puedo ir a eso, pero los mantengo con rezos.

> María Lucía: We have an announcement, about the Viacrucis at Federal Plaza. The representatives of the parish are going.
> Julio: It's not just about announcing, but getting people excited about going, no? Our parish Viacrucis is at 11:00–
> María Lucía: This Viacrucis is important because it's for Amnesty, no? But it's hard for us because each parish has to do its own Viacrucis and the parish can't end up without its faithful. Personally, I feel bad that I can't go, but I'll support it with my prayers.[4]

This exchange during the comité guadalupano's meeting at Saint John Parish reveals some of the tensions within the group. First, María Lucía makes an incomplete announcement about the event, naming it, without describing it or providing details, such as the time of the event. The married couple, Julio and Rosaura, were the delegates of this group to Tepeyac's general assembly, but their frequent attempts to bring the association's initiatives into the parish were met with resistance by the group's leader.

It was no secret that María Lucía mistrusted the director of Tepeyac, and even while frequently saying she wished to avoid conflict, "No quiero entrar en controversia," spared no opportunity to discredit the larger organization. While Saint John's central role in Tepeyac's formation and the role of the parish's pastor on its board meant the group could never fully secede from the association, in the frequent moments when an apparent conflict arose between needs of the parish and those of Asociación Tepeyac, María Lucía always sided with the parish and urged the group's members to do the same. Here, she made it clear that the church would not be unrepresented at the event: "our representatives will go," referring to Julio and Rosaura who were elected liaisons to Tepeyac by this group, but then she quickly implied that attendance by others could present a conflict with the members' assumed obligations to the parish and its Viacrucis. While María Lucía's statement infers a conflict between the two processions, in fact the parish Viacrucis was scheduled for 11:00 a.m. and Tepeyac's for 5:00 p.m. (which it seems Julio was about to point out when she interrupted him), thus causing no real logistical impediment to those who wished to attend both. While she acknowledged the importance of the event's link to the campaign for an immigration amnesty which was a key feature of the group's activism, she promised nothing more than her prayers in support.

Local Viacrucis at Saint John Parish

For its annual Viacrucis, Saint John convokes all of its parishioners. Participation in the procession is viewed as a strong indicator of loyalty to this particular church. Each year, there are several such events in addition to the Viacrucis: Ash Wednesday, Easter Sunday mass, Christmas Eve mass, and a mass held each year in celebration of Father Kenny's birthday. For these celebrations, the church's pews fill, not only with those who are currently active members but also with those members' extended family, former members who have moved out of the neighborhood, the pastor's twin brother and family who travel from Maine, and local activists, politicians, and pastors from other churches.

Each year, the Viacrucis at Saint John Church is preceded by a mass. At the end of the mass, the priest, followed by the altar boys and girls who carry candles, leads the procession into the street in front of the church. The participants gather together and begin to walk, making a circuit approximately six blocks square around the church's neighborhood.

This area was hard hit by the decimation of the fires in the Bronx in the 1970s and 1980s and decades of official neglect. While Mott Haven is only a short bridge away from Manhattan, and even, oddly, shares a Congressional and City Council district with East Harlem and Manhattan Valley, this is one of the neighborhoods continually presented as a case study of urban blight. From the fires and withdrawal of legal enterprise in the late 1960s to the crack epidemic of the 1980s, the South Bronx is legendary, even outside of the United States, as the worst kind of inner city neighborhood. In 1977, 1980, and 1997, Presidents Carter, Reagan, and Clinton, respectively, visited the South Bronx to promise aid and development. Carter called it "the worst slum in America" and Reagan compared it to bomb-scarred London during World War II, while Clinton was there to declare a victory for public and private sector cooperation (Raum 1997).

Between 1970 and 1980, the South Central Bronx lost 80 percent of its housing stock and population. Wallace and Wallace (1998) chronicle New York City's policy of "planned shrinkage," a local variation of Senator Daniel Patrick Moynihan's notion of "benign neglect," by which to combat the perceived pathology of inner city neighborhoods, relocation of populations was "encouraged" by the withdrawal of public services. Marshall Berman has called this "urbicide," the murder of a city (Berman 1987). The Rand Corporation Fire Project recommended the closing, in the South Bronx alone, of seven fire companies, more than any other neighborhood in the city, using a faulty calculus of response times, ratios of "arson" to "legitimate" fires, and racist social analysis of the lawlessness of poor neighborhoods. The area of Mott Haven was, furthermore, designated a target for "industrial development," with clearance of residential dwellings seen as the necessary precursor to the establishment of heavy and light industrial zones viewed as a more productive and profitable use of space than residences, and which would promote the reassertion of New York City's industrial identity (Wallace and Wallace 1998). Residents of the South Bronx during this period say that landlords hired arsonists to burn down their buildings in order to make insurance claims. Little effort was made by landowners to rebuild the destroyed housing. In the intervening decades, the result has been reimagined in some media and historical accounts as the demolition of its own habitat by a wantonly self-destructive and pathological urban community. However, as the Wallaces demonstrate, there was nothing spontaneous or unexpected about the destruction of the South Bronx by fire, nor could the blame rest with the area's residents. One of the legacies of this tragic period in New York City history is the ongoing association of the South Bronx with urban decay and danger, even as it is a site for many kinds of renewal: architectural, social, and, as we see here, religious. Orsi describes the South Bronx and similar "legendary" inner city neighborhoods as "locations cast by outsiders simultaneously as squalid dangerous slums and exotic locales for forbidden sensual delights" and reminds us that "part of the work of city religion is contending with the consequences of such fantasies" (1999: 7). It is in Saint John's local Viacrucis that we see some of this work accomplished.

When I began visiting this area in 2000, as part of my preliminary fieldwork, a few landmarks shaped my orientation. Just across the bridge from Manhattan was the Skate Key, one of the city's few remaining roller rinks; then the public housing projects, the police precinct across the street from them, the subway station, and nestled amidst all of this, Saint John Church. Across the street, a series of low-rise tenement buildings house a few storefront businesses: a bakery, a taco place, a small grocery, and a bodega (corner store). At that time, Saint John Church was in a state of advanced disrepair. There were buckets lining the aisles to catch the rain, and bits of falling plaster frequently punctuated Father Kenny's sermons. The rear exterior wall of the church was cracked, with one particularly large fault line bisecting the face of Christ in a large mural painted years before. Declining church membership and the church's physical state had led to it being slated for closure by the archdiocese. However, there were signs of change which varied in magnitude, but did not escape Father Kenny's notice. In my first interview with him in October 2000, Father Kenny remarked that the neighborhood was changing. The influx of Mexicans seemed exponential, with each person followed before long by a spouse, children, siblings, and parents. They filled his pews and challenged his pastoral skills, needing different kinds of counsel and assistance, and making different requests than prior waves of arrivals. He asked my husband and me to collect sleeping bags for the migrants who had arrived at his doorstep and to whom he offered a carpeted mezzanine as a sleeping space. He said the collection plate was heaping again on Sundays and that on festive days like the feast of Our Lady of Guadalupe, the church was filled to capacity. The building across the street was being renovated "for the first time!" Rumors had it that the "Clock Tower," a former piano factory a few blocks away, was being renovated into loft apartments for artists. Even though it would be a few years before real estate agents would start to crow about "SoBro," the new moniker they gave the Mott Haven section of the South Bronx, it was clear that the neighborhood was in transition (see Kugel 2004; Lee 2002).

However, for participants in the Viacrucis each year from 2001 to 2003, optimism about the future was tempered by anxiety. The Viacrucis and other rituals in this church served to illustrate the ways that Saint John served as a haven for its members, offering not only material succor (a food pantry, medical clinic, ESL classes, emergency shelter), but also spiritual re-assurance. In this neighborhood, it did not take much prying to find out that ethnic tensions and fear played an important role in the lives of members of this group. Julio, mentioned above, spoke at a meeting of the comité guadalupano about how he was pursued by two youths in the street who he thought wanted to mug him. He ran toward the precinct and knocked on the door of a police cruiser parked outside. The two officers inside said they could not understand him when he reported he was being followed. They told him that until he learned English, they could not help him. Don Mario, who lived in a boarding house around the corner, said that the men in his building, who arrive home late from jobs busing tables in Manhattan restaurants, were frequently mugged. Newspaper reports would later quote South Bronx residents referring to such workers as "walking A.T.M.'s" (Brady 2007). Landlords were known to threaten their tenants with a call to *la Migra*, immigration enforcement, if they complained about a lack of basic services. When the Viacrucis procession moved through the neighborhood, tracing an outline around the public housing projects, participants told me to be careful, that in years past people threw bags of urine, raw eggs, and garbage out of their windows onto the procession. I witnessed two eggs and many insults hurled from the windows of the buildings, but more important than the reality of the projectiles was the fear of them and the way that fear evoked solidarity among the participants.

The priest played only a minor role in the procession. It was the chorus and the readers who set the pace. The chorus was composed of an Irish woman in her sixties, an African American woman in her fifties, and two Puerto Rican women; all wore red smocks. Many of the most active members of the comité guadalupano, the cursillo movement, the Legion of Mary, and other lay groups accompanied them in their songs, often singing loudly and enthusiastically. The Stations of the Cross were read aloud in English and Spanish by people who took turns at a microphone. There were no actors or performances of the stations. The altar boys and girls walked, leading the way. The other participants gathered close, listening to the script, singing and praying at each station. The group grew in size as the procession moved, and the overall impression was of a closely knit community, shielding its members from the outside world.

Of the three important rituals that are held in Holy Week, the Viacrucis is the one that is most difficult for people in this parish to attend because it is held on a Friday morning. Members of the comité guadalupano frequently complained about the difficulty they experienced in complying with what they felt was an obligation of their faith—to participate in a Viacrucis—given that the larger society seemed unsupportive. They often remarked that in Mexico, to work on Holy Friday would be considered a sin and that participation in a public procession is not only a typical but expected way of spending the day:

> Man: Creo que eso se debe a que uno aquí está solo. No están las familias. No es que sea diferente. Tal vez la tradición es la misma. Pero no estamos reunidos en familia. Eso es lo que pasa.
>
> Woman: Yo creo que la diferencia entre aquí y en México es, como dice el señor, es que allá toda la gente es Católica. Toda la gente tiene la misma fé, la misma tradición. Pero aquí, vamos en procesión, sin embargo, la gente ni baja su música. Los señores están allí, hablando, no se perturba la gente. Mientras en nuestro país, toda la gente está haciendo lo mismo.
>
> Alyshia: ¿cuántos tuvieron que trabajar en la Semana Santa?
>
> All: sí, sí. [General agreement]
>
> Second woman: Uno tiene que trabajar hasta el viernes santo, tú sabes, que el viernes santo es un día tan sagrado. En el país de nosotros, no. Acá uno tiene que trabajar.
>
> Second man: Yo trabajo en una pescadería, y tu sabes que esos días no se come la carne. Entonces, nos pidieron trabajar extra. Tuvimos que trabajar todo el día el viernes santo. Se nos hace difícil aquí. Aquí uno tiene que trabajar, para la familia. Se hace difícil a los padres para educar a sus hijos, en las tradiciones. Yo creo que ha de ser difícil.[5]

> Man: I believe that it [the difference in celebrations between U.S. and Mexico] is that here, one is alone. Our families are not here. It's not that it's different, perhaps the tradition is the same, but we are not with our families. That is what happens.
>
> Woman: I believe that the difference between here and Mexico is, like the man says, that there everyone is Catholic. All of the people share the same faith, the same tradition. But here, we walk in procession, but people we pass do not even turn down their music. The people are there, talking,

they don't even bother [to make way]. But in our country, all of the people are participating in the same thing.

Alyshia: How many of you had to work on Holy Week?

All: Yes, yes. [general agreement].

Second woman: here one even has to work on Good Friday, and you know, Good Friday is such a sacred day. In our country, no, but here one has to work.

Second man: I work in a fish shop and you know that those days meat cannot be eaten. So, they asked us to work overtime. We had to work all day on Good Friday. It's difficult for us here. Here one has to work, for the family. It's difficult for parents to educate their children in the traditions. I believe it must be difficult.

Malenny, an altar girl, participated in Saint John's Viacrucis, in the Bronx. Several months later, she was fatally shot (The photograph mentioned in the text, in which the children's faces are visible, is not reproduced here due to privacy concerns.)

In these statements, we hear reiteration of some of the same themes mentioned above: Catholics as members of a closed community which protects its members from hostility and loss of tradition, the role of one's parish as surrogate family, and the difficulty of sustaining tradition when employers, outsiders, and others are perceived to attack or disallow it. The need for protection and community was especially poignant when I showed pictures from the Viacrucis the year before; attendees gasped when I showed a slide of the altar boys and girls. The little girl at the front of the group, hands joined in prayer, was fatally shot that August, outside a Lutheran Church where a cousin had been baptized. She was caught in crossfire between two Mexican youth gangs, some members of which had been at the baptism party. The danger felt by members of this church was described as indiscriminate, as likely to come from Mexicans as non-Mexicans and, in some ways, unavoidable, but the church community provided a haven from it. In this way, the larger parish community achieved what the comité guadalupano could not: offering its members the sense that they belong to a collectivity that would protect them from an unfriendly outside. As such, when members of the comité guadalupano like Rosaura and Julio frequently attempted to reassert the guadalupanismo they supposed to be at the core of the group's purpose, they were told they were generating controversy. The operational "we" in this parish was microlocal and multiethnic, not exclusively Guadalupano.

The Viacrucis at Our Lady of the Rosary Parish, April 18, 2003

Meanwhile, at Our Lady of the Rosary Parish, different kinds of negotiations were occurring that week. Founded with Tepeyac intervention and the continued material and moral support of the association, the comité guadalupano of Our Lady of the Rosary Parish was, by all accounts, a model comité. In 2003, its members had been chosen by the Asociación to play the roles of Jesus, the Romans, Mary, Veronica, and others in El Viacrucis del Inmigrante, a procession to be attended by comités from the five boroughs of New York City. This was an honor bestowed in part because the parish had invested a great deal of time, resources, and effort into the costumes and props necessary for such a performance (the realistic helmets and tunics of the Roman soldiers had been brought from Mexico, for example), but also because of the comité's close relationship to the leadership of Tepeyac. Their loyalty and their willingness to invest time, energy, and resources in Tepeyac's initiatives were being rewarded by offering them the most prestigious kind of participation. Thus, for many of the members of this comité, El Viacrucis del Inmigrante was the main focus of their Holy Week activities. Nonetheless, the comité could not shirk its duties during the Viacrucis in its home parish and was attempting to successfully fulfill multiple roles on this day.

Not long before, the much loved Irish-American priest, Father Byrne, who had led Our Lady of Rosary for decades, experienced a severe health crisis and was sent by the Diocese to recover at a retreat in upstate New York. He was replaced by a young priest whose family hails from the Dominican Republic, Father Castillo. When I asked the pastor at Saint John, who was a colleague and friend of Father Byrne, about this shift, Father Kenny criticized Father Byrne's successor and bemoaned what he perceived as the arrogance of young priests. He told me that Father Castillo refused to move into the rectory's living quarters, which for years had been suitable for Father Byrne, stating that it was uninhabitable. For Father Kenny's generation (of which Father Byrne was a member), the priesthood came with the expectation of sacrifice, and he felt the bourgeois interest of Father Castillo in comfortable living quarters was a sign of an insufficient commitment to the priestly life. Members of the comité guadalupano volunteered to quickly refurbish the pastor's quarters, but in spite of this dedication and their recent renovation of the church's exterior,[6] the Mexican parishioners felt Father Castillo did not appreciate them or treat them with the respect they felt they had earned. In contrast, Father Byrne had literally given them the keys to the church and allowed them to do almost any activities they wished inside its walls. He also ran interference between the different ethnic groups in the parish, trying to ensure they got along peacefully. Father Castillo, in contrast, wanted to charge the group rent for the use of church facilities for fundraisers or educational programs, even billing them to use a classroom they had built themselves in the basement to house the computers Tepeyac provided for classes. The priest also refused to speak to the members of this rather decentralized group, interacting only with the president of the comité and attempting to restrict the many subcommittees of the comité (such as the folkloric dance group) from using the church. This slow-building tension with the pastor was at a crisis point that spring of 2003, with the comité guadalupano considering abandoning the parish altogether and seeking out a more welcoming home elsewhere.[7]

The Way of the Cross in this parish was traditionally organized by the Legion of Mary, led in recent years by a woman in her sixties, Altagracia, an immigrant from the Dominican Republic. Shortly after its formation, the comité guadalupano showed an interest in participating in a very visible way in the Viacrucis, by acting out the stations. This participation was welcomed, but it was clear in 2003 that the two groups' cooperation was not fully harmonious.

I arrived at noon at the church on Holy Friday while the mass preceding the procession was in progress. It was an unseasonably cold 40 degrees, and the skies were overcast. The church was full and a man at the doors told me and another woman who also had a toddler in a stroller that we should wait outside. I wanted to hear the homily, but I obeyed and stood in the vestibule of one of the side doors.

In this church, prior to the formation of the comité and the arrival of a large contingent of Mexican parishioners, the congregation was composed largely of aging Puerto Rican and Dominican Catholics from the surrounding neighborhood. Indeed, most churches that experienced an influx of Mexicans over the last decade or so experienced a steep decline in attendance over the 1980s and 1990s, and typically only small numbers of older women came to the Spanish language mass regularly. Only on the most important holy days could entire families be seen in the pews. The priests almost universally welcomed the influx of young Mexican families and in some cases credited them with saving a parish that might otherwise have been closed by the diocese for dwindling membership. However, the incorporation of the new members was not always smooth. At Saint John Parish, a larger church which narrowly evaded closure by the diocese, the arrival of Mexicans was hailed as God's way to save the parish. Father Kenny welcomed the new arrivals and their children, and the sound of babies crying, playing, running in the aisles, and nibbling on snacks seemed never to interrupt his concentration during the homilies. On the contrary, he often organized his sermons around examples seemingly inspired by the young faces in the pews. In contrast, at Our Lady of Rosary Church, with its smaller number of seats and more numerous pre-existing congregation, Mexicans struggled to find their place. On any given Sunday in this parish, one is likely to notice that Filipino parishioners, who predominate in the choir, tend to sit in the front pews, stage left of the altar. Dominican and Puerto Rican parishioners sit in the center front pews. Mexicans tend to sit in the rear of the church, and in many cases, stand in the space behind the last pews and in the vestibules of the doors. This is true even of the masses "led" by the comité guadalupano, for which they have provided the flowers and volunteers to pass the collection baskets and to recite the biblical readings.

After noticing this, I asked several Mexican parishioners why they sat in the rear or why they thought others did. Most told me they had not noticed this tendency, but then laughed, sometimes sheepishly, and proffered an interpretation. The response of one couple to this inquiry is representative of most of the answers I received:

> Alberto: Bueno esa sí es una pregunta muy interesante. Nosotros no la podemos contestar. Pero en lo personal yo a veces he dicho cuando llego tarde una penitencia es no sentarme, en lo personal. No sé de las otras personas ¿sí? Porque creo yo que sólo una vez como decimos, sólo una vez, un día a la semana, es lo que Dios nos pide para estar con él, o para orarle. Si Dios nos dio, ahora sí, muchas cosas, por qué no darle un día nada más, o un rato nada más ¿sí? Eso en lo personal.
> Mirna: Bueno yo casi siempre me quedo en la parte de atrás por el niño, porque los niños corren, gritan, se ponen a llorar.
> Alyshia: Sí.
> Alberto: Pero aparte. . . . cada quien se va sentando de acuerdo como va sintiendo, como se va sintiendo en la iglesia, con su fe . . . Entonces conforme vas sintiendo, estás cada vez más cerca, más adelante.

> Alberto: Well, that certainly is an interesting question. We can't answer it. But personally, I have sometimes said that if I arrive late, as penance I will not sit—that's for me personally. I don't know about other people. Because I believe that only once, as we say, only once, one day a week, God asks us to be with him, and to pray to him. If God gave us so much, why can't we give him just one day, a little while, right? That's for me personally.
> Mirna: Well, I always sit in the back because of my son, because the kids run, shout, and start to cry.
> Alyshia: Yes.
> Alberto: But besides that . . . each person sits according to how he feels, how he feels about the church, in his faith . . . So according to how you feel, you start moving closer, closer to the front.

Here we see several possible explanations when applied to Mexicans as a group within the parish: that they are more likely to stand and sit in the rear as a form of penance, which could be perceived as their projection of heightened piety or a greater propensity to sin, or both; that they feel less close to their faith and God, and less comfortable in the church than other groups that cozy up to the altar; or simply that they wish not to disturb others with noisy children and late arrivals. Allowing for a great deal of variation for individual preference and chance, I am inclined to interpret seating patterns to each group's sense of their own legitimacy and status in the parish. It is possible that Father Castillo's prohibition of strollers in the aisles and frequent complaints from the altar about the noise caused by babies and children disproportionately impacts Mexicans, the youngest parishioners with the most young children, and causes them to huddle in the vestibule and struggle to hear the mass. The mass that day would not be the only time that Good Friday that those of us with young children and carriages would be asked to move to the margins or that the hierarchy among ethnic groups in the church would be made evident.

After the mass ended, the parishioners streamed out into the street, gathering around the doors of the church. Then, the man portraying Jesus emerged, carrying a large wooden cross, followed by the Romans and the women of Jerusalem. The costumed actors were followed by the statue of Our Lady of the Rosary carried on a wooden platform. The members of the Legion of Mary, all older women who wore pins on their lapels, unfurled strings which they used to create lines of demarcation around the image of the Virgin, inside which they processed, taking turns helping to carry the statue. Everyone else walked behind them or alongside them, outside of the strings. The priest came outside in his robes and climbed into a pick-up truck which was loaded with a large amplification system, driven by one of the members of the comité guadalupano. Altagracia moved around rapidly, ordering people into position and deciding when the procession would start. When it began to move, the actor playing Jesus walked while Roman soldiers shouted at him, "¡Camina, camina ladrón!" [Walk, walk thief!] and "¡Camina, rey de Judíos!" [Walk, king of the Jews!] and feigned whipping him with lengths of cotton rope.

Father Castillo, using a microphone and riding inside of a heated pick-up truck with windows partially rolled up, read the text of the Stations of the Cross. His script was a fairly generic one, emphasizing the trials of Jesus, but not making overt comparisons between them and the troubles faced by his faithful in this parish. The problems named were not ones that are structural or rooted in exploitation, but caused by sin: not listening to one's elders, failing to love one's neighbor, not taking good care of one's children.

The pacing and organization of the procession were controlled by Altagracia. She tried to keep the procession slow moving, "pá'que se vea bonito" [so it looks pretty], she said, but since the actors were leading the

Parishioners playing roles of Jesus and the Roman Soldiers in the Viacrucis at Our Lady of the Rosary Parish, April 18, 2003

procession and she was staying back, closer to the image of the Virgin, they were not able to communicate about pacing. The spatial divisions created by the strings served to reiterate the divisions between groups in this parish: Mexicans, many of them with baby strollers, walked outside the perimeter of devotion she had drawn. She commented on the procession in a loud stage whisper, and without ever saying anything about Mexicans or the comité guadalupano in particular, it was clear where her ire was directed: "¿Pá qué tienen micrófonos si no hacen caso?" [Why do they have microphones, if they don't listen?], "Estaría bien si no se estuvieran apurando ellos" [this would be nice if they weren't rushing], and "ellos caminan muy rápido" [they walk too fast].

After completing a circuit around the neighborhood, the procession arrived at the church for the final station, the crucifixion of Jesus. Here, the attention of those present was fully focused on the actors who play Jesus and the Romans. Three men, Jesus and two thieves, were tied with ropes to their crosses and the crosses lifted in the air. Having been stripped of their robes, the cold air and the realistic performance of the crucifixion created a moving spectacle. The members of the comité who were working to produce the theatrical event came face to face with the members of the Legion of Mary who held the image of the Virgin aloft on their shoulders, a clear vantage point for her to gaze on the crucified Christ. For a moment, no one complained or shouted orders, all were silent.

While this event resulted finally in an assertion of parish unity and piety, everything prior to the final crucifixion scene indicated significant fissures in this parish community. Because of the fraught nature of relations between groups in Our Lady of the Rosary Parish, and the availability of discourses of guadalupanismo, members of the comité guadalupano look outward, beyond their parish bounds to the larger Mexican population in New York City in their understanding of their community.

I turn now to *El Viacrucis del Inmigrante*, organized by Asociación Tepeyac.

El Viacrucis del Inmigrante

Despreciado y tenido como la basura de los hombres,
hombre de dolores y familiarizado con el sufrimiento,
semejante a aquellos a los que se les vuelve la cara,
estaba despreciado y no hemos hecho caso a él. (Isaías 53:3)

He was despised and rejected by men,
a man of sorrows, and familiar with suffering.
Like one from whom men hide their faces
He was despised, and we esteemed him not.

No maltratarás, ni oprimirás a los inmigrantes, ya que también ustedes fueron inmigrantes en tierra de Egipto. (Éxodo 22: 21)

Do not mistreat an alien or oppress him, for you were aliens in Egypt.[8]

These biblical verses grace the cover of the booklet created by Asociación Tepeyac each year for its Viacrucis del Inmigrante on Good Friday in the financial district of Manhattan and make clear the connections that this event draws between Jesus's path to execution and the mistreatment of immigrants in the United States. The Viacrucis makes its point in many modalities.

Just as la misión guadalupana and parish-based Viacrucis map the parish territory in a hyper-local way for each comité, El Viacrucis del Inmigrante is a mapping of a different sort. Participants leave their parishes, and in many cases their boroughs, to travel to what is perceived as the seat of power in New York City, the financial district in lower Manhattan, to conduct a Way of the Cross. This is explicitly both a devotional and a political performance, designed to awaken the consciousness of participants as well as spectators. This resignification of space, employing the theological power of the biblical narrative, is an important way that los comités guadalupanos communicate to outsiders as well as their members.

As in most performances of the Stations of the Cross, scripture is used to articulate particular moral arguments. The accessibility of biblical texts to this kind of application makes the script of the Viacrucis rich for analysis on its own. However, even more multivalent and powerful are the ways that the message of the Viacrucis is performed both by the actors who play Jesus, his followers, and his persecutors, but also by the noncostumed participants who attend. The Mexican community, as envisioned by Asociación Tepeyac, becomes visible in this event. It is at this event that the internal cohesion of the community is asserted at the same time as its difference from other groups, and the platform on which it is able to act is also described.

The procession begins at five in the afternoon. The time is strategic, scheduled so that as many people can attend as possible, after many of them get out of work and their children are dismissed from school. The timing also, as we saw in the prior sections, allows people to attend other Viacrucis processions in their home parishes, some of which are held early in the day. Finally, I was told by one of the organizers that the time is intended to provide maximum visibility, to allow the procession to occupy the streets at the same time that Wall Street's white collar labor force is spilling out of high-rise office buildings for the holiday weekend. The place is strategic as well. The procession begins at 26 Federal Plaza, the offices of the U.S. Citizenship and Immigration Services (formerly the Immigration and Naturalization Service, INS or "la Migra"), which for some represents the site of their most humiliating and yet most crucial interactions with the U.S. nation-state. Even routine immigration questions can only be asked by waiting in the elements, sometimes for four to six hours, outside the doors of this building. For the majority of Mexicans in New York who as undocumented immigrants are ineligible even for the privilege of this interaction with the state and are, instead *personae non grate* within U.S. juridical definitions, this place represents the seemingly unreachable goal of legalization.

During El Viacrucis del Inmigrante, the actor who plays Jesus is whipped along the entire route which culminates in his crucifixion. While Holy Week processions in Mexico are known to be macabre, this is not simply a recreation of a Mexican-style Viacrucis. If there is any doubt as to this fact, the signs held by participants declaring "No human being is illegal" dispel it.

In 2003, to see the same actors, members of Our Lady of the Rosary's comité guadalupano, perform two very different reenactments of the Viacrucis was striking. At their parish's Viacrucis, the Roman soldiers had shouted "¡Camina ladrón, rey de los judíos!" [Walk thief, king of the Jews!], and they had beaten Jesus with ropes with feeling, but without much muscle. Here they drew real blood through his tunic and they evoked comparisons between the Romans and U.S. border patrol agents by shouting, "¡Camina, camina ilegal!" [Walk, walk illegal!]. The semantic charge of the text and the closeness between the script's focus on the exploitation immigrants faced and the crucifixion of Christ were clearly deeply felt. This was not simply an event designed to make Christians contemplate the sacrifices their martyr had made for them but a performance of the ways that this population *felt* the pain Christ experienced in their own lives and on their own bodies. In the Bronx, the procession reiterated the differences between and among parishioners from the same church who participated, but in lower Manhattan, those who processed drew lines between "us" and the rest of the world, starting with the structural economic forces that pushed them from their homes and drew them to this world city.

Many of the participants work in the financial district, in delicatessens, or selling flowers or delivering lunches, those taken-for-granted workers whose lack of legal documents authorizing them to work makes them anonymous, even clandestine. In this procession, undocumented immigrants visibly and vocally decry their exploitation and the multiple injustices they suffer as a result of their efforts to earn a living for themselves and their families. What is more, they do so within the accepted idiom of Catholic faith. Here the Calvary, Jesus's path to the Cross and crucifixion, is performatively overlaid on the paths workers take to and from work, the zone of power from which the economic and political structures determining their fate are perceived to originate, and now, even the anonymous grave of dozens of their compatriots who died unaccounted for in the events of September 11, 2001.

Indeed, the appropriation of the space of this particular neighborhood by undocumented Mexican immigrants, who are such vital contributors to the city's economy in spite of not being considered legitimate members of its polity, is ultimately a symbolic gesture directed—like the stickers of the Virgin of Guadalupe on the doors of Mexican families in apartment buildings—to others in the same situation, other paisanos and guadalupanos. It, like the misión, is intended to galvanize the community and is made possible because religion is turned into a node for transformation and mobilization, on an individual and collective scale.

El Viacrucis del Inmigrante is offered "en memoria de los migrantes caídos en la lucha por sobrevivir con mayor dignidad, fuera de su tierra, lejos de sus familiares" [in memory of those migrants who have fallen in the struggle to survive with greater dignity, outside of their land, far from their families]. The document printed for the participants by Tepeyac and which includes the script for each station represents a theological defense for migration and argues that immigrants should be treated with the human dignity that their status as God's children affords them. In four introductory pages, the document quotes the U.S. Council of Catholic Bishops (USCCB) and Mexican Episcopate's jointly authored document, "Juntos en el camino de la esperanza: Ya no somos extranjeros" or "Strangers No Longer: Together on a Journey of Hope" (2003):

Nuestros diálogos han revelado el anhelo común de un sistema migratorio más ordenado, que reconozca la realidad de la migración y promueva la justa aplicación de la ley civil. Invitamos a todo Católico y a toda persona de buena voluntad a que se viva su fe y use sus recursos y dones para, verdaderamente, acoger al forastero entre nosotros.

[Our dialogue has revealed a common desire for a more orderly system that accommodates the reality of migration and promotes the just application of civil law. We invite Catholics and persons of good will in both nations to exercise their faith and to use their resources and gifts to truly welcome the stranger among us.][9]

The "Reflection" at the end of the introduction sets the tone for the Viacrucis:

La fe cristiana nos hace pensar que el Viacrucis o Camino de la Cruz de Jesús no solamente es semejante al camino de los millones de inmigrantes y refugiados en los países ricos. El camino de sufrimiento de los inmigrantes y refugiados es el mismo camino de Jesús.

[Our Christian faith makes us think that the Viacrucis, or Way of the Cross, is not just similar to the path of millions of immigrants and refugees in the rich countries. The path of suffering of the immigrants and refugees *is* the same path walked by Jesus.]

The Stations of the Cross make clear this equation between the suffering of Jesus and that of immigrants through examples. In the first station, Christ is condemned to death and in front of 26 Federal Plaza, a narrator reads, "Jesús pasó su vida trabajando y haciendo el bien, aunque era inocente, fue condenado a la muerte por Pilato" [Jesus spent his life working and doing right. Even though he was innocent, he was condemned to death by Pilate]. This was followed by a section entitled "Testimony" describing the case of Celestino and María Analco who, the text reads, planned and waited for their expected child with love. Two months after he was born, he began having health problems. After being turned away from the emergency room several times while suffering from a fever, the child died. The text says that although the official cause of death was "Cerebral death" that the real cause was "Medical negligence": "Nosotros sabemos que en varios hospitales no reciben la misma atención los inmigrantes como la reciben los ciudadanos" [We know that in many hospitals immigrants do not receive the same care as citizens]. This testimony is followed by a quotation from the document "Strangers No Longer" in which the Holy Family and immigrants are compared and described as similarly sacred. This is followed by the Lord's Prayer, the Ave María, and a third prayer: "give us a big heart to love and a strong heart to struggle."

The second station condemns the separation of families by immigration law and, with the same format as the first station, calls for Congress to pass comprehensive legalization for immigrants. The third station condemns gang violence and the solitude and separation from loved ones that precipitate it:

Jesús cae por el peso de la soledad y la falta de apoyo de los que fueron de su mismo pueblo, de su misma clase social, oprimidos por el imperio de los Romanos y la clase social alta de ese tiempo. Nosotros los inmigrantes somos todos parte del mismo pueblo inmigrante, de las minorías étnicas, quienes somos casi siempre discriminados. Sin embargo en momentos de confusión o dificultad abandonamos a nuestro propio pueblo.

[Jesus falls from the weight of loneliness and the lack of support from those who come from the same town, the same social class, oppressed by the Roman empire and the upper social class of that time. We, the immigrants, are all part of the same immigrant people, part of the ethnic minorities and we are the ones who are almost always discriminated against. Nonetheless, in moments of confusion or difficulty we abandon our own people.]

This narration is followed by testimony about a young man lost to gunfire in East Harlem, and the station ends with a hymn commonly sung in the churches to which the participants belong, "Perdona a tu pueblo, Señor" [Lord, forgive your people]. In the text of this station and others, people and town are one and the same: *pueblo,* a morally binding category of belonging. However, in tension with this unity are the forces of conflict and of isolation, oppression, and exclusion. Already by the third station, there are several mentions in this script of the "rich countries" and the "upper class." While there is an assertion of the ethical obligation of the oppressed to struggle together and support each other, this effort is countered at each turn by imperialism, discrimination, and exploitation. Thus, when immigrants enact the Stations of the Cross in lower Manhattan, the members of the community and those who would persecute them are vividly depicted. "Us," those who testify, pray, and perform Jesus's travails, are distinguished from "them," the uncomprehending citizens of Jerusalem, or, rather, the modern-day empire that is Wall Street and U.S. economic power. In this sense, it is not only happenstance but necessary to the narrative and its interpretation by the actors that passersby *not* understand.

Most of the signs and the script read by the participants are in Spanish and there is no one charged with answering the questions of the passersby who attempt to demand an explanation for the display or simply stare, mouths agape. In order for the actors to appropriately feel the suffering of Jesus and his followers which is, now, their own suffering, they must suffer publicly and be humiliated before unfeeling crowds.

One man said in response to a photograph of the event (which he did not attend):[10]

Para mí es chocante, no? Es significante para los que lo van haciendo, verdad? Pero para los autobuses, los negocios, creo que es impertinente. No dejan que tenga movimiento. Tal vez, hay gente que quiere moverse en ese momento. En nuestros países, en el lugar donde se hace eso, generalmente no van muchos vehículos, se cierran las calles. Tiene mucho

Viacrucis del Inmigrante, lower Manhattan, April 2003

significado en nuestro país. Aquí mucha gente no se da cuenta qué está pasando. Mucha gente no lo quiere comprender.

. . . Estamos pensando en lo que vino antes, los viacrucis que pasamos con nuestra familia . . . Significado tiene. Pero no es lo mismo.

[For me, it's a bit unsettling, no? It's meaningful for those who are doing it, right? But for the buses, the businesses, I think it is impertinent. They aren't letting people go by. Perhaps there are people who want to pass in that moment. In our countries, where these things are done, there aren't vehicles and the streets are closed [for the procession]. This has a lot of meaning in our country. Here, many people don't realize what is happening. Many people don't want to understand it . . .

We start to think about what came before, about the Viacrucis we spent with our family . . . This has meaning. But it's not the same.]

For Asociación Tepeyac's organizers, this event is meaningful precisely because of the nostalgia and sense of loss of those processions that have gone before, and it is the difference between this and the familiar, archetypal Viacrucis that moves participants toward a radical resignification of

Participants in El Viacrucis
del Inmigrante, lower Manhattan, dressed as the women of
Jerusalem

an old practice. The implication is that in Mexico, the faithful have the luxury of processing through the streets with their families, their com-patriots, *el pueblo*, and the meaning of the Viacrucis they perform can be limited to the traditional one: a contemplation of the suffering of Christ and its meaning for his faithful in the present. In New York City, however, the immigrant faithful do not have that luxury. Far from family, obliged to work on Good Friday, exploited by the larger economic and political structures and powers that be: the struggles of Christ are equated with their own. Thus, the discomfort—of traveling outside of one's comfort zone to the very centers of political and economic power to put on a dra-matic pageant of suffering—is, by design, unsettling for themselves and the anonymous members of the dominant population who their presence is assumed to discomfit. To translate the texts, offer bilingual spokespeople to explain, or to attempt to get out of the way of passersby would be to al-low "them" the opportunity to be sympathetic. Instead, the script calls for observers to be the angry mob of citizens, the rabble who jeer at Christ on his path to death. In contrast, the procession's participants, the many who are dressed in the robes of Jesus's following and all of those in street clothes who carry the script and understand it when it is read, are given the honor of comprehending and identifying with Jesus. It is precisely this identification which sets the stage for community to be imagined.

In analyzing culturally specific, faith-based activities like César Chávez's infusion of religious symbols into the United Farm Workers' actions, Phillip Hammond wrote, "César Chávez would have no hope of winning the moral support of Americans generally by offering a particularistic ideology, a creed so peculiar to farm workers that, in motivating them, it leaves everyone else unmoved" (1993: 171, quoted in Stevens-Arroyo and Díaz Stevens 1998: 44. See León 2005). Stevens-Arroyo and Díaz Stevens critique Hammond's assertion that ethnic expressions have no place in America's universalistic civil religion by noting that civil religion has always been "a creed historically prejudicial of Latino culture, nationality and religion, so much so that it encouraged invasion, subjugation, and colonialism" (1998: 44). The first time I presented ethnographic material on the Viacrucis del Inmigrante, in 2003, before an academic audience, one scholar remarked that in his opinion, the Viacrucis "would be alienating for the average American." Does the Viacrucis del Inmigrante emit a message broad enough to garner "the moral support of Americans"? Is that one of its goals? Would a performance accessible to outsiders remain meaningful for insiders? Indeed, like the melting pot and other metaphors of ethnic assimilation, civil religion's success is implicitly premised on the dilution of cultural particularism in favor of a generic brand of civically oriented ecumenism. The objective here seems to be quite different from that of "civil religion" as it has been historically defined.

In referring to Chicago's Pilsen district Viacrucis, Janise Hurtig writes that the procession is meaningful to its participants precisely because of its unassimilable Mexicanness: "Rosario made it clear that the inviting familiarity she encountered in many of the parish's ritual practices and religious symbols was due to their being specifically *Mexican*, not 'universally' *Catholic*" (Hurtig 2000: 39). In her analysis, "the passionate, public display of popular religion consolidates the community around symbols of local struggle which are made sacred as they become integral to Mexican-American ethnicity" (36). Thus, enduring symbols of the Viacrucis which are, on the one hand, accepted by Catholics as universal, traditional, and unchanging, by their insertion into a culturally specific celebration in the

United States, are "relocated, resacralized and relegitimated as 'native traditions'" (39). For Hurtig, this fosters the consolidation of an imagined common national heritage and the assimilation of Mexican immigrants into the ethnic category of "Mexican-Americans" (40). In New York City, given the shallow time-depth of Mexican migration, and the frequent assertion of the metropolis as a city of immigrants, Mexican-American is not a readily available ethnic category. Further, given the complicated relationship with other Latino groups that are not Mexican, ethnicity is not what I see being produced in the Viacrucis procession described here, at least not ethnicity as it has historically been constructed in the United States. In the twentieth century, ethnicity was largely imagined as a relatively static grouping referring to national origin, racialized categories, and frequently religion and language. While it has more recently been critiqued as never having worked as an analytical category in the way it was imagined to, and has been posited as more fluid and contingent, for Latino groups that may or may not share religion, language, racialized categories, or national origin (Sánchez 1995), it is perhaps so unconvincing as to be useless. In the Viacrucis, I see the contours of a community based on shared identity as Mexicans, guadalupanismo, and undocumented immigrants emerge, be refined, and become operationalized by practice, even while a fitting name for such a community continues to elude us. Just as the Christian Ecclesiastical Base communities in the Chicago parish described by Hurtig function to "replace the familial and fictive kin networks from which some parishioners apparently became dissociated in their migration to Chicago," the Guadalupan community asserted in El Viacrucis del Inmigrante promotes the formation of a community that can be mobilized for empowerment.

Communities can be entities that are self-designated, but frequently they are ascribed by outsiders for whom the internal differences of a group are less visible than the external signs of perceived commonality. Communities are also imagined in contradistinction to those who are different. By living in neighborhoods scattered throughout New York City and originating from many different places in Mexico, Mexican immigrants in New York City are not a community based on propinquity in their origin or their current settlement pattern. The comités guadalupanos and Asociación Tepeyac promote the feeling among their members that they belong to a single community that is frequently defined in contrast to those who are not guadalupano, Mexican, or undocumented. As such, performances of belonging and of exclusion like the misión guadalupana and the various

Viacrucis serve to delineate who "we" are for the members of various local and citywide groupings of Mexican immigrants. For parishioners at
Saint John Parish, the Alinsky-inspired discourse of community mobilization discourages the construction of a group sentiment among Mexican
immigrants. The problems that are identified and associated with each of
the Stations of the Cross are either not group-specific but local (such as
garbage pickup and crime) or transnational and vague (sexual violence
and poverty) and thus do not promote the consideration of Mexicans as
a group with specific qualities or problems. As the current numerical majority in a parish that has greeted them as saviors, they do not need to
negotiate with any other groups in order to obtain resources or services.
In fact, efforts to forge a mobilized Mexican identity in the parish which
could engage the citywide network of Tepeyac are countered by parish
lay leadership who cast such efforts as counterproductive and divisive. In
contrast, at Our Lady of the Rosary Parish, Mexicans struggle to achieve
and retain a place of respect where their tremendous energy and contributions can be matched by the pastor's esteem and fair dispersal of parish
resources. They perceive that other groups and the pastor look down on
them and attempt to constrain and control their expressions and their activities. In Tepeyac's citywide network, they not only find powerful allies,
but an outlet where their energies are rewarded (such as with the granting
of the premier roles in the citywide Viacrucis). As such, the space carved
out by the different Viacrucis processions is not, in all cases, a Mexican
or immigrant space, but is very differently projected outward to passersby
and other groups, as well as inward, in its work of defining an operative
"we." These dynamics work to produce certain kinds of actors who are,
depending on their location in the landscape I have described, more or
less likely to view their processional activities as community-building or
empowering.

6

La Antorcha Guadalupana/
The Guadalupan Torch Run
*Messengers for a People
Divided by the Border*

The Message

Sergio: Aquí en este país [la antorcha] se usa como un mensaje, es llevar el mensaje a toda esa gente de que lo que uno quiere es expresarse libremente y es como la luz de la esperanza de algún día tener la libertad, ¿no? . . . . El sentido que tiene en México, es llevar la luz de un lado a otro, ¿no?, ósea esto se viene realizando, tengo entendido, desde hace muchos años atrás, desde nuestros antepasados. Como no había forma de cómo comunicarse y para llevar el mensaje de un lado a otro tenían que usar la antorcha para poder ellos alumbrarse, ya que el mensaje tenía que llegar a como diera lugar, entonces iba, día y noche esa gente tenía que ir corriendo y este, con la luz, con la llama, era más que nada lo que se hacía anteriormente, después ya la tradición fue siguiendo y después se tomó sentido como la llama de la fe, ¿no? porque el llevar un mensaje de un lado a otro es como llevar la fe y la esperanza. Aquí en Nueva York, pues, el estar, digamos, un poquito oprimidos, el que no nos dejen, digamos, expresarnos o nos nieguen nuestros derechos, pues llevar la antorcha es la forma de expresarnos, ¿no?, de decir que lo que queremos es que nos tomen en cuenta y que pues nos den igualdad de derechos más que nada.

Alyshia: ¿Entonces para tí, la luz es un mensaje para los demás mexicanos, para que se enteren de sus derechos, o principalmente para los—

Sergio: No, no, el mensaje es doble, ¿no?, el mensaje es para nuestros paisanos, decirles que si todos nos unimos podemos lograr muchas cosas, y esa luz es una esperanza, para las demás personas es expresarnos y decirles que nosotros valemos y que necesitamos igualdad de derecho, pues el mensaje es para ambas partes, ¿no?

Sergio: Here, in this country the torch is a message, it's a way to carry a message to all of those people who wish to express themselves freely. It's like a beacon of hope that someday we'll be free, no? . . . The meaning the torch has in Mexico is to carry light from one part of the country to another, no, and this was been done for many, many years, since our ancestors' time. Since there was no way to communicate across distances, to carry a message from one place to another with a torch was a way for people to become enlightened. The message had to arrive to a certain location, so day and night they would run, with the light, with the flame. And as the years passed and the practice continued, well, it became a kind of tradition and took on meaning, as a beacon of faith, because to carry a flame from one place to another is like carrying a message of faith and hope, no? And here in New York, well, since we feel a bit oppressed and we feel, let's say, that we can't express ourselves freely and our rights are denied us, to carry a torch is a way to express ourselves. It's a way to say that we want to be taken into consideration and we want to have equal rights.

Alyshia: So for you the message is for your fellow Mexicans, for the most part or for the—

Sergio: No, the message is double, no? The message is for our compatriots, to tell them that if we are all united we can accomplish great things, and that the light represents hope. And for the rest, well, it's to express ourselves and to say that we are worthwhile and we need equal rights—it's a message for both groups. (interview with Sergio, staff member of Tepeyac and participant in Antorcha Guadalupana, January 2003)

The running of a torch was a pre-Columbian practice for carrying messages. Relay running is described in conquest-era codices as the means by which Moctezuma and his predecessors issued edicts and received news from all over the empire. Runners also brought the emperor fresh fish from the Atlantic and Pacific coasts on a daily basis, in addition to other foods, spices, and goods. It was the way that Moctezuma received news of the arrival of Hernán Cortés and his men at Veracruz, allowing him to prepare an elaborate reception for them. It was after the conquest of the Mexica empire that the practice became associated specifically with Guadalupan devotion. It is said that when Juan Diego appeared before the bishop to deliver the Virgin of Guadalupe's request for a shrine on the hill at Tepeyac and spilled roses at her feet, torch runners conveyed the news of the miraculous apparition throughout the land. On October 29, 2002, the first *Carrera Internacional de la Antorcha Guadalupana,* binational

Guadalupan torch run, was launched at the Basilica of Guadalupe. In it, a flame was carried by relay runners from the Basilica in Mexico City over land to Saint Patrick's Cathedral in New York City. This chapter examines the use of torch runs for conveying religious and cultural messages and the implications of running a torch across a border with a message about immigration reform, as Asociación Tepeyac has done each year since 2002. The previous chapters describe the performance of devotional practices by Mexican immigrants in New York City as means by which community is defined in contradistinction to other groups and on the basis of guadalupanismo, Mexican national identity, and undocumented immigration status. These activities may be microlocal in the space of a church or its parish neighborhood, or, in the case of El Viacrucis del Inmigrante, involve Mexican immigrants from New York's five boroughs in a citywide assertion of community identity. La Antorcha Guadalupana is binational, spanning thousands of kilometers and involving people who are immigrants along with members of their extended families that have not migrated. In this practice, the performance of guadalupanismo more assertively confronts U.S. immigration law and makes embodied incursions into contested legal territory, attempting to literally turn the space of the border into a Guadalupan space, and thus removing it from the jurisdiction of the punitive U.S. immigration landscape. In this chapter, I describe the logistical implementation of this, Asociación Tepeyac's most ambitious activity, with the meaning it has for participants and coordinators. It is in the run that we perhaps can see most vividly an assertion of an alternative definition of citizenship: one not arbitrarily constrained by borders and premised on a very particular kind of Catholic humanism articulated through Guadalupan devotion.

In La Mixteca region of Mexico, *carreras de antorcha*, torch runs, are a common way for young people to celebrate the feast day of the Virgin of Guadalupe. Torch runs are also used by social movements to create a sense of community.[1] When I asked participants in the binational antorcha whether they had ever participated in a torch run in the past, many recounted that as teenagers they ran from their hometowns to the Basilica of Guadalupe in the days preceding the feast day of Guadalupe on December 12. Organized by church-based youth groups, these runs are frequently one of the few excursions away from home and without family that young people are permitted to take. For many, running in an antorcha was like a rite of passage, an opportunity to bond with friends and also assert their individual identity as guadalupanos, outside of home-based devotional practices. For some, it was their first and only trip to the capital, and they spoke fondly of sleeping out in the *atrio*, the outdoor plaza surrounding the basilica, among like groups that had gathered from all over the republic.

La Antorcha Guadalupana was one of the first activities innovated by Asociación Tepeyac to draw together members of comités guadalupanos from all over New York City, and it would become its most spectacular. For a few years preceding the binational torch run, a local version was held each December 12. In previous chapters, I have traced how Mexican members of some parishes began to celebrate Guadalupe's feast day with a mass and mañanitas as early as the mid-1980s. In addition to local parish celebrations, the parish of Our Lady of Guadalupe on Fourteenth Street, down the block from Tepeyac's headquarters, had long been an epicenter for celebrations of the feast day. Founded as a national parish for the small Spanish expatriate community in New York City in the 1920s, the diminutive chapel was not designed to serve a robust congregation. Nonetheless, as home to what was perhaps the oldest image of Guadalupe in New York City and given its central location, it had always been a site where Guadalupanos left flowers, prayed, and heard mass on the Virgin's feast day. There is evidence that as early as 1937, the Guadalupan feast day included Mexican devotees, as a program for the mass that year included advertisements for food stores and restaurants specializing in Mexican cuisine located throughout Manhattan.[2] Until the parish was closed and its image transferred to a larger church two blocks west, Saint Bernard's, each December 12, the chapel's pews spilled over with devotees. It was from the Guadalupan chapel that Tepeyac launched torch runs starting around 1998. Brooklyn youth groups may have begun the practice as early as 1990 (Badillo 2006: 177–178; R. Smith 1995). Young people from parishes that house comités guadalupanos would come to a mass the morning of December 12 on Fourteenth Street, then light torches they had brought and run the flame back to their home parishes for an evening mass. For some young people, this was their only religious activity of the year outside of home.

In 2000, Asociación Tepeyac was granted the opportunity to organize the feast day mass at Saint Patrick's Cathedral. While the Cathedral typically dedicates each daily mass to a saint whose feast corresponds to the date, Tepeyac wanted, and worked for a few years to achieve, involvement in the Guadalupe mass: the ability to help program the mass, invite participants and attendees, and influence the meaning ascribed to the devotion. Upon achieving this, instead of launching the torch run from Fourteenth Street, bishops blessed the torch at Saint Patrick's and runners started out from Fifth Avenue and Forty-ninth Street. Upon exiting the cathedral, they extinguished the flame (the New York City Police Department had begun to prohibit them from carrying a lit flame), carried it in procession to Fourteenth Street, blessed it again outside the chapel there, and then the cold torches were symbolically "lit" from the one that had been blessed, and run to local parishes.

During the Guadalupe feast day mass the following year, on December 12, 2001, the Archbishop of New York, Edward *Cardinal* Egan, said that it would be nice for a flame to be brought all the way from the source of Guadalupan devotion, the Basilica at Tepeyac in Mexico City, for the following year's feast. Ironically, the idea for an international Guadalupan torch run actually did not come from a member of the Mexican community at all. Asociación Tepeyac answered the call and began the challenging logistical task of organizing people in dozens of parishes along the 4,500-kilometer route to run, house runners, obtain permits to circulate on streets and highways, and connect with Guadalupanos along the way. The run has occurred several times since, but here my focus is on the first one in 2002.

The Logistics

I observed preparations for the run in Mexico City and Puebla state in the weeks preceding the run and interviewed its organizers as well as members of collaborating organizations, and I also was present for the launch from the Basilica of Guadalupe on October 29, 2002. It is in the torch run that the deployment of Guadalupan devotion toward the project of humanizing Mexican migrants in the United States and making them subjects worthy of rights achieves its fullest elaboration. I asked one of the staff members of the Basilica who was serving as a liaison to the logistical coordinators of Tepeyac and its Mexican affiliates about publicity. Having witnessed the planning of so many events at Tepeyac, I knew that a good portion of the advance labor for any event was the writing and circulation of press releases, hosting of press conferences, and recruiting of leaders from the community to spread the word and bring their constituencies. I wondered whether a campaign had been undertaken to publicize the launch of the torch run to the media and potential attendees. "Oh no," I was told, "We don't publicize events at the Basilica."[3] I thought perhaps

Poster for the Antorcha Guadalupana, 2002

there was an anathemic relationship to the secular mass media. She went on to explain that when an event has to do with Our Lady of Guadalupe, the problem is crowd control and excessive turnout, not its opposite: "If we don't publicize events, thousands of people come, if word were to get out in the media, a million would come." The logistical conversations by the coordinators centered on organizing the thousands of people expected to attend, not inducing more people to come. This was indicative of the overall interpretation of the event among those affiliated with the torch run in Mexico. In Mexico City, Guadalupan devotion is, arguably, part of the landscape. Images of Guadalupe, as mentioned in previous chapters, are so ubiquitous as to be practically mundane. When I asked why a *Guadalupan* torch run, one coordinator of the run in Mexico City repeated an old saying: "In Mexico we are 95% Catholic, but 100% Guadalupan." It was assumed the event would be successful, highly attended, and comprehensible. No one seemed to question "Why?" as some affiliates of Tepeyac did in New York City. In spite of the herculean logistical implications, they viewed the event as a logical, expected expression of Guadalupanism undertaken by Mexicans living in the United States. Like the misión, it seemed self-evident that if one had a message to get out, in this case about inhumane immigration laws, Our Lady of Guadalupe was the most appropriate messenger to carry it.

The event was organized through social networks. An active organizer in a Queens parish-based comité guadalupano as well as a staff member at Tepeyac in the cultural affairs division, Heraclio, was the captain for the Mexican leg of the run. He told me he knew people at the Basilica and had some contacts in Puebla and in Hidalgo states, as well as other places. The executive director of Tepeyac, Joel Magallán, also boasted of a broad network of Jesuit brothers who were mobilized to the task. With virtually no budget, Heraclio traveled around Mexico in the summer of 2002 to map out the route, calling on community leaders, nonprofit organizations, and pastors to help. They sought to visit many of the communities from which Mexicans in New York originate, but those lie south of the capital, and they eventually needed to head north. They finally settled on a route that would take six weeks and cover 4,500 kilometers.

Members of some of the nonprofits that collaborated on planning told me they knew that Tepeyac had few funds to invest in the project, but as one organizer said, "we know that eventually our efforts will be reciprocated, perhaps not now, but someday, that's how we work here, amongst the NGOs" (interview with José Isaías Romero, October 18, 2002, Mexico

City). Heraclio asked the Basilica to schedule a mass for the launch. Marco Sotomayor, a beloved Jesuit brother in Puebla state, rallied community participation. People who planned to run in New York called their relatives and friends and told them to find out about and participate in the run.

On the morning of October 29, an unprecedented gathering sat in the pews of the Basilica of Guadalupe, before the most sacred object of Guadalupan devotion, the framed image of Guadalupe miraculously imprinted on Juan Diego's tilma, listening to mass. At the front of the altar was the recently commissioned official portrait of the newly canonized Saint Juan Diego. The controversial painting shows a man with markedly European features kneeling in the white homespun clothing archetypal of Nahua people at the time of the Conquest. On a banner hanging from the ceiling of this modern cathedral was a painting of Pope John Paul II blessing the new saint. Even during the formal masses and ceremonies that occur daily in the cathedral, the faithful are able to engage directly with the object of their devotion. An electric walkway runs behind the altar, just below floor level, carrying the faithful at a slow but efficient pace in front of the image, out of view of those gathered in the pews. In the rear of the basilica, young couples appear every few minutes carrying similarly sized bundles of blankets: according to custom, they bring their seven-week-old babies to receive the Virgin's blessing, which apparently can be obtained without interacting with clergy or other Basilica personnel. Aztec-style dancers perform on the atrio outside, and other pilgrims brave the capital's contaminated air to climb el Cerro Tepeyac, just to the rear of the basilica. Just adjacent to the new basilica is the original basilica. It is too small and decrepit to sustain the magnitude of contemporary devotion, and from a hundred meters it becomes clear why: it is sinking, off kilter, into the damp landfill on which this city rests. Just outside the atrio and the main gates of the basilica's grounds, a profusion of vendors line the main road leading to the *Villa*, as the basilica is known. Selling framed two- and three-dimensional images, snow globes, t-shirts, medallions, candles, scapularies, rosaries, ribbons, post cards, statues, and much more (including amaranth seed dough effigies, typical of pre-Columbian ritual offerings), they welcome pilgrims to this city within a city. Between the dozens of small shrines, the hill, the atrio, the basilica, and, of course, the image itself, the Basilica is practically a devotional theme park.[4]

On this day, those gathered here came from near and far. Priests from parishes located in the five boroughs of New York City gathered, along

Launch of the Torch Run. Luz María, widow of a victim of September 11, 2001, holds the torch, October 29, 2002

with many of the members of Grupo Timón, the founders of Tepeyac, as well as archdiocesan officials and bishops. Many of the staff members of Tepeyac who were able to travel were there. Most major news organizations in Mexico covered the event. The celebrity guests came, each with their own role. Alex Lora, lead singer of the popular folk rock band El Tri, would sing his famous ode to Guadalupe: "*Virgen Morena.*" Luz María, widow of a Mexican worker who perished in the World Trade Center on September 11, 2001, would hold the torch aloft in the Basilica, then pass it to Ana Gabriela Guevara, Olympic gold medal runner for Mexico, who would take the first steps of the run.

Joel Magallán announced from a stage outside the basilica that Our Lady of Guadalupe was carrying a message for the people divided by a border, and that she was carrying it to the family members that migrants leave behind, to migrants themselves, and also to the powerful in Mexico and in Washington, who could reform immigration law. She would carry this message across the border, and like the migrants she was to represent, she would do so without documents. Just as runners in pre-Columbian Mexico relayed messages to and from the imperial capital of Tenochtitlán, runners in the torch run, as their jerseys declared, imagined themselves running a message of dignity. Joel Magallán said at the launch of the torch run that like Saint Juan Diego, who knocked on the doors of the Bishop, imploring him to heed the request Guadalupe had entrusted to him, Mexican immigrants in the United States are knocking on the doors of the authorities, asking them to grant them the rights and dignity they deserve. I asked one of the community organizers in Puebla what the meaning of the binational antorcha was: "Esta carrera es un grito desesperado del inmigrante" [This run is the desperate shout of the immigrant] (interview with Amalia Cortázar, October 21, 2002). Referring to the 2007 antorcha, but relevant to each of the runs, María Zúñiga, first female *capitana* de la antorcha, wrote:

Esta es una Carrera de fé, durante el camino los que participamos no nos llamamos a nosotros mismos corredores, sino Mensajeros. Bajo el manto de la Virgen nos cobijamos. Y con ella como estandarte, Guadalupe ahora peregrina como nosotros, salimos a llevar su mensaje como lo hiciera el Indio Juan Diego. Todos los mensajes se entretejen en el manto de San Juan Diego que muestra en sus rosas las necesidades de nuestros pueblos y su lucha en la búsqueda de una vida más justa, digna y donde podamos caminar juntos como una gran comunidad humana, dispersa por el mundo.

[This is a run of faith. Along the way, those who participate do not call each other runners, but Messengers. Under the shawl of the Virgin we take shelter. And with her as our standard bearer, Guadalupe now walks amongst us [as a pilgrim]. We go out to take her message like the Indian Juan Diego did. All of the messages are woven into Saint Juan Diego's cloak that shows in its roses the needs of our people and our struggle in search of a more just and dignified life, where we can walk together as a great human community, spread out around the world. (2008)]

Torch run passes through Zapotitlán Salinas, Puebla, Mexico, 2007. Photograph by Joel Merino.

Leaving the Basilica, runners passed through parts of Puebla, Guerrero, Hidalgo, and Tlaxcala states, through towns from which thousands of migrants have left for New York. Following the eastern seaboard, they ran through Veracruz and Tamaulipas states, crossed at Brownsville into Texas, ran north through the new migrant communities in the southern United States, to Washington, DC, past the White House, all the way to New York City. The runners in Mexico were family members of migrants; those who crossed the border were, by necessity, those who had documents enabling them to cross; and those on this side of the border were mostly Mexican immigrants. Their shirts declared them and linked them all as "mensajeros de un pueblo dividido por la frontera" [messengers of a people divided by the border].

Los Comités Guadalupanos and the Torch Run

One exercise in contrasts between the two parishes in which I conducted my research was the way they organized their involvement in the torch run in the months that preceded it. At Saint John Church, Segundo had been the *capitán* of the antorcha for a few years, when the run had been local. Although he rarely attended the meetings of the comité guadalupano, María Lucía directed those who were interested in participating in the torch run to him, and as he was fairly known in the parish, it seemed most people were able to find him. Closer to the date, the nuns stationed at Saint John Parish also collected inscriptions, although they would not attend the events at Saint Patrick's Cathedral on December 12. It struck me as indicative of the fissures between Saint John and the larger association that the coordination of the Guadalupan torch run was handled outside of the comité guadalupano.

Already, on February 26, 2002, María José mentioned at a meeting of the comité that she was registered to run in the antorcha. She said she had made a promise to the Virgin to run for five consecutive years to ask for the Virgin to heal her liver. She was asked by María Lucía, Doña Rosario, and others present whether she had sought medical help for her liver. She said yes. Eyeing her belly, they then asked whether she was pregnant. María José lived across the street from the parish, sharing two rooms of a five-bedroom apartment with her husband and four of her children. Her eldest child remained in Guerrero state. While virtually everyone else who expressed sorrow or stress over medical and other difficulties in this setting was offered consolation, María José, notably, usually received skepticism and exasperation in response to her frequent troubles. This time, the women asked why she had gotten pregnant again, had she not protected herself, "¿no te cuidaste?" She reported that the doctor had not told her that medicine he prescribed for her hepatitis would lessen the effectiveness of her oral contraceptives. Doña Rosario took María's experience as fodder for a lesson on patient's rights: "¡Todos tienen derecho a un traductor en el hospital!" [Everyone has the right to a translator in the hospital!] The next time María José mentioned her *promesa* to the Virgin to run in the antorcha, Doña Rosario took it as an opportunity to comment upon the sinfulness of demonstrating faith in the Virgin in expectation of the fulfillment of requests: "Hacer promesas es pecado grave. Eso es lo mismo que prostitución, es lo que hizo Judas. Después cuando su petición se ha cumplido, en gracias, sí, hay que hacer algo" [To make promises is a grave sin. It's the same as prostitution. It is what Judas did. Only after your request is fulfilled, you must do something, in thanks." I do not recall that María José mentioned again her involvement in the torch run, but she was at the Cathedral on December 12, only a few weeks postpartum, dressed in the distinctive white sweatsuit of the antorcha, tied around her forehead a bandanna of the Mexican flag with an image of Guadalupe at its center. In spite of the treatment she had received in the comité, she was eager to run the flame back to her parish.

In spite of the involvement of some of its members as individuals, Saint John's comité guadalupano did not participate actively in the international torch run. Runners from the comité were not sent out of state to a leg of the route, and on December 12, the members of the Magaña family were nowhere to be seen. Some members of the comité, like María José, did run locally and others carried the comité's banner to the mass in Saint Patrick's Cathedral. In contrast, Our Lady of the Rosary's comité spent many months preparing for their participation, which was multilayered. The captain of the antorcha, Nancy, a woman who had organized it in the past, collected entry fees and sweatsuit orders from the comité's members over many months. She gave updates at each of the group's meetings, reporting the number of inscriptions that were paid in full, as well as the number of people who had expressed an interest but not yet paid their dues ($20 for inscription, including the uniform). At Saint John, the inscriptions were submitted the first week of December, so late that no sweatpants were left (a fixed number had been donated to Tepeyac and distributed in order of registration). In front of the group, María Lucía openly criticized what she viewed as excessive registration fees and asked the nuns, who had assumed the task of coordination, "the fee doesn't even include the sweatpants?" but no one made mention of the fact that the inscription period had closed weeks before. There was also no mention of the precise route, start time, or other details one would need to attend the event.

At Our Lady of the Rosary Church, meanwhile, at the meeting of the comité guadalupano on December 2, most of the group's time was spent on details surrounding "la fiesta para Mamá Lupita." The group's energies would be consumed that month not only by the Guadalupan festivities but also by the church's 150th anniversary celebration, involvement in which the priest made clear would be a testament to each lay organization's loyalty. The antorcha was described as one of the many activities the group was involved in to celebrate Guadalupe's feast. The group's members planned to decorate the church a little each day until the twelfth. One elderly woman had promised to walk on foot from her house, presumably some distance, carrying her offering of votive candles which she had requested be brought from Mexico. Others offered pots of *tamales* and *atole*. For the feast day, the comité was constructing a large realistic replica of the hill at Tepeyac complete with a water feature, but they could not install it until after the anniversary celebration on December 9, at the pastor's request.

That night, those who had participated in the antorcha in years past testified about what a beautiful experience it was and encouraged those who had not already registered to do so. Detailed instructions were given for those who would accompany the run in Philadelphia, to meet up with the torch in New Jersey to run it across the George Washington Bridge, meet the torch at the Cathedral, dance in the *atrio* of Saint Patrick's, or form part of the *cadena humana*, a human chain, on Fourteenth Street to run the flame to the parish. Members of the comité guadalupano were given multiple ways of participating in the Antorcha Guadalupana from which they could choose depending on their economic resources and time they could take from work or school. While the organizers hoped as many people as possible would travel to the comité's assigned segment of the route in Philadelphia, participation in local Antorcha activities was also valorized. The logistical difficulties encountered in organizing the event were presented here in great detail as problems pertinent to the people gathered here. It was evident on this, and on other occasions, that Tepeyac's problems were also the comité's problems. Further, in this comité the operational "we" includes Tepeyac, while at Saint John's grupo guadalupano, the association was invariably referred to as "they." Alberto said:

> Uno viendo la antorcha pensará que estamos muy organizados pero en Nueva York no tenemos permiso. Por ser ilegales, nos discriminan, hasta para pasar la antorcha por la Casa Blanca nos dieron permiso, pero en Nueva York, no. Hay que pensar en eso, y el lema de la antorcha, 'Mensajeros por la dignidad de un pueblo divido por la frontera.'

> [Looking at the antorcha, one might think that we are very organized, but here in New York we don't have permits. Since we're illegal, they discriminate against us. We were given permits even to pass in front of the White House, but not here. We have to think about that, and the message of the torch run: 'messengers for a people divided by the border.' (Meeting of the Comité Guadalupano, Our Lady of the Rosary Parish, December 2, 2002)]

Comités guadalupanos that volunteered to send numerous contingents of runners were assigned a segment of the route. Our Lady of the Rosary Parish was assigned to Philadelphia. Nancy reported that organization

had been difficult, "*un relajo*." She said people told her they would participate, but then failed to take into consideration the expense of traveling
to the part of the route where they would run or the arrangements they
would need to make to take off of work and other responsibilities. Her
roster of runners had been shifting: 14, 16, 20, back to 16. She said, "la carrera es para las cosas que queremos, amnistía, para tener el día libre el 12,
para celebrar la Virgen" [the run is for the things we want, for amnesty, to
have the day off on the 12th, to celebrate the virgin]. In spite of these difficulties, Our Lady of the Rosary sent one of the largest groups of runners
to the route of the antorcha. Within Tepeyac, Our Lady of the Rosary was
frequently referred to as a comité that could be counted on to participate
in the association's initiatives and fulfill the commitments that they made
to the organization of events, and in all senses *cumplir*.

I met up with the contingent from Our Lady of the Rosary in Philadelphia. Some members had remarked that the group had been lucky to
be assigned a not too distant segment of the route. Some parishes were
assigned relays in Mississippi, Alabama, or Virginia. Because many of the
participants are undocumented, flying was not an option and even boarding Greyhound or Amtrak was dicey. Some runners piled into someone's
vehicle and drove all night to reach their leg of the route in the deep
South. Social networks of immigrants in New York sometimes reach areas
of the Southeastern United States, especially North Carolina and Virginia,
that are just beginning to receive large numbers of Mexican migrants.
It is not unusual for a migrant in New York to have a cousin, brother,
or friend in the South, or for some families to have moved to New York
from the South, or vice versa. Even so, in addition to considerable travel
expenses and lost wages, participants shouldered a significant burden of
personal risk to participate in the run. This was described by participants
as one of the many opportunities the Virgin presented for one to demonstrate love and faith, and in return, it was said she would offer protection.
Indeed, one staff member of Tepeyac who lacks documents traveled to accompany the antorcha in Mexico and after praying to the Virgin, traveled
back across the border "de mojado," as he described it, with a coyote in
Arizona. Although I did not learn of anyone whose undocumented presence was detected as a result of participation, the shared exposure to risk
served to again reiterate the vectors of identity: guadalupanismo, Mexican
nationality, and undocumented status.

After tracking down the torch runners in Philadelphia, I hopped out
of a friend's car and into one of the vans that was dropping off runners

for their relays and picking them up at the end of them. There were more than ten people piled in the back of the van. They were a merry bunch, arms intertwined, laughing and chatting about the experience. Contrary to what I expected, they were not all from Our Lady of the Rosary Parish; some had joined the run on an earlier leg of the route. There were two staff members from Tepeyac including the driver, a woman from Wilmington, Delaware, running with her sixteen-year-old nephew, and a man from their parish; a woman from Immaculate Conception Parish in the Bronx; a man who was a paramedic from Matamoros; a teenage boy from Brooklyn who was born in Puebla but did not speak Spanish; and several men and women from Our Lady of the Rosary Parish. While they waited for their turn to run, I asked each of them why they were running: "*por devoción,*" out of devotion, was the most common response. One man from Puebla state, brother of the president of Our Lady of the Rosary's comité and a guitarist in a rock band, said he was running because his son suffers health problems. The paramedic said that he joined the run a month and three days before. He said his son had migrated to Queens eleven years earlier, and that although he visits him frequently, it is difficult to be separated. As we talked, runners were always within sight on the cold highway outside. As we traveled from the city center into more rural areas, the runners ran longer relays. When the torch's flame faltered, the Tepeyac staff member riding in the passenger seat passed a fuel-soaked rag out the window of the van to the runner, who squeezed it over the torch, then ignited it with a clicker.

The Symbolism

Despite the casting of the torch run as a means to knock on the doors of the authorities and demand amnesty, it was the transformation of runners into so many Juan Diegos, the chosen recipient of the Virgin's message, that was the principal goal and result of the run. I asked one of the organizers if he thought it was a problem that many of the runners joined purely out of devotional impulse, without an awareness of or interest in the political goals of the run. Each night, when the runners would break for the night or another group would arrive to take over the relay at a host parish, there would be a mass and he and others would make a presentation explaining the objectives of the run. In Mexico, the organizers wanted non-immigrants to be more aware of the situation of immigrants, that they are not living the easy life in the United

States, plucking dollar bills from the trees, but suffering exploitation and deprivation of their rights and dignity. At the stops in the United States, organizers wanted communities along the route to become more united, to be more aware of the suffering of the immigrants in their midst, and to politicize them with respect to immigration laws. For Heraclio, one of only two people who traveled the entire route of the antorcha, the torch created a chain of comités guadalupanos all along the route, like so many pearls, linking the Basilica and New York City in an embodied network of Guadalupan devotion. This chain bound the two countries, and specifically those towns and cities that are linked in the social networks of immigrants and their families, in a single space, a space of transnational or even post-national citizenship. Thus, while there were certainly recipients of the message who were non-Mexican, non-immigrant, and not Guadalupanos—and this was perceived as highly important— the main thrust of the antorcha was the effort to form a transnational Mexican community, asserting shared interests, culture, idioms, and objectives. Even while presentations and speeches were made in English and Spanish for non-Mexicans and Mexicans along the torch's route, the runners were primarily bringing their message to others who spoke in the same discursive idiom of Guadalupan devotion. Like the participants in the misión guadalupana in the Bronx, they entrusted the Virgin of Guadalupe to *abrir el camino* clear a path and bring along her faithful into a common cause for undocumented immigrants. María Zúñiga described the run's power to link families: although the border divides people who because of their undocumented status "cannot go home," the run can bring them together (2008). In Durham, North Carolina, during the 2007 antorcha, a young man approached her, requesting pictures of his mother. He said he was from Atlixtac, Guerrero. When the torch had passed through that town, María had taken pictures of some older women, and told them that when they spoke with their children in the United States to instruct them to find the antorcha and collect the pictures from her. In spite of these instructions, María was shocked when this young man succeeded in meeting up with the torch's route and requesting the photos. Nonetheless, he was momentarily saddened when he could not locate his mother in the photos. He had not seen her in seven years and could not pick her out from the crowd. María instructed him to close his eyes and see her with his heart. When he opened his eyes, she said, he immediately located his mother in multiple photos taken in Atlixtac.

The Torch passes through Progreso, state of Puebla, photograph by Joel Merino, Antorcha 2007

Like many members of los comités guadalupanos, the organizers of the torch run frequently described their relationship to Guadalupe as qualitatively different prior to their involvement. In fact, it was evident that some of the coordinators held a somewhat Marxian view of popular devotion prior to their experience with the torch run. When I asked Antonio, coordinator of the U.S. leg of the antorcha, "What were the big challenges you faced as coordinator?" he replied:

> Everything. Being American-born. Understanding the Mexican community. Certain dogmas and rituals, ways of thinking are hard to understand. Values. . . . How women stare seemingly for hours at the images seemed foreign. The continuous blessings. Non-stop. Why do they have to kiss the picture 500 times? [5]

Nonetheless, many of those involved in the torch run, including Antonio, developed a deep appreciation for the power of the image which in many cases transformed their own relationship to the Virgin of Guadalupe. Sergio said:

Pues, siempre he tenido la misma perspectiva de la Virgen de Guadalupe, pero el haber participado en esta carrera, sí, como que lo sientes mucho más, mucho más amor, pasas a ser como parte de ella, sientes que . . . no sé, ósea es un sentimiento que realmente es muy difícil de expresarlo . . . que si acaso estabas dudando, yo creo que se te hace muy fuerte el sentimiento . . . y más que nada por lo que te digo, ¿no?, el ver que la gente, por la Virgen de Guadalupe hace miles de cosas, es lo que más—es la satisfacción más grande que uno tiene.

[Sergio: Well, I've always had the same perspective on the Virgin of Guadalupe, but having participated in this run, yes, it's as though you feel it much more, much more love and you become a part of her, you feel that . . . I don't know, it's like a feeling that really is difficult to express . . . If you were doubting, I believe it makes your feelings stronger . . . and more than anything, as I say, to see that people, for the Virgin of Guadalupe, do a thousand things, it's what most—it's the greatest satisfaction one can have. (Interview with Sergio, staff member of Tepeyac and participant in Antorcha Guadalupana, January 2003)]

And at length, Rodrigo described the process by which he came to appreciate the power of the antorcha and its symbolism.

Alyshia: ¿Cómo te pareció la conexión entre la Antorcha y esta problemática [de la inmigración], viste inmediatamente el significado?
Rodrigo: Bueno, yo no lo vi inmediatamente, pero es como, es todo un significado . . . pues la Virgen de Guadalupe es este, pues digamos, es este, queridísima en la religión católica en México y digamos . . . cada año la adornan, entonces la peregrinación, entonces la confianza hacia la Virgen es muy grande y es un símbolo para los mexicanos, y para esto de la Antorcha, se utilizó a la Virgen de Guadalupe pues para pedirle el milagro de la amnistía, ¿no? para la comunidad mexicana y pues siempre va de la mano, eso de la lucha, la religión y pedirle a Dios a través de la Virgen . . . y en un principio tuve que pensarlo un poco para darle el significado pero a lo largo del tiempo sí entendí realmente el sentido de lo que era.
Alyshia: Y te asignaron el trabajo de colaborar con la Antorcha, ¿pero te dijeron inmediatamente que ibas a estar toda la ruta, y qué te pareció?
Rodrigo: No pues, no, no me lo imaginaba de hecho, este, pues los 45 días, un día en cada ciudad era diferente y todavía el día antes que estaba yo en el D.F., estábamos en el hotel, eran los 12 de la noche y no me imaginaba

lo que iba a pasar al día siguiente y pues, pero . . . no pues, una experiencia maravillosa, increíble, ver que toda la gente con sus corredores, sus devociones, sus iglesias, sus misas, ósea hay mil cosas, fue una experiencia increíble el haber participado, el haber estado a lo largo de la ruta.

Alyshia: ¿y tú te considerabas muy Guadalupano antes?:

Rodrigo: Pues nunca he pensado en eso de que soy guadalupano, pues de chiquito la Virgen de Guadalupe estaba presente en México, y pues toda mi vida la he tenido presente, pero nunca he pensado así como que "soy guadalupano." Y bueno . . .

Alyshia: ¿Ósea era como parte de tu identidad pero no lo pensabas mucho?

Rodrigo: No, porque era algo así como que ya venía arraigado

Alyshia: Como preguntarte porque tienes el pelo negro . . . ¿era como algo natural?

Rodrigo: Era algo ya arraigado en mí y pues a lo largo de la ruta, la Antorcha, digamos se fue fortaleciendo, aumentando . . .

[Alyshia: What did you think of the connection between the antorcha and the issue of immigration, did you get the significance immediately?

Rodrigo: Well, no, not immediately. But it's all part of the same meaning . . . The Virgin of Guadalupe is, let's say, so loved in the Catholic religion in Mexico and each year they decorate her, then they go on a pilgrimage. Then the trust that people have in her is very big and she's a symbol for Mexicans. Now for this, we utilized the Virgin of Guadalupe to ask for the miracle of amnesty, no? For the Mexican community. These things always go hand in hand, struggle, religion and asking God through the Virgin. And in the beginning, I had to think about it a bit to get the significance, but with time, I really understood the meaning.

Alyshia: And when they assigned you to work on the antorcha, did they tell you right away you'd be along for the entire route, and what did you think of that?

Rodrigo: No, in fact, I couldn't imagine the whole 45 days, being in a different city each day and even the day before, when we were in Mexico City, we were in a hotel and it was midnight and I still couldn't imagine what was going to happen the next day, but . . . well, it was a marvelous, incredible experience. To see all the people with the runners, their devotion, their churches, their masses. There are a thousand things. It was an incredible experience to be able to participate and be present for the entire route.

Alyshia: And did you consider yourself very Guadalupan before?

Rodrigo: Well, I had never thought about it, since I was little the Virgin of
Guadalupe was present in Mexico and well, my whole life she was present,
but I had never thought "I'm Guadalupan", and well . . .
Alyshia: So it was part of your identity but you never thought about it much?
Rodrigo: No, because it was like something that was just part of my roots.
Alyshia: It's like asking why you have black hair, it was something natural?
Rodrigo: It was something rooted in me and well, along the route, la antor-
cha, let's say it was strengthened and grew. (Interview, January 2003)

Some controversy centered on Tepeyac's "utilization" of the symbol of
Guadalupe. The basis of these critiques can be found in the general positioning of Guadalupe as the masthead of all of Tepeyac's activities and
in language that is frequently used to describe the Virgin's power. For example, Rodrigo remarks "se utiliza a la Virgen de Guadalupe," and Sergio
in the first quotation in this chapter, says "la antorcha se usa." Some critics accuse Tepeyac of exploiting people's faith in the Virgin for political
purposes. The director of another community organization which serves
Mexican immigrants in New York City, Jerry Domínguez, said about Tepeyac: "They are very powerful, very influential, they are very well organized which counts a lot and they don't pay rent, also that counts. It's a
church. How can you compete with a church and the Virgin of Guadalupe? Forget about it."[6] He went on:

The Virgin of Guadalupe goes beyond time, church and politics. . . . In
certain ways, it's bad because you are expecting something in the future
once you die. . . . And we need to get rid of it . . . that's why the Church
has able to market the Virgin of Guadalupe in such a way . . . everywhere
I see the Virgin of Guadalupe. It's so powerful. At the same time, it's so
weakening. (Interview with Jerry Domínguez, June 24, 2003)

For some, like Jerry Domínguez, Tepeyac's mobilization of Guadalupe is
cynical and instrumental. For others who do not share his Marxist vision of faith, but whose criticism is grounded in faith, it is presumptuous
and sinful to assume that the Virgin speaks for any one segment of the
population or cause, or to exploit her image for earthly gain. Examples
frequently cited by devotees of misuse of the Virgin's image include the
Cristero War (1926–1929), the spectacular visit of president-elect Vicente
Fox to the Basilica of Guadalupe in 2000 where he kneeled in thanks for
being elected, and the "mass of repentance" hosted at the Basilica by the

Partido Revolucionario Institucional (PRI) in October 2002, shortly after being routed from power after 71 authoritarian years. Indeed, following the Revolution, the 1917 Constitution ensured a very limited role for the church which would restrict public displays of religiosity associated with the state until 1992.[7]

While I never heard anyone question the sincerity of the faith of Asociación Tepeyac's staff or director, or that of anyone else associated with Tepeyac, cynicism about the use of such an irrefutably powerful symbol to recruit migrants to a specific political struggle was sometimes perceptible among non-participants. However, as is clear in the quotations above, the irreverent college students and staff who were involved in Tepeyac's campaigns, as well as the members of the comités, were moved by their experiences and rather than imply that they manipulated or exploited people's faith in their work, they say that observing people's faith and participation in a collective project organized around faith symbols changed them. What is more, the participants—migrants and their family members—never questioned Guadalupe's patronage of the torch run. In this, as in all of Tepeyac's successful activities, the linkage between popular devotion and the struggle for rights was viewed as logical and powerful, not instrumental. Sergio said:

No sé qué resultados va a tener el haberla traído desde México, pero pienso que lo que se está viendo es mucha unidad, pienso que al menos por la experiencia que yo tuve de que la fe mueve miles y millones de personas y que por esa fe podemos hacer miles de cosas si seguimos, este, uniéndonos, ¿no? Yo creo que por política o por otras cosas, nunca se ha llegado a unirse tanto la gente, sino en cambio por la Virgen de Guadalupe, la gente hace miles de cosas por estar ahí, ¿no?, participando en estos eventos, entonces para mí la satisfacción que me queda es . . . es que la gente le tiene mucha fe a la Virgen de Guadalupe, y que si queremos lograr algo, lo vamos a lograr, no utilizándola, digamos, pero si en nombre de ella vamos a lograr muchas cosas.

[I don't know what results it will have, to have brought the torch from Mexico, but I think what we're seeing is a lot of unity, that at least in the experience I had, that faith moves thousands and millions of people, and with that faith we can do a thousand things if we continue, you know, being united, no? I think that because of politics, or other things, we've never been able to unite so many people, however with the Virgin of Guadalupe, people will do anything to be there, no? To participate in these events. So for me, the satisfaction that remains with me . . . is that people have a lot of faith in the Virgin of Guadalupe and if we wish to achieve something, we're going to do it, not using her, per se, but in her name, we are going to achieve a lot of things. (Interview with Sergio, January 2003)]

Miracles

Each of the organizers that I interviewed in New York after the completion of the torch run also remarked on miraculous interventions on the part of the Virgin which reinforced their faith. Each of these young people said that, although in some cases they had faith in the Virgin of Guadalupe prior to the run, they were skeptical of her ability to effect earthly miracles. Nonetheless, they said, what they observed was difficult to explain without deferring to divine intervention. Heraclio said:

> Había cosas, experiencias que pasaron, donde creíamos que no se iba a lograr, fueron muchas millas y queríamos llegar y de alguna u otra forma llegábamos, entonces era muy chistoso, ¿no? Todavía lugares donde ibamos medido mal y que eran más las distancias, y por cualquier cosa que nos perdíamos pero llegábamos a la hora, vamos, era como decíamos, ¿verdad?, siempre llegábamos. Increíble todo eso porque la gente nos esperaba a tal hora y llegábamos a esa hora, entonces fue muy que la gente, que todos los coordinadores, pues, este, agarramos más fe, más fuerza, como la Virgen era muy milagrosa y nos apoyó, y como lo decíamos, ¿no?, creo que veníamos muy bien protegidos por que traíamos nuestra madre con nosotros . . . . La traíamos con nosotros y eso era muy importante.

[There were things, experiences that happened, where we didn't think we'd make it, where there were many miles and we wanted to cover them, and somehow we made it. So it was funny, no? There were places where we were having a bad time and the distances were long, and maybe we got lost, but we always made it on time. We were like "really?" We always arrived. It was incredible because people were expecting us at a given time and we arrived. So it was that people, that all of the coordinators, well, we had more faith, more strength, knowing that the Virgin was miraculous and helped us and supported us. And like we said, no, I believe we were very protected because we were bringing our mother with us . . . We brought her with us and that was very important. (Interview with Heraclio, January 2003)]

The day before the launch of the torch in Mexico City, Heraclio went to the Basilica to pick up the banner bearing an image of the Virgin of Guadalupe which had been promised. The staff member who greeted him said, "What banner? The Monsignor left those for you."[8] Leaning against the wall were two official portraits of Saint Juan Diego and Our Lady of Guadalupe, each painting measuring approximately two meters tall by one meter wide. Heraclio panicked. The torch would be accompanied by vans. Would the paintings fit in the vans? What if they were damaged? How would they carry these massive images? What if it rained? Ultimately, each day when the torch was carried by relay runners and two vans worked in concert to pick up and drop off the runners for their relays, the images were carried inside the vehicles. Sometimes rain fell on the runners all day long. However, miraculously, both Heraclio and Antonio recounted, the rain always stopped in the afternoon when they were arriving to their destination, and on the outskirts of town, the images were taken from the vans and carried into the town center in procession. In Virginia, there was one town where the organizers had not been able to obtain a permit, but the Virgin protected them from being stopped by the police. And of course, it was the Virgin's work that enabled them to deliver the torch across all 4,500 kilometers to Saint Patrick's Cathedral.

The painted images and the torch themselves became objects of devotion for their association with the Basilica and with the original image of Guadalupe which is at the center of her cult. The images, as mentioned above, were kissed by devotees along the route. People took photographs in front of them, threw flowers at them, and tried to touch them. To carry the torch was a deep honor for which people clamored. At the culmination of the run, the images were donated to Saint Bernard Parish in Manhattan, the new Guadalupan parish after the archdiocese closed Our Lady of Guadalupe Parish on Fourteenth Street. The following year, and every year since, a new pair of paintings was given to the parish of the comité guadalupano that recruited the greatest number of participants to the torch run.

After the launch of the torch in Mexico City, the most complicated planning surrounded the border crossing of the torch and its entourage. Joel Magallán made frequent mention of the fact that the Virgin would cross under cover of night, without documents, just as her children do when they migrate from Mexico to the United States. However, she—her image, the torch, and the painting of Juan Diego—and her entourage had to cross at a border checkpoint. Planners hoped to organize a *convivencia* at the border, a small gathering of people from both sides in which the family members and friends of migrants, those left behind, could bid farewell to the torch, which would be received by the immigrants themselves and carried all the way to New York where their family members had migrated. There was a certain degree of disingenuousness on the part of Tepeyac in making this event resemble in most ways the torch runs and other Guadalupan devotional practices (processions, worship of the images) with which many participants are already familiar rather than a protest vigil about immigration law.

As I describe in chapter 1, for some, there is nothing more expected than Mexicans engaging in devotion to Our Lady of Guadalupe. As such, even as the runners wore shirts declaring themselves a people divided by the border and as the torch run was punctuated by nightly teach-ins in which participants and host parishes were informed about immigration issues and the struggle for immigration reform, it was assumed that with Guadalupe as masthead, the runners could go where protestors could not. By couching politics within discourses and practices of devotion, Tepeyac hoped—and routinely hopes with many of its activities—to engage people who do not consider themselves activists or political. It was not a problem for the organizers that the runners frequently had no idea what the "message" carried with the torch was when they joined. It was important simply that they become involved, and they would be informed, and hopefully energized to the cause along the way. Similarly, the parishes in the Southeastern United States that were recruited to host the runners were not given much information in advance about the political message of the run. Likewise, border officials were asked for permission to transport sacred images in a procession originating at the Basilica of Guadalupe. Organizers told me that the Department of Homeland Security's office at the Brownsville/Matamoros crossing was open to the event and very cooperative, promising them that the convivencia could occur.

However, when the run reached the border, the act of opening the border to allow the images, the torch, and their entourage to cross which the convivencia implied, was seen by border officials in a different light. At the last moment, they refused to permit the performative spectacle in which Our Lady of Guadalupe was to open the border. The runners reached the border later that night than they had anticipated and than expected by the Department of Homeland Security. Feeling somewhat rushed, the organizers did not go ahead of the group to confirm the plan with officials. Instead, the mass of people and sacred objects arrived all together. Border agents came out and began to herd the group and sort them into separate contingents. A few agents told those carrying the images and the torch to step out of the main lines leading through the checkpoint and walk into a side door. Organizers initially thought the agents were doing the group a favor, enabling them the special time and space of reflection, prayer, and farewell that had been planned. Instead, they were told the images and torch would be inspected and carried across the dividing line between the United States and Mexico by border officials, not runners. After being accompanied on her long journey by her devoted followers, the Virgin really would travel like many migrants: utterly alone and at the mercy of the border patrol. The agents then began yelling out—as they do at immigration raids or when stopping immigrants at the border—"Papeles, papeles!" [documents, documents!]. In this way, they swiftly sorted the U.S. citizens and authorized immigrants from those who lacked documents—forcing the group to divide at the border. There would be no convivencia, not even time for a proper good-bye or a final kiss for the painting of Our Lady of Guadalupe.

Asociación Tepeyac had anticipated that, even in spite of the authorization they were given for a convivencia in the "no man's land" between U.S. and Mexican territory that is the border, officials would be careful not to allow anyone to use the cloak of the procession to cross without authorization. For this reason, they were careful to send only their staff members with impeccable legal status to the border and they discouraged undocumented immigrants from participating in the torch run anywhere in Texas. Organizers frequently commented that la Migra surely thought the torch run was a ruse to cross people "illegally," that such was the agency's inability to attribute humanity or credibility to anyone who is Mexican. People I spoke with also daydreamed about what a symbolic victory it would be if someone were able to cross, within the cloak of the Virgin's protection, right under the noses of the border officials, but they always added that no one would actually attempt such a thing and jeopardize the organization's reputation. The abrupt, even brutal separation of participants in the torch run at the border, into those who had documents and those who did not, was traumatic for those who experienced it. Sergio, Rodrigo, Antonio, and Heraclio, "captains" of the antorcha, all described being saddened about it, even as it powerfully reinforced the message of the run, calling attention to the people who are divided by the border.

7

Conclusion
Citizenship for Immigrants

It's Christmastime. Domestic tourism in New York has returned to pre-September 11 levels and since mid-November, red, green,
and anything sparkly have cloaked every available surface, especially on
Fifth and Madison Avenues, Fifty-seventh Street, Thirty-fourth Street,
and other shopping thoroughfares. I emerge from the subway, on a cold
day in the middle of a particularly cold December. I walk east on Forty-
eighth Street, turning my back on Radio City Music Hall and its Rockettes, nearly as synonymous with Christmas as Santa Claus. I turn up
Fifth Avenue, pass Rockefeller Center, thinking it is not at all ironic that
somewhere inside its vast lobby, under another painting Mr. Rockefeller
commissioned to cover it, is the mural Diego Rivera painted six decades
ago, celebrating the international workers' movement. I cross Fifth Avenue and am suddenly confronted with a crush of people, most moving
slowly, their expressions reflecting the combination of determined adven-
turousness and disorientation that distinguishes out-of-town visitors from
those of us who live here. Tourists gather outside of the window displays
at Saks, as carols waft out onto the sidewalk and intermingle with the jin-
gling of a bell by someone dressed in a Santa suit next to a Salvation Army
red bucket. Brass rails designating where and how one might pass by the
window displays appear to be a permanent feature of the landscape, but I
notice that they are inserted into neat sockets that lie flush with the sidewalk; in January, they, like many of the tourists, will be gone.

Standing mid-block, facing north on Fifth Avenue between Forty-ninth
and Fiftieth Streets, I suddenly encounter a startling image. The colors
of Christmas consumerism flow almost seamlessly into another effusive
visual display composed of red, green, white, and light. Is it possible that
some of the shoppers and tourists might have wandered between the two
displays without noticing that they were in fact categorically different? I

La Antorcha Guadalupana arrives to Saint Patrick's Cathedral, December 12, 2003

cross Fiftieth Street and find myself in the midst of banners, ribbons, flowers, costumes, and lights. But no longer are the colors indicative of Christmas, and the lights are not holiday lights or artificial candles. Instead, I see banners featuring Our Lady of Guadalupe, Mexican flags, and little bouquets of green, red, and white ribbons, and the vibrant living flame of a torch. I am standing on the steps of Saint Patrick's Cathedral, celebrating with thousands the arrival of a flame carried by relay runners all the way from the Basilica of the Virgin of Guadalupe in Mexico City. The run was timed to arrive today, for the Virgin's feast day, to this, the locus of the Catholic Church in a city that has received hundreds of thousands of Mexicans in the last two decades.

Each comité guadalupano present at Saint Patrick's Cathedal today is represented by *un estándarte*, a banner usually made of white satin with an image of the Virgin in her resplendent cloak of blue-green and stars, and her crown of sunlight, surrounded by roses, often standing on a crescent moon lofted by a little angel. The banner usually features the name of the comité embroidered in large letters, gold brocade framing the banner, and it is carried on a tall staff by one of the group's members.

Other members of the comités carry huge Mexican flags, some of them altered so that the mythical eagle standing on a cactus with a serpent in its mouth in the center of the flag is replaced by the Virgin of Guadalupe, who, for many, is the true symbol of the nation. Both versions of the tricolor flag are also on bandannas and scarves that are wrapped around people's heads and shoulders. Some of the women who will participate in the mass are dressed in the multilayered skirts and blouses, *a la sevillana*, associated with the state of Jalisco, origin of Mexico's most iconic folkloric dances. Their long hair is pulled back into dramatic buns with effusions of red, white, and green ribbons as adornment. Little boys are dressed as Juan Diego, and little girls as *inditas* [little Indians], with hand-woven, polychromatic dresses. The boys' flutes and sandals and the ties holding the girls' braids and their little woven purses again repeat the red, green, and white motif, referencing republican nationalism even while they are metonymic for a mythical, pre-Hispanic past.

Some runners ran with the torch across the Hudson River from New Jersey this morning, others traveled to accompany the torch across the border, or ran another leg in the Southeastern United States. Shortly, all

Dancers celebrate the arrival of the torch outside Saint Patrick's Cathedral, December 12, 2003

Participants in the
Torch Procession enter
Saint Patrick's Cathe-
dral, December 12, 2008

will run a torch from the Cathedral to their home parishes in Queens, Brooklyn, the Bronx, upper Manhattan, Staten Island, and even as far as the Hudson Valley and Jersey City. The official uniform of the Antorcha Guadalupana, white sweatpants and sweatshirts, features on the front the name of the torch run in a circle around a logo: a torch composed of red, green, and white flames, alongside the image of the Virgin in her cloak of "sky and stars," her head bowed, referencing her willingness to lend an ear to the humble and meek. On the back is another image of the Virgin, rays of light emanating from her image, and her hands in prayer. Instead of the angel, here it is the motto of the torch run that holds her up: Mensajeros por la dignidad de un pueblo dividido por la frontera Messengers for the dignity of a people divided by the border. Some runners wear sweatshirts printed in their own parishes. One notable shirt has a brightly colored image of the Virgin superimposed on the Manhattan skyline, prominently featuring the twin towers of the World Trade Center, the destruction of which marked a significant moment for everyone in New York, and its reverberations felt the breadth of the hemisphere. Many people carry signs, these featuring a vivid, polychromatic image of the Virgin, gazing out at the viewer and down at a prayer, in English, "Loving mother, please alleviate our exhausted steps, protect us with legalization." Other signs express support of HR 2899 for Legalization.[1] People chant "¡Sí, se pudo!" [Yes we could, *or* We did it!]. Others sing "Las Mañanitas" or "La Guadalupana" in tribute to the Virgin on her day. Reporters wielding massive cameras and notebooks press and jostle those gathered around the torch which is held by Heraclio, who has accompanied the torch along the entire route, now two years in a row. He stands in front of two massive images, reproductions of the official portraits of Saint Juan Diego and Our Lady of Guadalupe, brought from the Basilica, and objects of fervent devotion along the entire route of the run, to be housed now, fittingly, in Heraclio's home

Child dressed like Juan Diego being carried into Saint Patrick's Cathedral, wearing a pack full of objects meant to signify indigenous material culture (and a spare pacifier)

Man holding sign asking for legalization outside Saint Patrick's Cathedral,
December 12, 2003

parish in Queens, as a prize for having the greatest number of runners
participate in this year's run.

The many reporters are, virtually without exception, from Spanish-language media, including a significant contingent of correspondents from
Mexico. This, in spite of the fact that this year's torch run is dedicated to
promoting legislation in the U.S. Congress which, for the first time since
the "Amnesty" [Immigration Reform and Control Act] of 1986, would
enable undocumented workers to legalize their status from within the
United States without having to be highly skilled or to have an employer
sponsor. Most members of Congress do not speak or read Spanish. Nevertheless, "preaching to the converted" has the advantage of producing
an enthusiasm, an infectious and exuberant sense that a critical mass has

been achieved and that, now, it is only a matter of time before legislators and the general public come to the same, inevitable conclusion that legalization is a moral imperative. This exuberance, perhaps more than the visual spectacle of banners, flags, and costumes, the sound of thousands of voices shouting and singing, or the faint warmth of the flame, surely wafted from the steps of the Cathedral, across the street, and out into the city.

Guadalupanismo promotes a discourse of rights and dignity among many immigrants even while there is not a change in the juridical status assigned them by the state. Los comités guadalupanos and activities like the antorcha are where leadership and activism emerge. A community is formed which demands rights for the collective, even while politicians' promises, activist coalitions, and public sympathy may be fickle and fleeting. Rather than ceding to the state all of the power to define those within its borders and waiting for an amnesty to declare them citizens, residents, or some other enfranchised status, these activists claim a different kind of citizenship for themselves and posit it as the prerequisite to the struggle for a juridical acknowledgment of their rights. This citizenship rests both on their a priori status as human beings as well as the performance of acts and attitudes of dignity and belonging. Juan Diego, in the Guadalupan legend, resisted the Virgin's appeals, telling her the Bishop would never listen to someone of his lowly status as an indigenous and unlearned peasant. He even tried to avoid her by taking a different route, to avoid passing the site of the apparition. She had to reappear to him three days in a row, use soft and affectionate language with him, and speak in his own tongue, Nahuatl. She had to promise a miraculous sign, to fill his tunic with Castilian roses that spilled at the Bishop's feet, to give him some incontrovertible sign of her advocacy, in order to convince him to speak up. It is not what the authorities say or do when—or if—they open their doors, but the act of knocking, the transformation in personhood and collective identity produced by having a powerful and loyal advocate that is the important part of the story.

In this concluding chapter, we explore the relationship between the activities engaged in by the members of los comités guadalupanos and Asociación Tepeyac that have been discussed in preceding chapters in a larger national context, specifically as it is framed by the ongoing immigration debates. After tracing the current state of the movement for immigration reform, we will focus on the ways that the participants in these organizations imagine themselves as holders of rights and members of a community and act on those affiliations as citizens, if not in the juridical sense, in the substantive sense.

How are Mexican immigrants translating devotional practices into political activism and challenging dominant notions of citizenship through their involvement in confraternal religious organizations? This is the question that structured my research. I posited in the Introduction that los comités guadalupanos and Asociación Tepeyac redefine rights, citizenship, and identity by renegotiating the symbols of faith and nation, mobilizing the space of the church, and participating in activities normally reserved for citizens with very material aims such as immigration rights, social services, and political and economic equity. Just how effective are immigrants' efforts to improve the way that they are perceived and treated and the way they view themselves, their rights, and their community if the root cause of disenfranchisement faced by the majority of people involved in these organizations remains unchanged? Is achievement of a sweeping reform of U.S. immigration law, such as the general amnesty so ardently sought by these organizations, the only measure by which their efforts can be deemed successful?

Immigration Reform

In the first week of September 2001, general goodwill between then Mexican President Vicente Fox and U.S. President George W. Bush was fast turning into tangible plans and negotiations toward a "regularization" of the immigration status of an estimated 4.5 million undocumented Mexicans living in the United States. However, after the attacks of September 11, this effort was forgotten. During 2002–03, most people I spoke with felt any hope for an amnesty in the near future was lost. Then, in July 2003, Congressmen Jeff Flake (R-AZ) and Jim Kolbe (R-AZ) co-sponsored a bill (HR2899)[2] in the House of Representatives which in January 2004 was folded into then President George W. Bush's proposal for a new guest worker program (Greenhouse 2004). The various proposals that would follow were the first efforts to reform immigration law in a dramatic way since the mid-1980s.[3] While the 1986 Immigration Reform and Control Act, commonly referred to as "Amnesty," has largely been cast as a failure by lawmakers concerned with border security for not stemming the flow of unauthorized immigrants across the border, it was the employer sanctions it brought which chafed big business. Nonetheless, employment eligibility requirements under IRCA required employers only to request, not verify, documentation presented by employees. In many low-wage industries, the norm became a de facto "don't ask, don't tell" policy in which the burden of violating the law is shouldered by employees who routinely present false identity documents, not the employers who are complicit in the practice. In large corporations, employers ensure a further measure of protection from liability by hiring subcontractors who in turn hire workers, allowing large companies to feign ignorance and innocence regarding the employment eligibility of the workers doing a vast portion of the labor in their industries. A growing number of sectors complained that immigration law was out of sync with the U.S. economy's voracious appetite for low-wage workers.[4] Talk of guest-worker proposals was far from the complete package of a path to legalization for undocumented immigrants in the United States and mechanisms for future migration by workers desired by immigrants and their advocates, referred to glibly as "the whole enchilada" by then Mexican foreign minister Jorge Castañeda. Nonetheless, after the tarring undocumented immigrants received after September 11 in which anyone without papers could be associated with "terrorist sleeper cells,"[5] they responded enthusiastically to any talk of reform or of recognition of immigrants' contributions.

Optimism returned for many of the people with whom I conducted research. Asociación Tepeyac began to urge its members to gather and organize all of the documents that could prove their presence in the United States: children's birth certificates, apartment leases, check stubs, and more. They encouraged undocumented immigrants to apply for a Taxpayer Identification Number (TIN, issued by the Internal Revenue Service to any income-generating person not eligible for a social security number) and to file their personal income taxes retroactively for as many years as they could. They also suggested that families take day trips to the Statue of Liberty or the Empire State Building and take photographs holding a newspaper, to demonstrate presence as of a particular date. All of this advice was issued under the assumption that soon something like the amnesty of 1986 would enable anyone who was in the United States before a given date to regularize their status.

Bush's brand of Republicanism was in that period interpreted by many Mexican immigrants as pro-immigrant. As a former governor of a border state and unapologetic fan of big business, President George W. Bush was heard consistently characterizing immigrants as hardworking contributors to the national economy. He argued that control of the border went hand in hand with the establishment of regularized flows of immigrant workers across the border and also frequently insisted that most immigrants were simply trying to provide for their families in thankless, difficult jobs. This combination of enforcement, expanded worker visas, and "compassion" for undocumented immigrants already in the United States was referred to as comprehensive immigration reform. Public intellectual Tamar Jacoby wrote: "The most effective government in the world is no match for global economic forces. It's better to recognize those powerful currents and make the most of them" (2006).[6] However, soon, members of Bush's party, partly in response to the president's loss of political capital, began to split around the issue of enforcement. Joel Magallán, executive director of Asociación Tepeyac, observed to me that historically, any immigration reform has been accompanied by greater restriction, such as occurred with the IRCA amnesty, which was also the start of employer sanctions. While in 2001 it was thought that a humane approach might prevail, most activists came over the subsequent years to accept that reform, if it were to come at all, would only come bundled with stricter border enforcement and penalties for those who are undocumented.

In 2005 and 2006, immigration dominated the national consciousness. On May 1, 2006, the largest immigration rights marches in the nation's history occurred in large cities around the country: Washington, DC, Los Angeles, New York, Chicago, and Dallas among them. The marches in May 2006 were in large part a response to the Border Protection, Anti-terrorism, and Illegal Immigration Control Act of 2005 (HR 4437) sponsored by James Sensenbrenner (R-WI) and passed by the House of Representatives on December 16, 2005. Although the bill would die in the Senate, it nevertheless succeeded in pushing the immigration debate further in the direction of greater restrictionism. Among the items included in the lengthy bill were provisions that would make it a felony to assist migrants (even through humanitarian aid, such as water stations in the Sonora desert), build a 700-mile fence on the Southern border, require detention of immigrants awaiting deportation proceedings, and make unauthorized presence in the United States a criminal infraction. While Bush's State of the Union address in 2004 and the ensuing debates about immigration reform energized immigrants and immigrant advocates, Sensenbrenner's bill terrorized them. Surveys showed that even in the event of the passage of a guest-worker bill in which undocumented immigrants already in the United States might be eligible to participate, many immigrants were so terrified of mass roundups and deportations that they had already decided they would rather live further under the radar than sign up for any new program.

By decoupling border enforcement from the other major immigration issues, restrictionists managed to kill the potential for reform in an election year. They also managed to make the word "amnesty" an unutterable expletive in political discourse, and thus achieved the ability to condemn any proposal to address immigration simply by calling it an "amnesty," no matter how filled with penalties and fees it might be. By the summer of 2006, it became clear that immigration was too volatile an issue for most politicians to touch. Only the most vitriolic anti-immigrant politicians continued to address it and make it a key issue of their platforms.

A bipartisan bill for immigration reform combining border enforcement, a guest-worker provision, and a path to citizenship, punctuated by punitive fines and penalties, was crafted by a subcommittee of senators but failed in June 2006. Anti-immigrant groups like Numbers U.S.A., the Minutemen, and the Center for Immigration Studies[7] in concert with anti-immigrant politicians like Tom Tancredo (R-CO) and Peter King (R-NY) cleaved the Republican Party, dooming the bipartisan bill by arguing that immigration reform must be made to wait for a "secure border."

In the recent presidential campaign, most candidates sidestepped immigration reform during the primaries. The Republican candidates, still feeling confident in their efforts to distance themselves from Bush, accused each other of being too soft on immigration, they competed with one another to present the strictest proposals for immigration and border enforcement. Even Rudolph Giuliani, formerly a rather immigrant-friendly mayor of New York City, attempted to exceed his opponents in exclusionist proposals. While in the past, Senator John McCain had been a voice for comprehensive immigration reform, the anti-immigration majority of his party caused him to muffle his own voice, now premising any future reform on the securing of the borders. The Democratic candidates, meanwhile, while not competing to outdo one another's viciousness toward immigrants, spoke during the primaries of a path to citizenship while also pandering to restrictionists. Both Senators Barack Obama and Hillary Clinton voted to fund the border wall. Clinton distanced herself entirely from the issue after comments in November 2007 in which she said she thought New York State Governor Eliot Spitzer's effort to extend undocumented immigrants access to special drivers' licenses was a good idea. After she was attacked by restrictionists, she attempted to reframe and retract her words, and then was attacked by proponents of immigration reform for failing to articulate her views. Meanwhile, Spitzer was unable to pass the legislation in New York, and after that, and especially following the governor's own scandalous downfall, would-be reformers of immigration decided that it was prudent to stay out of the fray for a while. Only after the primary elections ended did Democratic nominee Senator Barack Obama begin to mention that he would favor comprehensive immigration reform early in his presidency. Somewhat unexpectedly, given the weighty problems on his domestic agenda, the White House indicated in April 2009 that President Obama was beginning a series of working groups to explore and debate immigration reform with an eye toward a legislative proposal in late 2009 or 2010 (Preston 2009). The almost immediate backlash in some sectors prompted White House spokespeople to temper their language regarding reform and posit that a massive reform would not be attempted prior to an improvement in the domestic economy (Yellin 2009), but as this book goes to press, "amnesty" is again on many immigrants' lips.

In the meantime, in this decade, immigration enforcement increased dramatically. In 2007, federal Immigration and Customs Enforcement agents arrested more than 35,000 undocumented immigrants, more than double the number in 2006, and deported 276,912 immigrants, a record number (Preston 2008). In a survey in the fall of 2007, the Pew Hispanic Center found that 53 percent of Latinos in the United States worry that they or a loved one could be deported (Pew 2007). The impact of raids on families has been particularly chilling. A large raid in Massachusetts in 2008 resulted in the separation of a mother from her nursing infant as well as other parents from young, U.S. citizen children. In many cases, those detained are immediately transported to detention facilities in other states, and immigrant advocates and family members have a difficult time even locating the detained in the vast system. On Long Island, local law enforcement officials collaborated with ICE agents to conduct a raid, deceiving day laborers into entering an enclosed area under the ruse that they would be given work. Then they were promptly processed and charged with immigration violations under a warrant issued to arrest "gang affiliates." Subsequent large raids in Postville, Iowa and Laurel, Mississippi indicated a dramatically heightened climate of enforcement, accompanied by less attention to immigrants' civil and human rights, with breathtakingly speedy trials and summary deportations causing alarm in immigrant and advocacy circles (Hsu 2008). Rather than taking pictures in front of the Statue of Liberty, organizations like Asociación Tepeyac began to hold workshops on how to write a declaration granting power of attorney and parental rights to a friend or relative in the event one is deported. Parents tell children what to say or do if they are not picked up from school. Some immigrant families avoid tourist attractions, commuter trains, long distance buses, marches, and other places where they fear a raid could occur or they might be asked to establish their identity. While President Obama has asked ICE to refrain from massive raids and detention and instead begin enforcing employer sanctions, many immigrants continue to be fearful. In the context of this stalemate on immigration reform, what are immigrants doing? How are they framing and articulating their demands for rights in light of their putative exclusion from the rights of citizenship? How does Guadalupanism contribute to an articulation of social citizenship?

La Virgen Quiere Amnistía [The Virgin Wants Amnesty]: The Virgin of Guadalupe as an Arbiter of Citizenship

As discussed in chapter 1, the Virgin of Guadalupe is often taken as a symbol of Mexicanness within and outside Mexico. As the song heard throughout the country and in many parts of the United States every December 12 declares, "Para el Mexicano, ser guadalupano es algo esencial" [For Mexicans, to be guadalupano is something essential].[8] Octavio Paz famously wrote in Labyrinth of Solitude that Mexicans only have faith in the national lottery and the Virgin of Guadalupe (1985). The entire Mexican national project is intertwined with la Guadalupana—from the divine election of Mexico and Mexicans as the recipients of the miraculous apparition of Guadalupe in 1531, to the lofting of her image on banners in the War of Independence and the Revolution, not to mention hundreds of other examples. Because of the turbulent relationship between church and state in Mexico, proclamations of Guadalupan devotion by politicians like former President Vicente Fox in recent years, or the mass of repentance by the PRI in the Basilica of Guadalupe in October 2002, are still greeted with astonishment; yet it is a fairly common assumption that Mexicans are Guadalupan.

This centrality of guadalupanismo to Mexican religiosity and identity is reiterated by members of Asociación Tepeyac as well as priests in New York City who have told me that to understand and serve the recent and massive influx of Mexican parishioners, pastors must recognize and honor Our Lady of Guadalupe. They do this by placing her image prominently within or on the exterior of the church, holding masses at dawn on December 12, and in many cases fostering a comité guadalupano. There is an assumption by many people within and outside the church, Mexicans and non-Mexicans alike, that Guadalupanism is an innate character trait of Mexicans, brought with them from home and virtually unchanged by migration.

The rooting of Guadalupanism in the United States is aided by her elevation to preferred status among Marian advocations in the Church. Pope John Paul II declared in 1999, "It is my heartfelt hope that she . . . will by her maternal intercession guide the Church in America, obtaining the outpouring of the Holy Spirit, as she once did for the early Church (cf. *Acts* 1: 14), so that the new evangelization may yield a splendid flowering of Christian life" (1999). Over the last two decades, the Church has attempted to conflate the vast diversity of Marian devotions in the Americas and to reiterate Mary's role as a "path to Christ" (and, by implication, not an appropriate object of devotion in and of herself). The selection of Guadalupe as evangelizer of the Americas and *the* chosen Mary reiterates her power as the quintessential advocation of Mary, and in turn, bestows on her most devoted, the Mexican people, a special centrality. The use of her image by Mexican immigrants reinforces the idea of Mexicans as chosen ones in relation to other Latino immigrants and casts them as especially needy and worthy of God and Mary's grace. The elevation of Guadalupe is not perceived by Mexicans I have spoken with as a dilution of her devotion but rather as a fitting recognition of her special power and their unique devotion. In U.S. churches with Latino congregations, this has served to anoint Mexicans as her appointed caretakers, even as pastors have stressed pan-Latino pastoralism.[9]

It is said that in the eighteenth century, Pope Benedict XIV saw a copy of the image of the Virgin imprinted on Juan Diego's *tilma*, and quoted Psalm 147: 20, *"Non fecit taliter omni natione"* [He has not done the like for any other nation] (Brading 2001: 6). The two main foundational myths of Mexico reiterate the notion of the nation and its people as chosen ones. The Mexica [Aztec] origins stories describe ages of migration which ended when Huitzilipochtli gave an incontrovertible sign: an eagle with a serpent in its mouth standing on a cactus on an island in a lake where Tenochtitlan and eventually Mexico City would be built. This not only augured the settlement of a nomadic people but their divine legitimation as eventual imperial rulers of Mesoamerica. Similarly, the Guadalupan apparition, as described above, has been interpreted as a special dispensation of grace to the Mexican people from the mother of God. As such, like all who view themselves as chosen people, Mexican Guadalupanos are cast as bearers of a universal mission, message, and morality. The mission, like Juan Diego's, is to carry a special message, the Guadalupan message, which we see in the Antorcha Guadalupana, la misión guadalupana, and El Viacrucis del Inmigrante; it is an assertion of a particular moral ethic: the essential personhood and attendant rights of all human beings. It is an assertion of citizenship.

For some Mexican immigrants crossing the border, devotion to Guadalupe is qualitatively transformed and transforming so that while they may have always believed in her, now they need her, and she, in new ways, is there for them. As described in chapter 4, crossing the border represents an initial transformation of self, as we expect to see in a ritual, especially a rite of passage. When immigrants arrive here, they see themselves vis-à-vis those they consider their community in a different way, and even the way they define "community" is different. To be Guadalupan in Mexico is to be *the same as*, to share commonality with, seemingly, everyone else, even if only on the Twelfth of December. To be Guadalupan in New York City is to be *different*: it signifies belonging to a community in need—at the moment, at least—of services, rights, and an end to immigration laws which allow their exploitation, discrimination, and the arbitrary separation of families. To define oneself as Guadalupan is also to belong to a community with a rich culture (the richest, they are not reluctant to insist), with a proud heritage and with the protection of the most powerful mother who has specially chosen to visit her grace upon them. The image of the Virgin of Guadalupe held at a rally is not for imagined mainstream "Americans" who are not supposed to have any real appreciation for her, but is a signal to other Mexicans, "*ánimo, paisano*, we're all in this together." To migrate is to be transformed, to carry a tattoo of the Virgin of Guadalupe on the inside (Cohen and Estrada 2002). Just as the Virgin of Guadalupe arrived at just the right moment, following the conquest, to soothe a wounded people, and to bless the Mexican earth with her presence, it is said she has chosen those who risk everything to come to this new land for the special dispensation of her advocacy.

Asociación Tepeyac posits that nearly every difficulty faced by the majority of Mexican immigrants is a result of being undocumented (interview with Estela Morales, November 14, 2000). The organization's rationale for its overarching emphasis on amnesty includes several arguments: that immigrants' minor children are often U.S. citizens; that they are contributing members of society with their labor, their family values, and high levels of church participation; and that they are not burdens to society. They cite the "sweat equity": that they spend their productive years in the United States, contributing to the U.S. economy, often in jobs native U.S. citizens reject, and then return, old and infirm, to their home communities.

In spite of these rationalistic arguments about immigrant workers' contributions which are common to many immigrant advocacy groups, Asociación Tepeyac anchors its claims for rights within notions of universal personhood drawn from discourses of devotion to the Virgin of Guadalupe, who is seen as the protector of Mexicans in general, but especially the poor, oppressed, and weak. Asociación Tepeyac's discourse is premised on a universal Catholic humanism that posits all human beings as equally deserving of rights and dignity, above and beyond the petty laws of nations and the injustices of men and women. The Catholic Church, which since Vatican II has supported popular religiosities and given special status to the Virgin of Guadalupe, is a transnational entity which both institutionally—in its global breadth and influence (especially as personified in the Pope), as well as its articulation of Catholic humanism—is a well-situated ally for immigrants' claims to rights irrespective of their legal status or membership in a nation-state. Indeed, the space of the church, where los comités gudalupanos meet, is, in effect, a sanctuary, enabling the collective mobilizations of people who often find it difficult to gather in almost any other space.[10] The Virgin of Guadalupe is also the figure around which a "Mexican community" is being imagined and mobilized. Goldring writes that it is in the experience of migration, as people get to know Mexicans from other localities and other Spanish speakers, that they "develop a sense of their shared 'Mexican-ness' and minority status" and that "they may be becoming members of the imagined national community of Mexicans, an identity that emerges in the process of being defined as a foreigner in the U.S." (1996: 86; see also Padilla 1985 on migrant identities as a product of conflict). The Virgin of Guadalupe, arguably more than language (some immigrants' first language is Nahuatl, Mixteco or another indigenous language), the flag, ethnicity, social class, or even Catholicism in general, is a symbol taken up by Asociación Tepeyac and los comités guadalupanos to galvanize and unite their membership.

They do this in the context of increased militarization on the border, heightened surveillance of those residing within U.S. borders, massive increase in immigration raids, and accelerated deportation proceedings. All of these are a resounding indication that the state, far from being on the decline,[11] is more virile than ever. The ever-increasing undocumented population in the United States is not a function of "broken borders" as many restrictionists would have us believe, but the dependence of the U.S. economy on undocumented labor as a "distinctly disposable commodity" (De Genova 2005: 8). As De Genova argues, "'illegality' is lived through a palpable sense of deportability whereby some are deported in order that most may remain (undeported) as workers" (ibid.). Nation-states perhaps always define themselves through a more or less violent process of inclusion and exclusion. However, membership in the United States is increasingly defined by ever more restrictive and exclusionary juridical categories that do not define "us" and "them" by those inside versus those outside our borders, but by defining the (legitimate) "us" in contradistinction to the (illegitimate) "them": undocumented immigrants who reside more or less permanently within the nation's borders. "Illegality" is no longer attributed simply to the act of border incursion but to the very being of undocumented immigrants. The efforts by Mexican immigrants to assert their claims to rights in the midst of this climate of xenophobia contains quite important implications for our conceptualization of citizenship.

Citizenship

My research with Mexican immigrant organizations in New York leads me to argue that the practices of members of these groups advance an alternative mode of citizenship founded upon notions of universal humanism enabled by and actuated by Guadalupan devotion. Their arguments—while political—supersede politics, and through the particular idiom of Guadalupan devotion posit membership in a polity defined by the belief that all people are equal in the eyes of the Mother of God, in her manifestation as the Virgin of Guadalupe. By anchoring the moral referent for their claims outside of the realm of national and international politics, they situate their demands for rights beyond the jurisdiction of the state.

This argument contains several implications that must be detailed. First, theories of cultural citizenship often assume that the juridical citizenship of minority social actors is uncontested even while they work in the cultural sphere to claim space and revindicate rights denied them because of racialized social structures and structural inequalities. Because cultural citizenship is an assertion of the rights of presence and expression that should always and already be assumed given the juridical membership of minorities in the polity, undocumented immigrants are sometimes deliberately excluded from analyses of cultural citizenship.

Participant holding sign at *El Viacrucis del Inmigrante,* lower Manhattan, 2003

But what of those who are new immigrants and whose juridical belonging in the nation-state, political citizenship, is not only contested but
largely nonexistent? Citizenship should never be a zero-sum game where
the exclusion of one group is seen to be to the advantage of another, but
the xenophobic rhetoric of the immigration debate in the United States
attempts to make it such. In New York City, where there is no evidence
of a sizable Mexican community until the latter quarter of the twentieth
century, being Mexican and undocumented go together more frequently,
and legitimately, than in other parts of the United States, but this does
not justify the denial of undocumented Mexican immigrants' claims to
cultural citizenship or the exercise of political rights. My notion of citizenship does not take for granted that social actors enjoy legitimacy in
their claims on the nation-state. Undocumented immigrants—in juridical
terms— are personae non grate in the U.S. polity. Asociación Tepeyac and
its members demand a general amnesty which would "legalize" undocumented immigrants, yet they do not do so by engaging in one-upmanship
about the economic contributions of immigrants and their labor or their
cultural contributions to social life in this country with the economists,

policymakers, and social scientists who set the terms of the immigration debate in the U.S. public sphere. Such debates inevitably are truncated by someone saying "they," undocumented immigrants, "broke the law" simply by coming here. Instead, through the idiom of citizenship based on rights associated with personhood, they situate the debate in a moral sphere in which the laws of the United States and the fickle lawmakers who write them are cast as petty, shortsighted, and inhumane. Even while they do make reference to the "sweat tax" paid by immigrants whose work sustains the economy and make reference to such scholarly findings as the fact that immigrants contribute more tax dollars than they receive in government benefits, their overall project is couched in an assertion of universal personhood.

Second, with my observation that in the comités guadalupanos citizenship is articulated through devotional practices, I wish to contest the teleological binaries that have been overly persistent in scholarship to date. First, religion has too often been seen as a precursor to other kinds of interventions, for example, playing the role of antithesis in dichotomies about tradition and modernity (e.g., "Old World" religion as something to be discarded and transformed as immigrants assimilate to U.S. civil religion and civic life). This kind of analysis is logical given the way even those scholars who contest Durkheimian safety-valve theories of festival and popular devotional practices and acknowledge the "world-shaking" properties of religious practice note that *sometimes* festival *may* turn into "real" rebellion, without acknowledging that revolution may be always already contained in the festive practices themselves.[12] This is related to the binary constructed by Werbner (among others) that I discussed in chapter 4, which posits that devotional practices, like procession, may enable social actors to imagine getting involved in "real politics," by planning, say, a protest. Real citizenship, real political involvement is deferred to a later date and acquisition of another status, and, barring comprehensive immigration reform, it is deferred indefinitely. In this way, the state and the social theorists become complicit in "making citizenship count for more, by making it harder to obtain, or both" (Bosniak 1998: 26). What if we instead recognize as citizens those who behave as citizens? There are available and operational narratives about citizenship and its requisite behaviors, including the willingness to stand up for and pursue one's rights, liberty, justice, and happiness. Perhaps these can guide us to a more inclusive notion of citizenship.

Demonstration for general amnesty, midtown Manhattan, October 2000

In a talk about New York City, Saskia Sassen remarked, "By god, you can be an undocumented immigrant and get involved in street politics, doing the work of citizens." She said that through immigrants' "emergent informal politics in the city . . . a space is produced with micro-architectures for global civil society" (Sassen 2002). She challenged scholars and activists to invent a politics that would formalize these networks. Nevertheless, she continues here to reproduce the notion of graduated empowerment. Sassen said that "long-term undocumented migrants" through "unauthorized but recognized activism" contribute to the emergence of an informal social contract through which they can make claims for legalization, outside of the frame of "big amnesties" (ibid.).

While the activities of devotees of the Virgin of Guadalupe may indeed have long-term effects which are still only emergent, and I applaud the optimism—and evocative imagery—of Sassen noting that their practices may "produce micro-architectures for a global civil society," I contest the notion that what they accomplish will *only* be realized in the future and with their transformation into something else. Undocumented Mexican immigrants do not have the luxury to forget their very literal exclusion from the nation-state by making claims for citizenship solely in a cultural realm. Through practices that assert personhood, they perform their claims for rights. They do not claim space in order to "eventually" claim rights as posited by Flores and Benmayor (1997); their claiming of space is in itself a claim for rights. While these practices may not immediately lend themselves to quantifiable civic processes like electoral participation, petition-signing, and lobbying of elected officials, they create dispositions that transform the posture of immigrants and their interactions with others. This embodied practice may be as mundane as sweeping a chapel of the Virgin of Guadalupe on a Bronx street, thumb-tacking an image of Guadalupe on the door of a fifth-floor walkup apartment, preparing food that is ingested daily by people of all social strata in New York City, or constructing the buildings in which many of us live and work. It is also as performatively spectacular as remapping the space of the community in procession with the misión guadalupana, resignifying the space of Wall Street with El Viacrucis del Inmigrante, or carrying a torch and images of the Virgin of Guadalupe and Saint Juan Diego across the border, physically connecting "home" and "host" loci of Guadalupanismo in la Antorcha Guadalupana. It is a stance that makes exploitation less feasible at the same time that it has the snowball effect of leading to ever larger and more public assertions of rights and cultural expression.

While Asociación Tepeyac, the comités guadalupanos and their participants never give up hope that an amnesty will "regularize" their status, they do not imagine that an eventual amnesty is the day when they will be empowered, included in the polity, or emancipated. In the comités guadalupanos, members describe a process of realization: that there were other Mexicans, that others were undocumented and shared similar challenges and aspirations, and that guadalupanismo provided an idiom for expressing and transforming their own posture toward the world. Unlike what they depict as their grandmothers' church in Mexico, in some New York Catholic parishes they describe finding a place where their stories are heard and echoed by the experiences of others, where they learn what rights they already have and develop plans for activism to gain greater rights. This process is not formulaic, as the Alinsky-style process of the formation of community leaders is imagined, but instead emotional, sometimes mystical, and told in the language of a faith conversion. By coming into a community, guadalupanos assert that they are Juan Diego: someone who has been excluded and ignored by the dominant society, but who has an important prophetic message to tell. By insisting that their message is heard, they are turning themselves into citizens. In this formulation of citizenship, a citizen is as a citizen does. The nation-state, while able to exercise its privileges of sovereignty, including control of the border, does not, in this formulation, get sole jurisdiction over the realm of citizenship which has, I dare say, been recast as sacred.

This is an assertion of personhood couched within Christian humanism's understanding of the inherent rights and dignity of human beings. Asociación Tepeyac promotes this model, arguing that all human beings are children of Mary and equal in the eyes of God. While this may contain resonances of Catholic natural law which can be easily refuted by a positivist approach to the law,[13] for immigrant activists these assertions have an important purpose. Never forgetting for a moment that a reform of current U.S. immigration law is the main goal, Asociación Tepeyac and its members assert that such reform can only be demanded by people who have already assumed the mantle of the rights of citizenship. Without such a disposition, legal reform can never be achieved. Because the essential rights of personhood are so often denied to undocumented immigrants whose very identity is obfuscated in the journey to *el norte*, this is a profoundly political assertion. This is the same discourse that underlies the theologically founded argument of the United States Council of Catholic Bishops and the Mexican Episcopate's declaration "Strangers no longer," which makes comparisons between contemporary immigrants and biblical migrations including the Exodus and Mary and Joseph's search for shelter. They state:

> The Church recognizes that all the goods of the earth belong to all people. When persons cannot find employment in their country of origin to support themselves and their families, they have a right to find work elsewhere in order to survive. Sovereign nations should provide ways to accommodate this right. (USCCB 2003)

This discourse refers to a higher authority than the nation-state and thus allows for the possibility that the laws controlling immigration are trivial, vindictive, and superseded by a higher moral law. Yasemin Soysal writes, "human personness constitutes the normative basis of an expanding citizenship, [it] has become an imperative in justifying rights and demands for rights, including those of nonnationals in national polities" (1994: 42; also Jacobson 1996: 9). It is premised on Judeo-Christian principles, which closely echo the same principles on which the Constitution and Bill of Rights are based. It also inserts nicely into what Pease Chock calls "immigrant opportunity narratives" in which aliens are transformed into American "persons" (1994: 47).

However, there are, unfortunately, pitfalls in this argument too. First, it lends itself to paternalism. The UCCSB document reads: "We judge ourselves as a community of faith by the way we treat the most vulnerable among us." And, "Under the light of the apparition of Our Lady of Guadalupe to the littlest of her children, who were as powerless as most migrants are today, our continent's past and present receive new meaning." In these formulations, immigrants are cast as needy children, to be protected by a benevolent state and populace. Benevolence can easily run over into paternalism and infantilization of immigrants.

Further, these narratives sometimes foster romanticized visions of model immigrants who are honest, hardworking, god-fearing, and family oriented, and can result in an implicit denigration of anyone who does not ostensibly fit that profile. This narrative is often couched within oft-repeated statements like "they're just doing the jobs that no American wants to do." As social scientist Judith Adler Hellman argues, being considered a model immigrant is not necessarily an advantageous position (2008). Notions of model minorities are often folded into visions of docility and might only last until someone speaks up against ill treatment or low wages. Further, it pits groups that in many cases share similar socioeconomic conditions against each other, rather than fostering solidarity between them. If migrants are "the vulnerable among us" who must be protected, where does that leave other groups? African Americans, documented immigrants and immigrant groups that do not receive the model immigrant designation are not likely to fall over themselves in solidarity for people perceived as docile, submissive, and willing to undercut the labor rights achieved through decades of struggle. Further, this kind of dynamic complicates relationships within the Catholic Church, as discussed above, in which other groups sometimes resent pastors' accommodation of Mexicans' requests for special observance of Guadalupe's feast days or the placing of an image near the church's altar.

The late social psychologist Jocelyn Solís wrote of Asociación Tepeyac's organizational methods that they promote the transformation of an "illegal identity" into an "undocumented" one, which she argues is an oppositional, resistant positionality, which, even while immigrants' legal status remains unchanged, transforms their understandings of their own condition and willingness to defend themselves against exploitation (Solís 2002: 8–9). It is the Virgin of Guadalupe, advocate of the poor and oppressed, who guarantees and oversees these demands. This is because, just as immigrants claim to have drawn strength from the Virgin in their most trying moments, they, in the consolidation of devotion and activism in her image and name, have strengthened her. In this cycle of empowerment, those who are juridically disenfranchised come to believe they have rights.

In all versions of the apparition legend, it is stressed that Our Lady of Guadalupe spoke to Juan Diego in Nahuatl, his own language, using diminutive terms of affection. The language Juan Diego used to communicate to the Bishop is not emphasized: after all, it was not Juan Diego's words that the Bishop heeded. It was only when Juan Diego demonstrated evidence of the divinity of his message, material proof in the form of roses, that the Bishop believed him. Guadalupanos in New York City speak to one another in a common language: Spanish inflected by Guadalupan symbolism and theology, but offer as proof of the veracity of their message what they consider to be incontrovertible signs for the dominant population: Christian humanism, hard work, dignity, and family values. These two discourses, as incommensurable as they may be and even as they generate certain misunderstandings, are each necessary and mutually constitutive. One serves to generate a community, and the other to assert its rights before those who would deny them. It is the Guadalupanos' hope that as the divinity of the Virgin's message was sustained through the process of reception, translation, and transmission by Juan Diego, likewise the power and truth of their message as it is translated, transmitted, and performed, will prevail. If it does not, if, ultimately, they are standing like Juan Diego with a tilma full of roses, but their message is not heeded, it is arguable that by having accessed the zones of power, they will not again be silently oppressed. At that moment, they are citizens: a status not endowed by law but earned through embodied practice.

In spite of the potential pitfalls, hazards, and limitations, ultimately, for many Mexican immigrants in New York, participation in los comités guadalupanos and in the activities of Asociación Tepeyac accomplishes several things. First, it enables the articulation of a new spiritual identity in which guadalupanismo takes on new import and new valences in the context of the experience of migration and adaptation to life in the United States. As a result of this renewed or redefined guadalupanismo, many people then come to understand themselves as part of a larger Mexican community composed of people who not only share the same national background but similar experiences as a result of being undocumented. This recognition of commonality premised on guadalupanismo, Mexican national identity, and undocumented immigration status enables the articulation of arguments for rights. The staff and community leaders of Asociación Tepeyac and members of the comités guadalupanos promote this articulation and mobilization. In these shared experiences of organizing, worshipping, and recruiting new members, participants imagine themselves to belong to the same community and set to work to promote the rights of their members, asserting a shared humanity and worthiness vouchsafed by Our Lady of Guadalupe. Because these efforts are situated on a moral plane in which the immigration laws of the United States are rendered petty and unethical, the achievement of the concrete goal of legalization is not the measure of these organizations' success. Rather, it is the realization by participants that they are worthy of rights, their willingness to defend them, and the ways that such efforts constitute acts of citizenship that are the groups' most notable and enduring achievements.

Appendix

A Note on Methodology and the Use of Pseudonyms

The relationship of undocumented immigrants to the state is by nature vulnerable, and it became even more vulnerable after September 11, 2001, when legislation like the Patriot Act and heightened enforcement of some previously existing but rarely enforced provisions of immigration law (such as indefinite detention of immigrants who have not been formally arrested or charged with a crime) threw into doubt whether researchers could ever again guarantee their subjects' privacy or that their notes and other materials would not be subpoenaed and used in the courts in ways that might harm participants and their families. Federal regulations regarding research involving human subjects call for special provisions when research subjects include "vulnerable populations" such as pregnant women, minors, and prison inmates. While undocumented immigrants are not specified as such, in my research design and methodology I decided to make similar provisions in order to ensure that my research would not be used against those who participated in it.

As such, I use only a very small number of real names in this study; instead, I use pseudonyms for most participants as well as the churches where the two comités guadalupanos I focus upon are housed. I do not use pseudonyms for the neighborhoods in which the churches are found for two principal reasons. First, there are many Catholic churches in these neighborhoods, such that without extensive first-hand knowledge of the neighborhoods and the churches themselves, it would be difficult to identify them precisely. While the parish priests and many parishioners know that my study focuses on groups within their churches, given the long precedence of the notion of sanctuary within the Catholic Church, I am confident that this knowledge will not circulate from the churches themselves back to federal agencies in such a way that would prejudice the undocumented immigrants who are congregants. Second, the need to protect research participants must always be responsibly balanced with the scholarly goal of verifiability. Since the only detailed information I give about the neighborhoods is demographic, I do wish for the information I have gathered about the population composition in these neighborhoods to be available in a broadly applicable form to other scholars.

I only use the proper names of the public spokespersons and directors of large community organizations, such as Joel Magallán Reyes, executive director of Asociación Tepeyac. As a known public figure who frequently appears in the press, Joel's name is no secret. Moreover, he opposes my use of pseudonyms, telling me it is important for people's stories to be heard and accredited to them. He also regularly tells Tepeyac's members, "La migra nunca vino a buscar a nadie porque salió en el diario" [The INS never came after anyone because their name appeared in the paper], encouraging them to have no fear of making their stories known and to put names and faces on the troubles and triumphs of immigrants as a group. While I agree with him (in spite of some recent events like then Representative Tom Tancredo of Colorado's attempt to deport an undocumented high school valedictorian following accolades in the press), given the status of individual liberties after the Patriot Act and unprecedented collaborations occurring across the nation between local law enforcement and federal immigration officials on non-criminal immigration violations, I felt it was ethically necessary to protect the identity of all other participants in my study, most of whom are undocumented, in order to avoid my work jeopardizing their fragile position in the United States as individuals, even while hoping my work might contribute to their objectives as a group. The promise of confidentiality was made to participants when they agreed to take part in the study and thus may also have given them a greater degree of comfort in speaking to me freely.

Studies and nonscholarly publications related to similar populations take very different approaches to confidentiality. Some authors subscribe to Joel Magallán's reasoning, seeing the proper identification of participants in Tepeyac as a means of supporting their activism, making their claims public and symbolically bringing all undocumented Mexicans "out of the shadows" and recognizing them as identifiable, named individuals. Others use pseudonyms even for Asociación Tepeyac and other organizations. I have chosen a middle path and view myself primarily accountable toward my research participants as individuals and the protection of their privacy. Since Asociación Tepeyac has become known throughout New

York City via English-language media and among charitable and service foundations and agencies, as well as internationally in Spanish-language media as an advocacy organization dedicated precisely to the situation of undocumented immigrants, to use a pseudonym for it at this date is unnecessary and would be naïve. Further, by using its actual name, I hope to contribute even in a small way to its well-deserved prominence, to serve as another historiographer of its work, and to lend support to its activist project of making the difficulties faced by undocumented immigrants more known and visible.

Notes

1. From heaven one beautiful morning,
   From heaven one beautiful morning,
   La Guadalupana, La Guadalupana, La Guadalupana came down to Tepeyac.
   Beseechingly she pressed her palms together; her clothes and face were
      Mexican.
   Her arrival filled all of Anáhuac with light and harmony. [Anahuác is an
      ancestral name for the land now known as Mexico.]
   Juan Diego was passing by the hill and when he heard singing, approached.
   The Virgin told Juan Diego, I choose this hill for my altar.
   On his cloak she deigned to leave her image among painted roses
   Since that time, for the Mexican
   To be Guadalupan is something essential,
   And when he has troubles, he kneels down and raises his eyes to Tepeyac.

2. My deep gratitude to Miguel Díaz-Barriga for articulating this framing
of my project.

3. The Reconquista refers to Spain's campaign to expel non-Christians
from the Southern part of the Iberian peninsula and reclaim the territory which
ended in 1492; the Conquest is the violent imposition of Spanish rule in the
Americas which began the same year.

4. The "traditional" cargo system has been defined as "a hierarchy of
ranked offices that together comprise a community's public civil and religious
administration" (Chance 1985: 1, citing DeWalt 1975: 91).

5. As such, in this book, I use a variety of demographic sources, both
because there is no single source that is entirely reliable and because triangula-
tion of data may be one means of addressing the inadequacies of single sources.
While I sometimes cite census and other figures, I do so with these shortcomings
in mind and a measure of caution.

6. The growing demographic impact of Mexicans in New York City is augured by the group's high birth rate. In 2006, 6.7 percent of all live births in New
York City were to Mexican mothers, while Mexicans constitute only 2.2 percent

of the total population (Schwartz et al. 2007, table 35: 50). This translates into a birth rate of 31.8 per 1,000 persons, well more than double the citywide birth rate of 15 per 1000. Birth rates are misleading, given that they are derived using data from two sources: the Summary of Vital Statistics from the Health Department which accounts for all live births in the city, and the Census, from which the "per 1,000" is drawn. As long as the total population of Mexicans is unknown, given the vast undercount of the Census, even knowing the exact numbers of births to Mexican mothers will not give us an accurate idea of the birth rate among Mexicans. Nevertheless, if my calculation that the population is closer to 350,000 is correct, the birth rate for Mexicans is still high: 23.96 per 1,000. Further, in terms of total births, the number of births to Mexicans is fourth among all groups (after African American, Puerto Rican, and Dominican), respectively, and second among immigrants (Schwartz et al. 2007).

7. To give a specific example, the NAFTA agreement, ratified in 1994, gave certain protections to Florida avocado growers and in effect ended the ability of avocado growers in La Mixteca to competitively export their goods to the United States. Thank you to Liliana Rivera Sánchez for her description of this phenomenon (personal communication 2002).

8. Reading early analyses of Mexican migration to New York, it was easy to imagine that it was composed overwhelmingly of men from Puebla state. According to Census figures, in 2000, 42 percent of Mexicans in New York City were female, and 58 percent male (U.S. Census 2000: SF2). The Mexican Consulate asserted as late as 2003 that 51 percent of those Mexicans soliciting the Consular identification card, *la matrícula consular,* in the tristate area hailed from Puebla state and that they continued to be disproportionately male. In 2002, the Mexican consulate issued 50,000 passports to citizens living in New York, half of them from Puebla (Cortina 2003), but Mexican government officials estimate that 35 percent of the 4.5 million estimated undocumented Mexican immigrants in the United States have never visited a consulate (Diestra 2003). Because of problems inherent in all of the available statistics, it is likely that dramatic changes in the composition of the Mexican community—like the shift toward much broader diversity of origins and the gender composition—might take years to be reflected in these figures. And in fact, changes in the gender makeup of the community might never be reflected in statistics originating at the Consulate for other specific reasons. First, women are more likely to access services for themselves and their families without documents, such as prenatal care with emergency Medicaid or the New York State–subsidized insurance program Child Health Plus, and are more likely to be in charge of their children's education and health care, two spheres where migratory status does not often come to bear (not least because their children are often U.S. born). Second, men more frequently undertake financial transactions, such as opening a bank account or visiting the consulate on behalf of their families than women. In fact, in my research, I found the organizations

and households I worked with to be composed of nearly equal numbers of men and women and to feature a remarkable diversity of place of origin in Mexico.

9. In spite of being home to one of the wealthiest per capita zip codes in the United States (found in the western edge of the borough, Riverdale), the Bronx is the poorest of New York City's five boroughs, with an average per capita income of only $15,235 (U.S. Census Bureau: American Community Survey 2004). Its population is 1,317,547, or slightly less than 17 percent of the city's total. About 13 percent of the borough is White non-Hispanic, 31 percent Black non-Hispanic, and 52 percent Hispanic or Latino (ibid.). Of the Hispanic or Latino population in the Bronx, 9.1 percent, or 67,764, are from Mexico (American Community Survey 2006).

10. Time spent together, sometimes implying convivial food, drink, and conversation on a particular occasion, but also used to refer to the time spent together by friends, family, or neighbors, a process of building trust and relationships over time as lives are shared. To refer to a bond built over time with others, one might say, "*hemos convivido.*"

11. The names of the parishes have been changed; however, the neighborhoods are referred to by their real names. See Appendix.

CHAPTER 2

1. See, for example, Powell 2008; also the website of Humane Borders for links to more statistics and resources: http://www.humaneborders.org/about/about_bibliography.html.

2. I am grateful to my colleague in the Mellon funded seminar on "The Sacred and the Secular," historian Greg Downs, for reminding me of some of the historical antecedents through which citizenship was defined in inclusive and exclusive ways in the 19th century. He signals as an important landmark the infamous Dred Scott decision (1857) while he points out that rights associated with citizenship were largely determined and guaranteed by states, not the federal government through the late 19th century.

3. In recent years, many scholars have returned to T. H. Marshall's mid-century notion of graduated citizenship, divided into civil, political, and social realms progressively granted in stages, as well as his positing of citizenship as membership in a community, not solely a nation (Marshall 1950; see also Baubock 1994; Jacobson 1996; and Yuval-Davis 1997).

4. This is similar to Appadurai's notion of culturalism: "the conscious mobilization of cultural differences in the service of a larger national or transnational politics" (1996: 15). See also Young (1989, 2000), although her work is problematic for her failure to discuss immigrants and the fact that she takes as her point of departure the resolution of criteria for inclusion in "universal citizenship" in the United States.

5. Jacobson implies that in part because of the shift of the referent of rights to universal personhood, citizenship in any given state is no longer important or relevant to migrants who, for example, do not naturalize when given the chance (1996: 9). More recent research points to the opposite, that when given the chance to naturalize without losing their Mexican citizenship, Mexican nationals see U.S. citizenship as a means of ensuring rights, mobility, and access to services (Boehm 2000; and Ortega and Obsatz 2002). The European Community is perhaps a laboratory par excellence for an experiment in postnational membership, as a supranational governing organization that has assumed many of the former roles of the nation-state by issuing currency, allowing the free flow of EC citizens between countries, and regulating trade, thus reducing, arguably, the nation's role to the preservation and promotion of "culture" and language. It is not clear, however, that the same model could be applied to North and Latin America, where, in spite of "free" trade agreements, and even the proliferation of the dollar, the United States maintains a vested interest in its borders and sovereignty, ceding little to its less powerful neighbors. Further, Soysal's methodology and argument that immigrant or guest-worker incorporation is a function of the kinds of political structures found in host societies, e.g., corporatist (Sweden), liberal (Great Britain), and statist (France), takes no account of variability between immigrant groups, nor does it allow that collective mobilizations could alter immigrant status, rights, or entitlements. As such, exclusionary policymakers could use her argument to imagine successfully suppressing immigrant initiatives by closing them out of political processes.

6. Domínguez's statement about driver's licenses is no longer true in New York State and most other states in the United States.

7. The Bracero Accord was a guest-worker treaty with Mexico in which laborers were recruited to work in the United States for temporary stints from 1942 to 1964.

8. Illegal immigrants, in purely legal terms, have no legitimacy being in the United States and either entered the country surreptitiously (more frequently the case of Mexican immigrants in this study), or overstayed their visas, becoming "illegal." Foreign nationals who are in the United States legally are visa holders or Lawful Permanent Residents (LPRs). Most visas are "non-immigrant" visas, meaning they allow someone to work, study, or visit the United States as a tourist for a given time period or multiple entries, but do not imply any long-term right to settle. LPRs are people who have adjusted their migratory status to allow them to stay permanently, e.g., they qualified under the Immigration Reform and Control Act of 1986 (IRCA), married a citizen, or are an immediate relative of an LPR or citizen who can sponsor them under family unification provisions. Asylees are another category able to obtain LPR status. After holding LPR status for a given number of years (currently 3 or 5 depending on status), residents can apply for naturalization, a process which involves

swearing allegiance to the United States, registering for Selective Service (for men), passing a citizenship exam, demonstrating moral character, and not having a criminal record, among other things. In spite of the fact that it is more arduous to become a naturalized citizen than to have U.S. citizenship as a birthright, naturalized citizens are supposed to enjoy all of the rights accorded native-born citizens, except for a few exceptions, such as eligibility to run for president of the United States.

9. Of course, not all of those who claim to be able to find a means for immigrants to *arreglar papeles* or obtain legal status are doing so under false pretenses. There are, in many cases, some loopholes and programs which immigrants, even when undocumented, can exploit. For example, prior to the Patriot Act, a lawyer could serve as sponsor for a client's student visa application, demonstrating the ability to provide at least $20,000 annual support of the client while he or she studied at any number of institutions, from four-year colleges to fly-by-night ESL schools, that were federally authorized to grant student visas. Another means is for a worker to seek an employer-sponsored work visa. Options like these require savvy and social networks. Nevertheless, most existing means of permanently overcoming "illegal" status require immigrants to already qualify for an adjustment of status, an impossibility for many. See also Coutin (2000) and Hagan (1994).

10. An exception to this is Immigration amendment 245i, signed at the very end of President Bill Clinton's administration, allowing those who could make a legitimate claim for adjustment of status (e.g., being married to a U.S. citizen, or having a valid claim to family reunification) to file by December 31, 2000 and overcome the bar of having been undocumented by paying a fine of $1,000.

CHAPTER 3

1. Mexico, dear and beautiful
   If I die far from you,
   May they say that I'm sleeping
   And may they bring me back here.

2. "Las Mañanitas" is the name of the serenade sung in Mexico to wake someone celebrating a birthday. It is sung to Our Lady of Guadalupe the evening of December 11, or at dawn on December 12, her feast day.

3. These theories were developed and reached their peak before the influx of large numbers of non-Christian or Jewish immigrants after 1965. In part it is the increasing religious diversity of immigrants in the last few decades which has obliged a revision of assimilationist theories (see Leonard et al. 2005; Warner and Wittner 1999; Ebaugh and Chafetz 2000; Kniss and Numrich 2007; Foley and Hoge 2007).

4. In parishes with multiple pastors, the church might be spatially subdivided, with the main space dedicated to the English mass, and a basement or smaller rectory chapel home to the Spanish-language mass. This separation, which seemed to many to be visibly hierarchical, offended many Puerto Ricans, who complained of being relegated to basement churches (Díaz-Stevens 1993a). A monsignor I interviewed in a very large parish in the northernmost section of the Bronx justified this division—which remarkably still persists in his parish— by saying that the Latino parishioners do not like the austere, modern design of his church with its emphasis on the sculptural formality of the altar and architecturally maximized play of natural light, preferring the basement chapel to which the statuary of saints and the Virgin Mary were relegated after the renovation. In many parishes, however, Spanish-speaking parishioners quickly outnumbered English-speaking ones, so sheer demographics, as well as, in many cases, a change of heart on the part of clergy, altered the spatial arrangements of the masses.

5. Spellman and Illich differed on whether the integrated Hispanic mass was the ultimate goal, or a transitional one, leading to the ultimate integration and assimilation of Hispanics into English-language worship and "American" culture.

6. Juan Diego was only canonized in 2001, but some parishes, including Saint John, have been celebrating his feast on December 10 for much longer.

7. A dj-performer who works with music, lights, smoke, his or her own voice, and amplified and recorded messages of greeting for loved ones whether present or in Mexico (see Ragland 2003).

8. Mott Haven is 73 percent Hispanic or Latino, among whom 11 percent are Mexican. In the Census tracts which include and surround Saint John Church, Mexicans number 3,125, and represent about 16 percent of the population (U.S. Census 2000: SF1).

9. Goods donated to a community food pantry.

10. Even though the comités guadalupanos are composed predominantly of Mexicans, there are a few members from other countries who consider themselves guadalupanos. While, on the one hand, this fact complicates my analysis, which is focused primarily on Mexican immigrants in New York City, it is another indicator that devotion to Guadalupe provides powerful idioms of empowerment and participation which are meaningful even to non-conationals. In this case, this Guatemalan family explained that they were long devoted to Our Lady of Guadalupe in their home country, so when they heard about an organization dedicated to her that also offered information useful to immigrants, they became eager members of the group and were welcomed by the other members.

11. Wood writes that "old-style" Alinsky organizing declined in popularity in the 1970s at the same time that grassroots faith-based organizing began to rise in prominence and breadth (2002: 146).

12. Although I must note that I never observed elections or knew of them occurring in my absence, during the fall of 2000 and the year from fall 2002 to fall 2003, when I attended or obtained information about all of the group's meetings. María Lucía is not an elected officer of the group even though she runs its meetings, organizes its weekly agenda, and plans its activities.

13. The elected officers during the second part of my field research were Doña Rosario, president, Don Julio and his wife Doña Rosaura, treasurer and secretary, and Segundo, captain of the torch run. While the president is required by the Asociación to attend all of its business meetings and to relay messages and initiatives in both directions, Doña Rosario did not seem to visit Tepeyac at all in 2002–3, during my formal research, although previously, in the fall of 2000, I knew her to attend some meetings at Tepeyac and to bring newsletters and other information back to the group. I only saw the captain of the torch run attend a single meeting of the grupo guadalupano in the fall of 2000, just before December 12, although people were directed to speak to him about matters related to it.

14. This and other translations, except where noted, are mine.

15. The Virgin of Guadalupe is notable, Father Byrne told me, as an image of the Virgin Mary pregnant, and so after being named patroness of the Americas by Pope John Paul II, she was taken up as an icon by many Catholic anti-abortion activists in the United States.

16. Compadrazgo is the system of fictive kinship found in many parts of Latin America, but particularly pronounced in rural Mexico, in which families become bound to each other in ties of mutual assistance, reciprocity, and affection through being designated godparents for one another's children. Compadres and comadres may be siblings or cousins, but in rural settings, where children might have many aunts and uncles, it is the godparents who are seen to have a special relationship to them and their parents. With migration, these ties have come to take on new valences, as one's compadre or comadre may be the most likely candidate to lend money for the migration journey, or to receive the new migrant at their destination. Immigrants residing in the United States sometimes find themselves favored as candidates to be *padrino* or *madrina* for their nieces, nephews, cousins, and other children they may have never met, remitting money for the child's baptism outfit, party, or photographs, as well as other needs the child may have.

17. Literally co-brother-in-law, the relationship between spouses of siblings. The relationship which is one degree closer, between a person and his/her sibling's spouse, is referred to as cuñada or cuñado. All of these terms are translated as brother- or sister-in-law in English.

18. The *caja de ahorro* was profiled in a *New York Times* article on July 30, 2003 (Barry 2003), where it was described as the latest in a long line of efforts by immigrant groups to define themselves and their legacy.

19. Much has been written about the "hometown associations" formed by Mexican migrants in the United States that sometimes collect hundreds of thousands of dollars for public works projects in their hometowns, such as potable water plants, stadiums, or bridges (see Smith 1995, 2005, and Alex Rivera's 2003 film *The Sixth Section* for New York–area examples of this). The *caja* is substantively different because its members do not all originate from the same hometown (the concentration of elaborate family and social networks in a single small town helps ensure compliance and good management of funds in the associations), and are dedicating themselves to capital projects in New York City.

20. "*Endrogarse*," while a cognate of "to drug oneself," in English, in Mexico City slang refers to falling into debt. Thank you to María José Gómez for this information.

21. During the period of my dissertation fieldwork, Joel Magallán was referred to as Hermano Joel. In 2006, he left *la Compañía de Jesús*, the Jesuit Conference, and is now referred to by those who know this simply as Joel. Others continue to call him Hermano Joel.

CHAPTER 4

1. Gruzinski notes that "the early church was hostile to the miracle which, it affirmed, played only a secondary role in the conversion of the Indians," and that they favored "a religion without miracles, reserved on images and saints, animated with a concern to go to the essential and avoid confusions between the faith and paganism." However, the Franciscans welcomed indigenous visions as a sign of nascent, if naïve, faith (1993: 188–190). On Dominican, Augustinian, and to a lesser extent Franciscan opposition to the cult of Guadalupe, see Ricard (1966).

2. She is associated particularly with the nagvioli flower, "which represented Huitzilipochtli, the great ferocious sun god of the Aztecs. Guadalupe is mother of Huitzilipochtli" (Castillo 1996).

3. Gachupín is a colloquial and slightly derogatory term used in colonial Mexico for Spaniards residing in the colony. The term criollo, or Creole, is a synonym that was used self-referentially by Spaniards born in the colony.

4. Figueroa Deck, likewise, in a review of Our Lady of Guadalupe, throws into question Poole's project of questioning historical sources, to ask what is more important, "the factual events or the people's mythos that envelops their faith?" (1995).

5. Since Saint Thomas traveled in India and is said to have introduced Christianity there, it is possible that the same confusion which led Columbus to believe he had found an alternative route to "The Indies" led to the belief that Thomas had made the same trip centuries earlier. This was a belief perpetuated into the eighteenth century, as in Fray Servando Teresa de Mier's infamous "Sermón Guadalupano" at the Basilica of Guadalupe in 1794 (Mier Noriega y Guerra

1982). Dominican Juan de la Puente also argued that Saint Thomas preached from Mexico to Brazil (Brading 2001: 36).

6. Until Joel's late confession in 2008, described in chapter 3.

7. On Durkheim's notion of disenchantment in our contemporary globalized age, see Franco 2007.

8. This is changing, as a recent CIESAS survey indicates that the number of Catholics in Mexico has dropped from 99 percent of the population in 1950 to 88 percent in 2000 (Universo Cristiano 2008).

9. As a point of comparison, in the United States, there is one priest per 1,510 Catholics, while in Mexico the number is one per 6,276 (Statistical Yearbook of the Church, graphic reproduced in Goodstein 2008).

10. This is not to say that it is not possible to have a theologizing experience without migrating.

11. Ironically, while this mode of referring to fellow members of the group certainly implies fellowship and communitarian bonds, as opposed to traditional understandings of compadrazgo, I also observed that given the oft-fluctuating membership roles of the comités, sometimes the term was used when people could not remember the name of the person to whom they were speaking.

12. Also called El Apostolado in other parishes.

13. Carolina, mentioned earlier in this chapter.

14. "Lupe" and "Lupita" are nicknames, and in this case a term of endearment, for the Virgin of Guadalupe. It is also used for anyone named Guadalupe, which includes a great number of Mexican men and women.

15. Nuns of the Dominican order who were brought by the parish priest from Puebla to minister to fellow poblanos with what he hoped would be a culturally specific pastoralism.

16. This conversation occurred with Rubén, choreographer of the ballet folklórico of Our Lady of the Rosary Parish, who is also a staff member of Asociación Tepeyac. I did not record the conversation, but it is vivid in my mind and I took notes shortly after it occurred. Nevertheless, I write it here in English so as not to give the impression that it is a direct quotation. The translation of the phrases that I left in Spanish is "You [plural] go first," "No, you," "No, I insist, after you."

CHAPTER 5

1. Text read at the Second Station of *el Viacrucis del Inmigrante,* the Stations of the Cross of the Immigrant, organized by Asociación Tepeyac, April 2003. Translation my own.

2. Via Crucis is the Latin term for the Way of the Cross. The term is also used conventionally in Spanish, but spelled *Viacrucis.* It is also called the Stations of the Cross or the Via Dolorosa and is the site, often, for performances of Passion Plays. I use the spelling used by the organizations with which I conducted research, Viacrucis.

206 Notes to Chapter 5

3. Not all Viacrucis processions include a fifteenth station, the resurrection of Jesus, which for some cannot be depicted until the Sunday of Holy Week, Easter Sunday.

4. This was the only time I heard someone say "la Viacrucis" as opposed to "el Viacrucis" in Spanish.

5. After beginning preliminary research at the church in the fall of 2000, attendance at events was one way that I kept in touch with the members of the church and the clergy in the interval of time while I completed the preparations for intensive field work (obtaining funding and institutional review). One of my main roles in the church in that period was as a photographer of events. I took photographs for my own purposes (I created several photo essays) as well as for use by the church and individuals, volunteering to photograph baptisms, weddings, church events, protests, and the church building for use in a fundraising campaign to renovate the church. After several months of shooting pictures, I went to the parish to show a slide show of the images and also asked people to comment upon them. I recorded their comments, and this experiment in "photo elicitation" yielded rich commentary on the way that members of this church view their participation in rituals like the Viacrucis.

6. The first time I met Father Byrne and told him I wished to talk to him about the comité guadalupano, he spent the first part of our conversation taking me on a tour around the church, proudly showing me the new shrine to Our Lady of Guadalupe outside of the rectory, the freshly whitewashed exterior of the church, and the repaired roof, all of which had been accomplished by members of the comité guadalupano who volunteered on their days off from construction jobs.

7. In the last few years, I have been told that Father Castillo and the comité guadalupano have come to appreciate each other. They get along well now and I have even seen Father Castillo officiating at the mass of Our Lady of Guadalupe at Saint Patrick's Cathedral along with other priests from around the city who are highly regarded by the Mexican community. It is important to note that I approached Father Castillo several times in person, by phone, and even a letter to request an interview with him for this book, but each time he refused or did not reply.

8. The Spanish texts here are from the booklet distributed by Asociación Tepeyac. The English verses are from the New International Bible. There are some discrepancies in emphasis in the translation. For instance, in the Spanish, Christ is said to have been treated like "garbage," and in the English it is said he was "rejected."

9. Translation in original USCCB document, but not in excerpts reprinted in Tepeyac's pamphlet.

10. At the photo elicitation group at Saint John Church.

CHAPTER 6

1. Thank you to one of the anonymous reviewers of this manuscript for this information.

2. I located this program in the archives of the New York Historical Society.

3. I have reproduced this dialogue from notes, not transcribed audio recordings, so I do not include the original Spanish here. The same is true of other quotations in this chapter that are represented in English.

4. I adapted this term from Jerome Krase's notion of "ethnic theme parks" (2006).

5. Antonio was unusual among Tepeyac's staff, which was largely composed of immigrants. He was born in Brooklyn and was thoroughly bilingual. He told me he came to Tepeyac as an activist and only later came to consider himself *guadalupano*, and to appreciate the meaning of the Virgin for the organization's members and mission.

6. This interview was conducted in English and this excerpt is from transcribed audio recordings.

7. Thank you to one of the anonymous reviewers of this manuscript for this information.

8. Translation from audio recording of an interview with Heraclio.

CHAPTER 7

1. HR2899 was the failed Land Border Security and Immigration Improvement Act of 2003.

2. This bill would have established two visa programs. The H-4A program would allow foreign workers to apply for jobs posted in an electronic job registry and work under three-year work visas, at the end of which they could apply for permanent residency with or without an employer sponsor. The H-4B visa program would allow undocumented workers already in the United States to obtain a work visa, and at the end of a three-year period, apply for an H-4A visa for another three years (after paying a fine of $1,500), after which they would be eligible to apply for permanent residency. Holders of both visa categories would be able to travel outside of the country and enjoy all of the protections afforded workers under U.S. labor law.

3. Of course, there was the Illegal Immigration Reform and Immigrant Responsibility Act of 1996 (IIRIRA). However, this did not extend legalization to immigrants but was rather more an "enforcement only" law, making many more categories of crimes, including many misdemeanors, "aggravated felonies" under immigration law, triggering automatic deportation. It increased border enforcement and also increased detention of immigrants and deputized local law enforcement officials to enforce immigration law.

4. Frequently the term "low wage" is coupled with "unskilled" in discussions of the labor sectors in which unauthorized immigrants are most frequently employed. I avoid this term because even though immigrant workers frequently do not boast the training, skills, or safety equipment necessary to butcher cattle, build skyscrapers, re-point mortar, or many of the other dangerous jobs in which they are hired, that does not seem to stop employers from assigning them such tasks and paying them a fraction of the wages commanded by unionized, trained laborers doing the same work.

5. The perpetrators of the September 11, 2001 attacks were not undocumented immigrants but holders of active visas, especially student visas. A further sign of cognitive dissonance and paranoia about some immigrants has been the obsession with the "openness" of the Southern border even while the much longer Northern border has received little attention.

6. Jacoby, formerly of the Manhattan Institute, a conservative think tank, is now President and CEO of ImmigrationWorks USA, and is one of the public intellectuals working to make lawmakers recognize what she described as the need to bring the immigration system (mainly the number of visas issued to workers each year) into agreement with the number of available jobs so that people do not feel compelled to enter illegally.

7. CIS is a think tank which describes itself as nonpartisan. Its mission is "to expand the base of public knowledge and understanding of the need for an immigration policy that gives first concern to the broad national interest. The Center is animated by a pro-immigrant, low-immigration vision which seeks fewer immigrants but a warmer welcome for those admitted" (http://www.cis.org/aboutcis.html). Its directors, Steven Camarota and Mark Krikorian, are among the most frequent commentators on immigration, always advocating for reduced immigration, in mass media, Internet media, large immigration conferences, and more. They are frequently featured in debates, advocating "greater restrictions on immigration."

8. http://usuarios.lycos.es/acjm/canc/cantosmarianos.html.

9. One example of this is the annual Marian Parade on the Upper West Side of Manhattan which ends at the Church of the Ascension. At the culmination of a large parade in which representatives from every country in the hemisphere march, dance, and process with effusive floats, banners, and statues of their national patroness, Father Duffell beseeches all to remember that there is only one Mary and that she is the path to Christ. Further, he insists that only by turning their faith to devotion to Our Lady of Guadalupe, Queen of the Americas, and voting (the parade is always held shortly before November elections) will Latinos come together in unity and faith in the United States.

10. Recently the "New Sanctuary" movement has worked to turn Catholic and other churches into literal sanctuaries for immigrants at risk of deportation.

11. As was once posited exuberantly, and apparently, prematurely, by Arjun Appadurai (1996), among others.

12. For literature on festival, see Bristol 1985; Burke 1978; Caillois 1959; Girard 1977; and Ladurie 1979.

13. Thanks to Jill Stauffer of the Mellon funded seminar on "The Sacred and the Secular" for calling my attention to these distinctions.

References

Abercrombie, Thomas. 1992. "La Fiesta de Carnaval Postcolonial en Oruro: Clase, Etnicidad y Nacionalismo en La Danza Folklórica." *Revista Andina* 10: 279–352.

———. 1996. "Q'Aqchas and the Plebe in 'Rebellion': Carnival vs. Lent in 18th-Century Potosí." *Journal of Latin American Anthropology* 2: 62–111.

———. 1998. *Pathways of Memory and Power.* Madison: University of Wisconsin Press.

Alba, Richard, Albert Raboteau, and Josh DeWind. 2009. *Immigration and Religion in America: Comparative and Historical Perspectives.* New York: New York University Press.

Alonso, Ana. 1994. "The Politics of Space, Time and Substance: State Formation, Nationalism and Ethnicity." *Annual Review of Anthropology* 23: 379–405.

———. 2004. "Conforming Disconformity: 'Mestizaje,' Hybridity, and the Aesthetics of Mexican Nationalism." *Cultural Anthropology* 24 (19, 4): 459–490.

Altman, Ida. 1989. *Emigrants and Society: Extremadura and America in the Sixteenth Century.* Berkeley: University of California Press.

Anzaldúa, Gloria. 1987. *Borderlands/La Frontera.* San Francisco: Aunt Lute Press.

Appadurai, Arjun. 1996. *Modernity at Large: Cultural Dimensions of Globalization.* Minneapolis: University of Minnesota Press.

Arendt, Hannah. 1994. *The Origins of Totalitarianism.* San Diego: Harcourt Brace Jovanovich.

Asociación Tepeyac de New York. 2004. "Mission." Electronic resource: http://www.tepeyac.org, accessed 12/1/2004.

Badillo, David. 2006. *Latinos and the New Immigrant Church.* Baltimore: Johns Hopkins University Press.

Barry, Dan. 2003. "About New York; Mexican, but the Dream Is American," *New York Times,* July 30.

Basch, Linda, Nina Glick Schiller, and Cristina Szanton-Blanc, eds. 1994. *Nations Unbound: Transnational Projects, Postcolonial Predicaments and Deterritorialized Nation States.* New York: Gordon and Breach Science Publishers.

Baubock, Rainer. 1994. *Transnational Citizenship: Membership and Rights in International Migration.* Brookfield, VT: Edward Elgar.

Bellah, Robert. 1970. *Beyond Belief.* New York: Harper and Row.

Bergad, Laird. 2007. "Mexicans in New York 1990–2005," and "Mexicans in New York City, 2007: An Update," Latino Data Project, Center for Latin American, Caribbean & Latino Studies, City University of New York, Electronic resource: http://web.gc.cuny.edu/lastudies/pages/latinodataprojectreports.html.

Berman, Marshall. 1987. "Among the Ruins." *New Internationalist* 178, http://www. newint.org/issue178/among.htm, accessed 12/1/04.

Berryman, Phillip. 1987. *Liberation Theology: The Essential Facts about the Revolutionary Movement in Latin America and Beyond.* New York: Pantheon.

Beyer, Peter. 1994. *Religion and Globalization.* Thousand Oaks, CA: Sage Publications.

Boehm, Deborah A. 2000. "'From Both Sides': (Trans)Nationality, Citizenship, and Belonging among Mexican Immigrants to the United States." In *Rethinking Refuge and Displacement*, ed. Elzbieta Gozdiak and Dianna Shandy. New York: American Anthropological Association.

Bosniak, Linda. 1998. "Citizenship of Aliens." *Social Text* 56: 15–30.

Bossy, John. 1970. "The Counter-Reformation and the People of Catholic Europe." *Past and Present* 47(1): 51–70.

Brading, David. 2001. *Mexican Phoenix: Our Lady of Guadalupe: Image and Tradition across Five Centuries.* Cambridge: Cambridge University Press.

Brady, Emily. 2007. "For Mexican Workers, a Long Walk Home." *New York Times,* October 21, 2007.

Brentano, Lujo. 1870. *On the History and Development of Gilds, and the Origin of Trade-Unions.* London: Trübner & Co.

Bristol, Michael. 1985. *Carnival and Theater: Plebeian Culture and the Structure of Authority in Renaissance England.* New York: Methuen.

Brown, Jonathan. 1998. *The Word Made Image: Religion, Art, and Architecture in Spain and Spanish America, 1500–1600.* Hanover, NH: University Press of New England.

Brown, Peter. 1981. *The Cult of the Saints: Its Rise and Function in Latin Christianity.* London: SCM Press.

Burdick, John. 1993. *Looking for God in Brazil: The Progressive Catholic Church in Urban Brazil's Religious Arena.* Berkeley: University of California Press.

Burke, Peter. 1978. *Popular Culture in Early Modern Europe.* New York: Harper Torchbooks.

Burkhart, Louise. 2001. *Before Guadalupe: The Virgin Mary in Early Colonial Nahuatl Literature.* Albany: State University of New York Institute for Mesoamerican Studies.

Caillois, Roger. 1959. *Man and the Sacred.* Glencoe, IL: Free Press.

Campese, Gioacchino. 2007. "Beyond Ethnic and National Imagination: Toward a Catholic Theology of U.S. Immigration." In *Religion and Social Justice for Immigrants,* ed. Hondagneu-Sotelo. New Brunswick, NJ: Rutgers University Press.

Carmona, Alicia. 2008. "*Bailar con fe*: Folkloric Devotional Practice in a Bolivian Immigrant Community." *e-misférica 5.1*, www.emisferica.org.

Castillo, Ana. 1996. *Goddess of the Americas: Writings on the Virgin of Guadalupe*. New York: Riverhead Books.

Castillo y Piña, Jose. 1945. *Tonantzin: Nuestra Madrecita*. Mexico, DF: Siluetas.

Celestino, Olinda, and A. Myers. 1981. *Las Cofradías En El Perú, Región Central*. Frankfurt/Main: Verlag Klaus Dieter Vervuert.

Chance, John K. 1985. "Cofradías and Cargos: An Historical Perspective on the Mesoamerican Civil-Religious Hierarchy." *American Ethnologist* 12: 1–26.

Chávez, Leo. 1991. "Outside the Imagined Community: Undocumented Settlers and Experiences of Incorporation." *American Ethnologist* 18: 257–278.

———. 2001. *Covering Immigration: Popular Images and the Politics of the Nation*. Berkeley: University of California Press.

———. 2008. *The Latino Threat: Constructing Immigrants, Citizens, and the Nation*. Palo Alto, CA: Stanford University Press.

Christian, William. 1981. *Local Religion in Sixteenth-Century Spain*. Princeton, NJ: Princeton University Press.

Cohen, Sandro, and Josefina Estrada. 2002. *De cómo los Mexicanos conquistaron Nueva York*. Mexico DF: Colibrí.

Connerton, Paul. 1989. *How Societies Remember*. Cambridge: Cambridge University Press.

Cortes, Sergio. 2003. "Migrants from Puebla in the 1990s." In *Immigrants and Schooling: Mexicans in New York*, ed. Regina Cortina and Mónica Gendreau. Staten Island, NY: Center for Migration Studies.

Cortina, Regina. May 6, 2003. Paper presented at conference on Mexican Migration, New York University.

Cortina, Regina, and Mónica Gendreau, eds. 2003. *Immigrants and Schooling: Mexicans in New York*. Staten Island, NY: Center for Migration Studies.

Coutin, Susan Bibler. 2000. *Legalizing Moves: Salvadoran Immigrants' Struggle for U.S. Residency*. Ann Arbor: University of Michigan Press.

Curcio Nagy, Linda. 1994. "Giants and Gypsies: Corpus Christi in Colonial Mexico City." In *Rituals of Rule, Rituals of Resistance: Public Celebrations and Popular Culture in Mexico*, ed. Ed Beezley. Wilmington, DE: Scholarly Resources.

Davalos, Karen Mary. 2002. "The Real Way of Praying." In *Horizons of the Sacred*, ed. Timothy Matovina and Gary Riebe-Estrella. Ithaca, NY: Cornell University Press.

Davies, Victoria M. 1995. *St Peter Claver's Parish (Brooklyn) African American Mission Way-Station or Home?* MA thesis, New York University.

Dean, Carolyn. 1999. *Inka Bodies and the Body of Christ*. Durham, NC: Duke University Press.

De Certeau, Michel. 1984. *The Practice of Everyday Life*. Berkeley: University of California Press.

De Genova, Nicholas. 1998. "Race, Space, and the Reinvention of Latin America in Mexican Chicago." *Latin American Perspectives* 25: 87–116.

———. 2005. *Working the Boundaries: Race, Space and "Illegality" in Mexican Chicago.* Durham: Duke University Press.

Delgado-Gaitan, Concha. 1994. "Consejos: The Power of Cultural Narratives." *Anthropology & Education Quarterly* 25: 298–316.

Del Paso y Troncoso, Francisco. 1979. *Códice Borbónico: Manuscrito Mexicano De La Biblioteca Del Palais Bourbon.* Mexico: Siglo Veintiuno.

DeWalt, Billie. 1975. "Changes in the Cargo Systems of MesoAmerica." *Anthropological Quarterly* 48, no. 2 (April): 87–105.

Díaz-Barriga, Miguel. 2008. "Distracción: Notes on Cultural Citizenship, Visual Ethnography, and Mexican Migration to Pennsylvania." *Visual Anthropology Review* 24, no. 2: 133–147.

Díaz Del Castillo, Bernal. 1963. *The Conquest of New Spain.* J. M. Cohen, trans. London: Penguin Books.

Díaz-Stevens, Ana M. 1993a. *Oxcart Catholicism on Fifth Avenue: The Impact of the Puerto Rican Migration upon the Archdiocese of New York.* Notre Dame, IN: University of Notre Dame Press.

———. 1993b. "The Saving Grace: The Matriarchal Core of Latino Catholicism." *Latino Studies Journal* 4 (September): 60–78.

Diestra, Mario. 2003. "Facing Our Current Challenges." Presentation at City College of New York.

Dolan, Jay P. 1985. *The American Catholic Experience: A History from Colonial Times to the Present.* Garden City, NY: Doubleday.

———. 1994. *Hispanic Catholic Culture in the United States.* Notre Dame, IN: University of Notre Dame Press.

Driessen, Henk. 1984. "Religious Brotherhoods: Class and Politics in an Andalusian Town." In *Religion, Power, and Protest in Local Communities the Northern Shore of the Mediterranean,* ed. Eric Wolf. Berlin: Mouton.

Durand, Jorge, and Douglas Massey. 1992. "Mexican Migration to the United States." *Latin American Research Review* 27: 3–42.

Durkheim, Emile. 1947 [1915]. *The Elementary Forms of Religious Life.* New York: Free Press.

Eade, John, and Michael Sallnow. 1991. *Contesting the Sacred: The Anthropology of Christian Pilgrimage.* New York: Routledge.

Ebaugh, Helen R., and J. Chafetz. 2000. *Religion and the New Immigrants: Continuities and Adaptations in Immigrant Congregations.* Walnut Creek, CA: Altamira Press.

Elizondo, Virgilio. 1981. *La Morenita, Evangelizadora de las Americas.* Liguori, MO: Liguori Publications.

———. 1986. "Popular Religion as Support of Identity: A Pastoral-Psychological Case-Study Based on the Mexican-American Experience in the USA." In

Popular Religion, ed. Norbert Greinacher and Norbert Mette. Edinburgh: T. and T. Clark.

———. 1997. *Guadalupe: Mother of the New Creation*. Maryknoll: Orbis Books.

Fernández Hervás, Enrique. 1992. *Fiestas de Moros y Cristianos en España y su Estudio en la Provincia De Jaén*. Jaén: Gráficas Catena.

Figueroa Deck, Allan. 1995. "Review of Our Lady of Guadalupe by Stafford Poole." *America* 30 September.

Flores, William, and Rina Benmayor, eds. 1997. *Latino Cultural Citizenship*. Boston: Beacon Press.

Flynn, Maureen. 1989. *Sacred Charity: Confraternities and Social Welfare in Spain 1400–1700*. Ithaca, NY: Cornell University Press.

Foley, Michael, and Dean Hoge. 2007. *Religion and the New Immigrants*. Oxford: Oxford University Press.

Foster, George. 1960. *Culture and Conquest: America's Spanish Heritage*. Viking Fund Publications in Anthropology, no. 27. New York: Wenner-Gren Foundation for Anthropological Research.

Franco, Jean. 2007. "The Second Coming: Religion as Entertainment." In *Performing Religion in the Americas*, ed. Alyshia Gálvez. London: Sea Gull Books.

Fraser, Valerie. 1990. *The Architecture of Conquest: Building in the Viceroyalty in Peru, 1535–1635*. Cambridge: Cambridge University Press.

Gálvez, Alyshia. 2010 (in press). "Resolviendo: How September 11th Tested and Transformed a New York City Mexican Immigrant Organization." In *Politics and Partnerships: The Role of Voluntary Associations in America's Political Past and Present*, ed. Elisabeth Clemens and Doug Guthrie. Chicago: University of Chicago Press.

Gálvez, Alyshia, and José Luque Brazán, eds. 2008. "Traveling Virgins/Virgenes Viajeras." In *e-misférica*, electronic resource: http://www.hemisphericinstitute.org/journal/5.1/eng/en51_index.html, April 2008.

García Ayluardo, Cesar. 1994. "A World of Images: Cult Ritual and Society in Colonial Mexico City." In *Rituals of Rule, Rituals of Resistance: Public Celebrations and Popular Culture in Mexico*, ed. Ed Beezley.Wilmington, DE: Scholarly Resources.

Geertz, Clifford. 1973. *The Interpretation of Cultures*. New York: Basic Books.

Gibson, Charles. 1966. *Spain in America*. New York: Harper Torchbooks.

Girard, René. 1977. *Violence and the Sacred*. Baltimore: Johns Hopkins University Press.

Glazer, Nathan, and Daniel Patrick Moynihan. 1963. *Beyond the Melting Pot: The Negroes, Puerto Ricans, Jews, Italians, and Irish of New York City*. Cambridge, MA: Harvard University Press.

Gleason, Philip. 1987. *Keeping the Faith: American Catholicism, Past and Present*. Notre Dame, IN: University of Notre Dame Press.

Glick Schiller, Nina, Linda Basch, and Cristina Szanton-Blanc, eds. 1992. *Towards a Transnational Perspective on Migration: Race, Class, Ethnicity, and Nationalism Reconsidered.* New York: New York Academy of Sciences.

Goizueta, Roberto. 2002. "The Symbolic World of Mexican American Religion," In *Horizons of the Sacred,* ed. Timothy Matovina and Gary Riebe-Estrella. Ithaca, NY: Cornell University Press.

Goldring, Luin. 1996. "Blurring Borders: Constructing Transnational Community in the Process of U.S.–Mexico Migration." *Research in Community Sociology* 6: 69–104.

González, Juan. 1997. "Cultures Clash at Church in El Barrio." *New York Daily News,* January 10. Electronic resource: http://www.nydailynews.com/archives/news/1997/01/10/1997-01-10_cultures_clash_at_church_in_.html. Accessed July 20, 2008.

Goodstein, Laurie. 2008. "Serving U.S. Parishes, Fathers without Borders." *New York Times,* December 27.

Greenhouse, Steven. 2004. "Plan for Illegal Immigrant Workers Draws Fire from Two Sides." *New York Times,* January 8, p. A28.

Gruzinski, Serge. 1993. *The Conquest of Mexico: The Incorporation of Indian Societies into the Western World, 16th–18th Centuries.* Cambridge: Polity Press.

Guarnizo, Luis Eduardo, and Michael P. Smith. 1998. "The Locations of Transnationalism." In *Transnationalism from Below,* ed. M. P. Smith and L. E. Guarnizo. New Brunswick, NJ: Transaction Publishers.

Guerrero, Andres G. 1984. *The Significance of Nuestra Señora De Guadalupe and La Raza Cósmica in the Development of a Chicano Theology of Liberation.* Ph.D. dissertation, Harvard University, Cambridge.

Gupta, Akhil, and James Ferguson. 1992. "Beyond 'Culture': Space, Identity and the Politics of Difference." *Cultural Anthropology* 7: 6–23.

Hagan, Jaqueline. 1994. *Deciding to Be Legal: A Mayan Community in Houston.* Philadelphia: Temple University Press.

Halbwachs, Maurice. 1992. *On Collective Memory.* Chicago: University of Chicago Press.

Hammond, Phillip. 1993. "Religion and Nationalism in the United States." In *Religion and Political Power,* ed. Gustavo Benavides and M. W. Daly. Albany: State University of New York Press.

Hellman, Judith Adler. 2008. *The World of Mexican Migrants: Between the Rock and the Hard Place.* New York: New Press.

Herberg, Will. 1960. *Protestant, Catholic, Jew: An Essay in American Religious Sociology.* Garden City, NY: Anchor Books.

Holston, James, and Arjun Appadurai. 1999. "Introduction: Cities and Citizenship." In *Cities and Citizenship,* ed. James Holston. Durham, NC: Duke University Press.

Hondagneu-Sotelo, Pierrette. 2007. *Religion and Social Justice for Immigrants*. New Brunswick, NJ: Rutgers University Press.

Honig, Bonnie. 1998. "How Foreignness 'Solves' Democracy's Problems." In *Social Text* 56: 1–27.

———. 2001. *Democracy and the Foreigner*. Princeton, NJ: Princeton University Press.

Hsu, Spencer. 2008. "Raid's Outcome May Signal a Retreat In Immigration Strategy, Critics Say." *Washington Post*, September 2, p. A13.

Hunter, James Davison. 1991. *Culture Wars: The Struggle to Define America*. New York: Basic Books.

Hurtig, Janise. 2000. "Hispanic Immigrant Churches and the Construction of Ethnicity." In *Public Religion and Urban Transformation: Faith in the City*, ed. Lowell Livezey. New York: New York University Press.

Ibarra, Marcela. 2003. Paper presented at Mexican Migration conference, New York University.

Industrial Areas Foundation. 2008. "Who Are We?" Electronic resource: http://www.industrialareasfoundation.org/iafabout/about.htm, accessed July 18, 2008.

Jackson, Robert. 1999. *Race, Caste and Status: Indians in Colonial Spanish America*. Albuquerque: University of New Mexico Press.

Jacobson, David. 1996. *Rights across Borders: Immigration and the Decline of Citizenship*. Baltimore: Johns Hopkins University Press.

Jacoby, Tamar. 2006. "What to Do on Immigration." *Council on Foreign Relations*, June 2. Electronic resource: http://www.cfr.org/publication/10910/, accessed January 23, 2008.

John Paul II. 1999. *Ecclesia in America (The Church in America)*. Washington, DC: U.S. Catholic Conference, available electronically at: http://www.vatican.va/holy_father/john_paul_ii/apost_exhortations/documents/hf_jp-ii_exh_22011999_ecclesia-in-america_en.html.

Johnson, Harvey L. 1980. "The Virgin of Guadalupe in Mexican Culture." In *Religion in Latin American Life and Literature*, ed. Lyle C Brown and William F. Cooper. Waco, TX: Baylor University Press.

Katz, Melissa. 2001. *Divine Mirrors: The Virgin Mary in the Visual Arts*. New York: Oxford University Press.

Kearney, Michael. 1991. "Borders, Boundaries of State and Self at the End of Empire." *Journal of Historical Sociology* 4: 52–74.

———. 1995. "The Effects of Transnational Culture, Economy, and Migration on Mixtec Identity in Oaxacalifornia." In *The Bubbling Cauldron: Race, Ethnicity and the Urban Crisis*, ed. M. P. Smith and J. Feagin. Minneapolis: University of Minnesota Press.

Klor De Alva, Jorge. 1995. "The Postcolonialization of the (Latin) American Experience: A Reconsideration of 'Colonialism,' 'Postcolonialism' and 'Mestizaje.'"

In *After Colonialism*, ed. Gyan Prakash. Princeton, NJ: Princeton University Press.

Kniss, Fred, and Paul Numrich. 2007. *Sacred Assemblies and Civic Engagement.* New Brunswick, NJ: Rutgers University Press.

Koopmans, Ruud, and Paul Statham. 1999. "Challenging the Liberal Nation-State? Postnationalism, Multiculturalism, and the Collective Claims Making of Migrants and Ethnic Minorities in Britain and Germany." *American Journal of Sociology* 105: 652–696.

Krase, Jerome. 2006. "Seeing Ethnic Succession in Little Italy: Change Despite Resistance." *Modern Italy* 11 (1): 79–95.

Kugel, Seth. 2004. "In the South Bronx, the Arts Beckon." *New York Times*, January 30, p. E1.

Kurtz, Donald. 1982. "The Virgin of Guadalupe and the Politics of Becoming Human." *Journal of Anthropological Research* 38: 194–210.

Ladurie, Emmanuel Leroy. 1979. *Carnival in Romans.* New York: G. Braziller.

Lafaye, Jacques. 1993. *Quetzalcóatl y Guadalupe: La Formación de la Conciencia Nacional en México.* Mexico: Fondo de Cultura Económica.

Lahiri, Tripti. 2003. "In Death, Homeward Bound; Most Mexican Immigrants Are Sent Back for Burial." *New York Times*, June 26, 2003, p. B1.

Leach, Edmund. 1976. *Culture and Communication: The Logic by Which Symbols Are Connected.* Cambridge: Cambridge University Press.

Lee, Felicia. 2002. "The South Bronx: Music Changes, but Never Stops." *New York Times*, March 24, p. E1.

León, Luis. 1997. *Religious Movement in the United States-Mexico Borderlands: Toward a Theory of Chicana/o Religious Poetics.* Ph.D. dissertation, University of California, Santa Barbara.

———. 2005. "César Chávez and Mexican-American Civil Religion." In *Latino Religions and Civic Activism in the United States*, ed. Gastón Espinosa, Virgilio Elizondo, and Jesse Miranda. Oxford: Oxford University Press.

León, María. 2008. "Migrant Deaths up on Arizona-Mexico Border." *La Oferta.* January 4. Electronic source: http://www.laoferta.com/index. php?option=com_content&task=view&id=3992&Itemid=38.

Leonard, Karen, Alex Stepick, Manuel Vasquez, and Jennifer Holdway. 2005. *Immigrant Faiths: Transforming Religious Life in America.* Walnut Creek, CA: Alta Mira Press.

Light, Ivan. 1981. "Ethnic Succession." In *Ethnic Change*, ed. Charles Keyes. Seattle: University of Washington Press.

Limonic, Laura. 2008. "The Latino Population of New York City, 2007." *Latino Data Project*, Report 20, December.

Livezey, Lowell. 2000. *Public Religion and Urban Transformation: Faith in the City.* New York: New York University Press.

Lockhart, James. 1972. *The Men of Cajamarca: A Social and Biographical Study of the First Conquerors of Peru.* Austin: University of Texas Press.

Magallán, Joel. 2002. Press Conference Preceding Launch of Guadalupan Torch Run, Mexico City, Mexico.

Mahler, Sarah. 1998. "Theoretical and Empirical Contributions toward a Research Agenda for Transnationalism." In *Transnationalism from Below,* ed. Michael P. Smith and Luis Eduardo Guarnizo. New Brunswick, NJ: Transaction Publishers.

Marroni, María Da Gloria. 2003. "The Culture of Migratory Networks: Connecting New York and Puebla." In *Immigrants and Schooling: Mexicans in New York,* ed. Regina Cortina and Mónica Gendreau. Staten Island, NY: Center for Migration Studies.

Marshall, T. H. 1950. *Class, Citizenship and Social Development.* New York: Doubleday.

Massey, Douglas. 1999. "Why Does Immigration Occur? A Theoretical Synthesis." In *The Handbook of International Migration,* ed. Phillip Kasinitz and Josh De Wind. New York: Russell Sage Foundation.

Matovina, Timothy. 2005. *Guadalupe and Her Faithful.* Baltimore: Johns Hopkins University Press.

Matovina, Timothy, and Gary Riebe-Estrella. 2002. *Horizons of the Sacred.* Ithaca, NY: Cornell University Press.

McGreevy, John T. 1996. *Parish Boundaries: The Catholic Encounter with Race in the Twentieth-Century Urban North.* Chicago: University of Chicago Press.

Mier Noriega y Guerra, Fray Servando Teresa de. 1982. "Sermón Guadalupano." In *Testimonios Históricos Guadalupanos,* ed. Ernesto De La Torre Villar and Ramiro Navarro De Anda. Mexico: Fondo de Cultura Económica.

Miller, Toby. 2001. "Introducing...Cultural Citizenship." *Social Text* 69 (19): 4.

Milliken, Elizabeth. 1994. *Beyond the Immigrant Church: The Catholic Sub-Culture and the Parishes of Rochester, New York, 1870–1920.* Ph.D. dissertation, Cornell University, Ithaca.

Mitchell, Timothy. 1990. *Passional Culture: Emotion, Religion and Society in Southern Spain.* Philadelphia: University of Pennsylvania Press.

Mittleberg, David, and Mary C. Waters. 1992. "The Process of Ethnogenesis among Haitian and Israeli Immigrants in the United States." *Ethnic and Racial Studies* 15: 412–435.

Monaghan, John. 1994. *The Covenants with Earth and Rain: Exchange, Sacrifice and Revelation in Mixtec Sociality.* Norman: University of Oklahoma Press.

Moreno Navarro, Isidoro. 1985. *Cofradías y Hermandades Andaluzas: Estructura, Simbolismo, e Identidad.* Sevilla: Biblioteca de la Cultura Andaluza.

———. 1997. *La Antigua Hermandad de los Negros de Sevilla: Etnicidad, Poder y Sociedad en 600 Años de Historía.* Sevilla: Universidad de Sevilla.

220   *References*

Motolinía, Toribio De. 1950. "Of the Festival of Corpus Christi and Saint John
    Which Were Celebrated in Tlaxcala in the Year 1538." In *History of the Indians
    of New Spain*, ed. Elizabeth Andros Foster. New York: The Cortés Society.
New Advent Catholic Encyclopedia. 2007. Electronic resource: http://www.
    newadvent.org/cathen/15569a.htm, accessed December 1, 2007.
Norget, Kristin. 2006. *Days of Death, Days of Life*. New York: Columbia Univer-
    sity Press.
Ochs, Elinor, and Lisa Capps. 1996. "Narrating the Self." *Annual Review of An-
    thropology* 25: 19–43.
Ong, Aihwa. 1996. "Cultural Citizenship as Subject-Making." *Current Anthropol-
    ogy* 37: 737–762.
———. 1999. *Flexible Citizenship: The Cultural Logics of Transnationality*. Dur-
    ham, NC: Duke University Press.
Orsi, Robert Anthony. 1992. "The Religious Boundaries of an Inbetween People:
    Street Feste and the Problem of the Dark-Skinned Other in Italian Harlem,
    1920–1990." *American Quarterly* 44: 313–341.
———. 1999. *Gods of the City*. Bloomington: Indiana University Press.
Ortega, Jazmin, and Sharyn Obsatz. 2002. "Seeking Clout South of Border: Some
    Immigrants and Their Descendants Want to Vote in Mexican Elections." *The
    Press-Enterprise and La Prensa*, July 8.
Padilla, Felix. 1985. *Latino Ethnic Consciousness*. Notre Dame: University of Notre
    Dame Press.
Palacios, Joseph M. 2007. *The Catholic Social Imagination: Activism and the
    Just Society in Mexico and the United States*. Chicago: University of Chicago
    Press.
Parker, Kunal. 2001. "State, Citizenship, and Territory: The Legal Construction
    of Immigrants in Antebellum Massachusetts." *Law and History Review* 19 (3):
    583–643.
Paz, Octavio. 1985. *The Labyrinth of Solitude*. New York: Grove Press.
Pease Chock, Phyllis. 1994. "Remaking and Unmaking 'Citizen' in Policy-Making
    Talk about Immigration." *PoLar* 17 (2): 45-56.
Peña, Elaine. 2008. "Beyond Mexico: Guadalupan Sacred Space Production and
    Mobilization in a Chicago Suburb." *American Quarterly* 60, 3 (September):
    721–747.
Pew Hispanic Center. 2007. *National Survey of Latinos: As Illegal Immigration Is-
    sue Heats Up, Hispanics Feel a Chill*. Electronic resource: http://pewhispanic.
    org/reports/report.php?ReportID=84, accessed January 24, 2008.
Poole, Stafford. 1995. *Our Lady of Guadalupe: The Origins and Sources of a Mexi-
    can National Symbol, 1531–1797*. Tuscon: University of Arizona Press.
———. 2005. "History Versus Juan Diego." *The Americas* 62 (1): 1–16.
Pottenger, John. 1989. *The Political Theory of Liberation Theology*. Albany: State
    University of New York.

Powell, Stewart. 2008. "ICE Defends Workplace Raids: Democrats Rip Tactics as GOP Backs Agency on Immigration Issue." *Houston Chronicle*, May 21; available online: http://www.chron.com/disp/story.mpl/politics/5793319.html.

Preston, Julia. 2008. "Facing Deportation but Clinging to Life in U.S." *New York Times*, January 18.

———. 2009. "Obama to Push Immigration Bill as One Priority."*New York Times*, April 8.

Ragland, Cathy. 2003 "Mexican Deejays and the Transnational Space of Youth Dances in New York and New Jersey." *Ethnomusicology* 47 (3): 338–354.

Raison, Eva Blom. 2007. *Pidiendo la palabra: Immigrant Narratives and Spanish Literacy in New York City*. MA thesis, New York University.

Ramírez, Daniel. 2007. "Más allá de Azusa: The Construction of Transnational Pentecostalism in the U.S.-Mexico Borderlands." Paper presented at Latin American Studies Association, Montreal, Canada, September 6.

Raum, Tom. 1997. "Clinton Visits Revitalized South Bronx." *CNN*, Atlanta. Electronic resource: http://www3.cnn.com/ALLPOLITICS/1997/12/10/bronx.visit/, Accessed 12/15/07.

Reed-Bouley, Jennifer. 1998. *Guiding Moral Action: A Study of the United Farm Workers' Use of Catholic Social Teaching and Religious Symbols*. Ph.D. dissertation, Loyola University, Chicago.

Reu, Tobias. 2008. "Urqupiña Travels: A meditation on the Virgin Mary, displacement, and agency." *e-misférica 5.1, Vírgenes Viajeras/Traveling Virgins*, ed. Alyshia Gálvez and José Carlos Luque Brazán. Electronic resource: http://www.hemisphericinstitute.org/journal/4.2/splash/en_index.html. April 2008; accessed September 1, 2008.

Ricard, Robert. 1966. *The Spiritual Conquest of Mexico: An Essay on the Apostolate and the Evangelizing Meghods of the Mendicant Orders in New Spain*. Berkeley: University of California Press.

Ricourt, Milagros. 2003. *Hispanas de Queens: Latino Panethnicity in a New York City Neighborhood*. Ithaca, NY: Cornell University Press.

Rivera Batiz, Francisco L. 2002. "The Socioeconomic Status of Hispanic New Yorkers: Current Trends and Future Prospects." Pew Hispanic Center Study. Electronic Resource: http://pewhispanic.org/files/reports/5.pdf; accessed June 20, 2006.

Rivera Sánchez, Liliana. 2004. "Expressions of Identity and Belonging: Mexican Immigrants in New York." In *Indigenous Mexican Migrants in the United States*, ed. Jonathan Fox and Gaspar Rivera-Salgado. Berkeley: Center for Comparative Immigration Studies University.

Rivermar Pérez, María Leticia. 2003. "Santa Maria De La Encarnación Xoyatla: A Nahua Community of Peasants and Migrants." In *Immigrants and Schooling: Mexicans in New York*, ed. Regina Cortina. Staten Island, NY: Center for Migration Studies.

Rodríguez, Jeanette. 1994. *Our Lady of Guadalupe: Faith and Empowerment among Mexican-American Women*. Austin: University of Texas Press.

Rosaldo, Renato. 1989. *Culture & Truth: The Remaking of Social Analysis*. Boston: Beacon Press.

———. 1997a. "Cultural Citizenship and Educational Democracy." *Cultural Anthropology* 9: 402–411.

———. 1997b. "Cultural Citizenship, Inequality and Multiculturalism." In *Latino Cultural Citizenship*, ed. Flores et al. Boston: Beacon Press.

———. 1999. "Cultural Citizenship." In *Race, Identity and Citizenship: a Reader*, ed. Rodolfo Torres et al. Oxford: Blackwell.

Rouse, Roger. 1991. "Mexican Migration and the Social Space of Postmodernism." *Diaspora* 1: 8–23.

———. 1995. "Thinking through Transnationalism: Notes on the Cultural Politics of Class Relations in the Contemporary United States." *Public Culture* 7: 353–402.

Rubin, Miri. 1991. *Corpus Christi: The Eucharist in Late Medieval Culture*. Cambridge: Cambridge University Press.

Rudolph, Susanne Hoeber and James Piscatori. 1997. *Transnational Religion and Fading States*. Boulder, CO: Westview Press.

Sahagún, Fray Bernardino De. 1950. *Florentine Codex: General History of the Things of New Spain 1561–82*. Santa Fe, NM: School of American Research and the University of Utah.

Sánchez, George J. 1995. *Becoming Mexican American: Ethnicity, Culture, and Identity in Chicano Los Angeles, 1900–1945*. New York: Oxford University Press.

Sánchez Herrero, José. 1974. *Las Fiestas de Sevilla en el Siglo XV*. Madrid: Editorial DEIMOS.

Sassen, Saskia. 2002. "New York City: The Intersection of Global Circuits. Presented at New York City: An American Metropolis," Lecture September 23, New School University, New York.

Schuck, Peter H., and Rogers M. Smith. 1985. *Citizenship without Consent: Illegal Aliens in the American Polity*. New Haven, CT: Yale University Press.

Schwartz, Steven, Regina Zimmerman, Rosalyn Williams, Wenhui Li, Flor Betancourt, and Richard Genovese. 2007. *Summary of Vital Statistics 2006*. New York: New York City Department of Health, electronic resource: http://www.nyc.gov/html/doh/html/vs/vs.shtml.

Seltzer, Robert. 2008. "Religious Liberty and the American Creed." Multinational Institute Panel, New York University, June 25.

Siu, Lok. 2001. "Diasporic Cultural Citizenship: Chineseness and Belonging in Central America and Panama." *Social Text* 69: 4.

———. 2005. *Memories of a Future Home: Diasporic Citizenship of Chinese in Panama*. Palo Alto, CA: Stanford University Press.

Smart Girl Technologies. 2002. *Local Demographic Analysis*. New York: Professional Workshop Series.

Smith, Michael P., and Luis Eduardo Guarnizo. 1998. *Transnationalism from Below*. New Brunswick, NJ: Transaction Publishers.

Smith, Robert C. 1995. *"Los Ausentes Siempre Presentes"*: *The Imagining, Making and Politics of a Transnational Migrant Community between Ticuani, Puebla, Mexico and New York City*. Ph.D. dissertation, Columbia University.

———. 1997. "Transnational Migration, Assimilation and Political Community" In *The City and the World: New York's Global Future*, ed. Margaret Crahan and Alberto Vourvoulias Bush. New York: Council on Foreign Relations.

———. 2001. "Mexicans: Social, Educational, Economic and Political Problems and Prospects in New York." In *New Immigrants in New York*, ed. Nancy Foner. New York: Columbia University Press.

———. 2002. "Issues Facing the Mexican Community in New York." Asociación Tepeyac's 5th Anniversary Conference, September 6.

———. 2003. "Imagining Mexican Educational Features in New York." In *Immigrants and Schooling: Mexicans in New York*, ed. Regina Cortina. Staten Island, NY: Center for Migration Studies.

———. 2005. *Mexican New York*. Berkeley: University of California Press.

Smith, Timothy. 1978. "Religion and Ethnicity in America." *American Historical Review* 83: 1155–1185.

Solís, Jocelyn. 2002. *The Transformation of Illegality as an Identity: A Study of the Organization of Undocumented Mexican Immigrants and Their Children in New York City*. Ph.D. dissertation, City University of New York.

Sommer, Doris. 1991. *Foundational Fictions: The National Romances of Latin America*. Berkeley: University of California Press.

Sousa, Lisa, Stafford Poole, and James Lockhart. 1998. *The Story of Guadalupe: Luis Laso De La Vega's Huei Tlamahuicoltica of 1649*. Palo Alto, CA: Stanford University Press.

Soysal, Yasemin. 1994. *Limits to Citizenship: Migrants and Postnational Membership in Europe*. Chicago: University of Chicago Press.

Starr-Lebeau, Gretchen D. 1996. *Guadalupe: Political Authority and Religious Identity in Fifteenth-Century Spain*. Ph.D. dissertation, University of Michigan.

Stevens-Arroyo, Antonio M., and Ana María Díaz-Stevens. 1998. *Recognizing the Latino Resurgence in U.S. Religion*. Boulder, CO: Westview Press.

Tamez, Elsa. 1987. *Teólogos de La Liberación Hablan Sobre la Mujer*. Yorktown Heights, NY: Meyer-Stone Books.

Tomasi, Silvano M. 1970. "The Ethnic Church and the Integration of Italian Immigrants in the United States." In *The Italian Experience in the United States*, ed. Sylvano Tomasi and Madeline Enge. Staten Island, NY: Center for Migration Studies.

———. 1975. *Piety and Power: The Role of the Italian Parishes in the New York Metropolitan Area, 1880–1930*. Staten Island, NY: Center for Migration Studies.

Turner, Victor. 1969. *The Ritual Process: Structure and Anti-Structure*. Chicago: Aldine.

———. 1974. *Dramas, Fields, and Metaphors: Symbolic Action in Human Society*. Ithaca, NY: Cornell University Press.

Turner, Victor, and Edith Turner. 1978. *Image and Pilgrimage in Christian Culture*. New York: Columbia University Press.

U.S. Census Bureau. 2000. *American Community Survey*.

———. 2002. *American Community Survey*.

———. 2004. *American Community Survey*.

———. 2006. *American Community Survey*, electronic resource: http://www.census.gov/acs/www/.

U.S. Citizenship and Immigration Services. 2004. "How Do I Become a Lawful Permanent Resident While in the United States?" http://www.uscis.gov/portal/site/uscis/menuitem.5af9bb95919f35e66f614176543f6d1a/?vgnextoid=8b76194d3e88do10VgnVCM10000048f3d6a1RCRD&vgnextchannel=4f719c7755cb9010VgnVCM10000045f3d6a1RCRD , Electronic resource, accessed 6/1/04.

U.S. Conference of Catholic Bishops, Inc. and Conferencia del Episcopado Mexicano. 2003. *Strangers No Longer: Together on a Journey of Hope*. Electronic resource: http://www.usccb.org/mrs/stranger.shtml, Accessed 9/29/08.

Universo Cristiano. 2008. "El número de cristianos evangélicos según el INEGI." Electronic resource: http://www.universocristiano.com/noticias.phtml?id=402, accessed 7/22/08.

Vásquez, Manuel, and Marie F. Marquardt. 2003. *Globalizing the Sacred: Religion Across the Americas*. New Brunswick, NJ: Rutgers University Press.

Verdery, Katherine. 1998. "Transnationalism, Nationalism, Citizenship and Property: Eastern Europe since 1989." *American Ethnologist* 25: 291–306.

Vidal, Jaime, and Jay P. Dolan. 1994. *Puerto Rican and Cuban Catholics in the United States, 1900–1965*. Notre Dame: University of Notre Dame Press.

Wakin, Daniel. 2003. "Latino Church Greets Its New Home with a Procession of the Faithful." *New York Times*, April 14.

Wallace, Rodrick, and Wallace, Deborah. 1998. *A Plague on Your Houses: How New York Was Burned Down and National Public Health Crumbled*. London: Verso.

Warner, Stephen R., and Judith Wittner. 1999. *Gatherings in Diaspora: Religious Communities and the New Immigration*. Philadelphia: Temple University Press.

Webster Verdi, Susan. 1998. "Processional Sculpture." In *Art and Ritual in Golden-Age Spain: Sevillian Confraternities and the Processional Sculpture of Holy Week*. Princeton, NJ: Princeton University Press.

Werbner, Pnina. 1996. "Stamping the Earth with the Name of Allah: Zikr and the Sacralizing of Space among British Muslims." *Cultural Anthropology* 11: 309–338.

———. 2001. "The Limits of Cultural Hybridity: On Ritual Monsters, Poetic License and Contested Postcolonial Purifications." *Journal of the Royal Anthropological Institute* 7: 133–152.

Williams, Rhys. 2007. "Liberalism, Religion and Immigrant Rights." In *Religion and Social Justice for Immigrants*, ed. Hondagneu Sotelo. New Brunswick, NJ: Rutgers University Press.

Wolf, Eric. 1958. "The Virgin of Guadalupe: Mexican National Symbol." *Journal of American Folklore* 7: 134–139.

Wood, Richard L. 2002. *Faith in Action: Religion, Race, and Democratic Organizing in America*. Chicago: University of Chicago Press.

Yellin, Jessica. 2009. "WH won't push immigration issue this year." CNN News, electronic resource: http://politicalticker.blogs.cnn.com/2009/04/09/wh-wont-push-immigration-issue-this-year/, published April 9.

Young, Iris Marion. 1989. "Polity and Group Difference: A Critique of the Ideal of Universal Citizenship." *Ethics* 99 (January): 250.

———. 2000. *Inclusion and Democracy*. Oxford: Oxford University Press.

Yuval-Davis, Nira. 1997. *Gender and Nation*. Thousand Oaks, CA: Sage.

Zolberg, Aristide, and J. Casanova. 2002. *Religion and Immigrant Incorporation in New York: Analytical Summary and Findings of RIINY Project*. Presented at concluding conference of RIINY Project, New School University.

Zúñiga Barba, María. 2008. "Guadalupe, Madre de los Inmigrantes." *e-misférica* 5.1, *Vírgenes Viajeras/Traveling Virgins*, ed. Alyshia Gálvez and José Carlos Luque Brazán. http://www.hemisphericinstitute.org/journal/4.2/splash/en_index.html, April 2008.

Index

245i amendment of the Immigration and Nationality Act (2000), 201n10

Acapulco, 47m
Aggregation, 86
Alabama, 162
Alberto, 53, 55, 90–91, 100, 126, 153
Alinsky, Saul, 44, 139, 185–186, 202n11
Allende, Salvador, 52
Alonso, Ana, 104
Al otro lado, 83. See also *Coyote*
Altagracia, 124, 127
Amnesty, 29, 42, 116–117, 154, 172, 174, 177, 178, 181, 185. *See also* Immigration Reform and Control Act (IRCA)
Ana, 54
Anáhuac, 197n1
Analco, Celestino and María, 133
Antonio, 157, 162, 164, 166, 207n5
Antorcha Guadalupana, La, (Guadalupan Torch Run), 5, 15, 55, 102, 140–167, 181; capitána/es of, 55, 149; tradition of running, 142; uniform, 170
Apostates, 77
Appadurai, Arjun, 199n4, 209n11; and James Holston, 18
Archdiocese of Brooklyn, 60
Archdiocese of New York, 35, 46, 60, 62, 162; Committee for Hispanic Affairs, 60. *See also* Diocesan clergy; Egan, Edward Cardinal; Priests; Spellman, Francis Cardinal

Arizona, 154
Arraigo, 23
Arthur Avenue, 51
Asociación Tepeyac de New York, 4, 6, 13–15, 16, 23, 25, 29, 31, 54, 60–71, 95, 107; formerly known as El Centro Guadalupano, 62; funding, 64–65; institutional expansion of, 64; mission, 63, 65, 67
Aspirations, 13, 189. *See also* Superarse
Assimilation, 3, 24, 34, 185; critiques of, 86
Atlixtac, Guerrero, 156
Ave María, 114, 133

Badillo, David, 94
Ballet Folklórico, 54
Basilica of Our Lady of Guadalupe. *See* Our Lady of Guadalupe, Basilica of
Bellah, Robert, 33
Benedict XIV, Pope, 180
Benign neglect, 118
Berman, Marshall, 118
Beyer, Peter, 37
Bolivia, Bolivians, 82
Border, 17, 80; "broken," 182; crossing of, 87, 142, 150, 154, 164, 165; enforcement of, 80–81, 164, 188; governors of states on, 175; patrol of, 80, 162; spectacle of, 164–165; surveillance of, 182; violence on, 87, 115. *See also* Immigration and Naturalization Service (INS); *Migra, la*

Bosniak, Linda, 17
Bracero Accord, 27, 41, 60, 200n7
Bronx, 1, 10, 12, 13, 41, 113–115, 118, 131, 199n9
Brooklyn, 12, 65, 155, 170
Brownsville, Texas, 150, 164
Bundle of years, 8
Bush, George W., 29, 174–176
Buxó i Rey, María Jesús, 79
Byrne, Father Quincy, 50–53, 63, 124, 203n15, 206n6

Caja de ahorro, community chest, 57, 203n18
Calvary, 108, 131
Camarota, Steven, 208n7
Cárdenas, Lázaro, 22
Cargo. *See* Mayordomía
Carolina, 4
Carter, Jimmy, 118
Cartography, 101
Casa Mexico, 7, 26
Castañeda, Jorge, 175
Castillo, Father Jonathan 124, 127, 206n7
Catholic(s): identity, 89, 205n9; German, 33; Italian, 36–60; social teaching, 63; Spanish, 143
Catholic Church; 32–36, 189; attendance, 99; as the "immigrant" church, 32–33; in Mexico, 78, 81, 85, 98; in the U.S., 79–80, 111, 167, 182
Catholic natural law, 188
Catholicism: popular, 81–82; public, 78, 131
Center for Immigration Studies, 177, 208n7
Centro Guadalupano. *See* Asociacion Tepeyac de New York
Chávez, Cesar, 38, 78, 137
Chiapas, 113, 115
Chicago, Illinois, 4, 61, 104, 137, 138, 176

Chicano Rights Movement, 38, 78
Chile, 52
Christ, Jesus, 73, 81, 107, 129, 131,133, 137
Circuits, 7, 29, 128
Citizenship, 4, 6, 7, 17, 103–105, 142n, 173n, 174n, 181, 183–191, 199n3, 200n5; "first class," 18, 20; "second class," 18; cultural, 17, 102, 183; flexible, 19; juridical, 17, 104, 174, 183, 184; liberal, 22; post-national, 20, 156, 200n5; practiced, 38, 174; universal, 199n4
Civil Religion, 33–34, 38, 112, 137
Civil Rights Movement, 38–39. *See also* Chicano Rights Movement; Puerto Rican Rights Movement
Clinton, President Bill, 118, 201n10, Clinton, Hillary, 177
"Clock Tower," 119
Coatlicue, 8, 9
Coatlicue Theater Company, 112
Cofradías, 23; *de la Pasión,* 108
Colombia, 43
Colorado, Hortensia and Elvira (performance artists), 112
Comités guadalupanos, 3, 13–16, 25, 29, 39, 40
Communitas. See Community
Community, 3, 6, 25, 37–38, 87, 98; 103, 123, 129; building, 8, 37, 57–59, 89, 111, 139, 182; definition of, 92, 138, 142. *See also* Pueblo
Compadrazgo, 54, 203n16, 205n11
Concuño, 55, 203n17
Confianza, 55, 67, 87
Confraternal, 3, 39. See also *Cofradías*
Congregation, 3, 108; congregationalism, 34
Conquest, 76–77, 147; of New Spain, 75
Consejo de honor, honorary council, 56

Convivencia, 14, 164–165, 199n10
Co-op City, 50
Corpus Christi, 105
Cortes, Hernán, 141
Council of Trent (1545–1563), 81.
    See also Counter- or Catholic
    Reformation
Counter- or Catholic Reformation,
    81–82
Coyolxauhqui, 9
Coyote (immigration trafficker), 68, 83,
    87, 154
Crime, 84, 113, 120, 139
Criollos, 76. *See also* Gachupines
Cristero War, 160
Crossing, 83–84. *See* Border
Cursillo, 35, 112
Cuzco, Peru, 105

Davalos, Karen Mary, 104
De Certeau, Michel, 101, 104–105
De Genova, Nicholas, 26, 30, 86, 183
de la Puente, Juan, 205n5
de las Casas, Fray Bartolomé, 77
Death, 69
Democracy, 103–104
Deportation, 17, 176, 178, 182; de-
    portability, 183
Devotional practices, 3, 10, 73, 98,
    155, 164, 185
Devotional theme park, 147
Díaz, Bernal, 75
Díaz Barriga, Miguel, 18, 197n2
Díaz-Stevens, Ana María, 34, 76, 79,
    137
Diocesan clergy, 46–47, 50, 64. *See
    also* Archdiocese of New York
Disenchantment, 82
Dominguez, Jerry, 26, 160
Dominican order, 205n15
Dominicans, Dominican Republic, 51,
    124–125

Don Roberto, 90–91
Downs, Gregory, 199n2
Dred Scott decision, 199n2
Drugs, 113
Duffell, J. P., 208n9
Durkheim, Emile, 82, 185, 205n7

East Harlem, 134
Ecclesia in America, 75
Ecclesiastical base communities. *See*
    Liberation Theology
Edson, 43, 96
Egan, Edward Cardinal, 48, 143, 144
Egypt, 84, 129
Ejido, 23, 39
El Tri (rock band), 148
Elizondo, Virgilio, 77, 79
Encomienda, 77
Enlightenment, 82
Erasmus, Erasmian humanism, 77. *See
    also* Humanism
Ethnic succession, 32
Ethnographic research, 23, 24, 92
Eurocentrism, 82
Evangelization, 77–78
Exodus, 84, 87, 138, 188
Extremadura, 8

Federal Plaza, 116, 130, 133
Felipe, 43
Fictive coethnicity, 32
Fictive kin, 138
Figueroa Deck, Allan, 204n4
Filipino, 124
Flake, Jeff, 174
Florencia, Francisco de, 75
Florentine Codex, 8
Florida, 198n7
Flowers, 1–2, 32, 39, 40, 50, 61, 72–73,
    74, 141, 143, 173, 190
Flows, 7
Focus of book, 13

Fordham Road, 50
Fordham University, 50
Fox, Vicente, 160, 161, 174, 179
Francisca, 42
Fuentes, Omar, 53, 55, 91, 95
Funeral rites, 69

Gachupines, 75–76, 204n3; and Castil-
    ians, 79. See also *Criollos*
Gangs, 53, 123
Geertz, Clifford, 79
Gender, 42–43, 53–54
Gibson, Mel, 111
Ginés de Sepúlveda, 77
Giuliani, Rudolph, 50, 177
Globalization, 82
Goizueta, Roberto, 81–82, 104
Goldring, Luin, 182
Good Friday, 108, 121, 124, 129, 136
Gossip, 59
Great Britain, 101–2
Grito de Dolores, 75, 78
Grupo Timón, 46, 52, 60, 148
Guadalajara, Jalisco, 66
Guadalupanismo (Guadalupan devo-
    tion), 2, 6, 7, 75, 89, 142, 146, 154,
    156, 173, 179, 181, 186, 187, 190;
    guadalupanos, 144; as aspect of
    identity, 160, 179
Guatemala, Guatemalans, 43, 96, 202n10
Guelaguetzas/tequios, 23
Guerrero, Andrés, 79
Guerrero, state of, 9, 41, 150, 151, 156;
    Atlixtac, 156
Guest worker proposals, 174–175,
    207n2. See also Bracero Accord
Guevara, Ana Gabriela, 148
Gútierrez, Gustavo, 63. See also Libera-
    tion Theology

Habbakuk's lament, 113
Hammond, Phillip, 137

Health, problems, 151, 155; insurance,
    198n8
Hellman, Judith Adler, 189
Heraclio, 146–7, 156, 161–163, 166,
    171, 207n8
Hermanas Colorado (Colorado sis-
    ters). *See* Colorado, Hortensia and
    Elvira
Hidalgo, Miguel de, 75, 79
Hidalgo, state of, 146, 150
Holy Week, 108, 121
Homeland Security, Department of,
    164–165
Housing, 11
HR2899, 174, 207n1
HR4437, 176
Hudson River, Hudson Valley, 169, 170
*Huei tlamahuicoltica. See Nican
    Mopohua*
Huitzilipochtli, 8, 180, 204n2
Humane Borders, 199n1
Humanism, 179–191. *See also* Erasmus
Hurtig, Janise, 137–138

IAF. *See* Inter Areas Foundation
Identity, vectors of, 7, 21, 25, 45, 56,
    138, 139, 154, 190
Idolatry, 82
"Illegality," 7, 17, 26, 27, 30, 87, 102,
    183, 200n8
Illich, Ivan, 35, 202n5
IIRIRA, 207n3
Im/migrant, 26, 27
*Imagen de la Virgen María, Madre de
    Dios de Guadalupe*, 75
Immigration and Customs Enforce-
    ment, (ICE), 178–179
Immigration and Naturalization Ser-
    vice (INS), 130
Immigration reform, 3, 6, 30, 133, 164,
    171, 173, 174, 177–179, 185; stale-
    mate on, 179

Immigration Reform and Control Act (IRCA), 1986, 29, 42, 172, 174, 176. *See also* Amnesty
Indigenous people: costumes of, 169; humanity of, 76–78, 80
Industrial development, 118
Infidels, 77
Inquisition, the, 77
INS. *See* Immigration and Naturalization Service
Inter Areas Foundation (IAF), 44–45, 112
Irish, the, 31–32, 46, 50
Israel, 114; Israelites, 84
Italians, Barrio Italiano, 51. *See also* Catholics, Italian
ITESO (Instituto Tecnológico de Estudios Superiores del Occidente), 66–71
Iturbide, Agustin, 75

Jacob, 114
Jacobson, David, 188, 200n5
Jacoby, Tamar, 176, 208n6
Jalisco, state of, 169
Jerusalem, 108, 134
Jesuits, 46, 50, 60, 61, 63, 146, 147, 204n21
Jews, 77; cultural identity, 87
John Paul II, Pope, 146, 147, 180
Josefa, 68
Josefina, 43
Joseph, 188
Juan, 43
Juan Diego, Saint, 6, 20, 39, 72, 75, 80, 81, 141, 149, 155, 163, 171, 173, 180–181, 185, 186, 190, 202n5; costumes of, 169; image of, 171
Judeo-Christian, 38, 188
Julio, 46, 116, 120, 123, 203n13
Kenny, Father John, 40, 46–49, 63, 117, 124, 125

King, Peter, 177
Kolbe, Jim, 174
Krase, Jerome, 207n4
Krikorian, Mark, 208n7
Kurtz, Donald, 76

Lasso de la Vega, Luis, 75, 97
Latino Cultural Studies Group, 18
Laura, 42, 96, 99
Leadership, 40–49, 56–57, 91–92
Lefebvre, Henri, 104
Legalization, 4, 27, 29, 131, 133, 171–172, 174–175, 184,185
Legion of Mary, 112, 124, 126
Lerins, Vincent of, 75
Liberation Theology, 7, 37, 46, 52, 62–63, 78, 79; comunidades eclesiales de base (CEBs), 62, 138
Lima, Peru, 105
Liminal, liminal phase, 86–87
Lisette, 91–92
London, 118
Lora, Alex, 148
Los Angeles, 176
Luther, Martin, 81
Lutheran Church, 123
Luz María, 148

Magallán Reyes, Joel, 11, 31, 45, 60, 63–64, 72–73, 146, 149, 163, 176, 194, 204n21
Magaña family, 40–46, 55, 61–62, 114–117, 152; María Lucia, 123, 151, 203n12; Rosario Martínez de, 40–43, 96, 114, 151, 203n13
Malenny, 96
Manuel, 43
Manuela, 55
Mañanitas, las, 31; as song, 171, 201n2
Mapping. *See* Space
Marco, 1–2, 10, 24, 58–59
Margin (limen), 86

María Jose, 151–2
Maríanism, 94
Mario, 43
Marshall, T. H., 18, 199n3
Martínez de Magaña, Rosario. *See* Magaña family
Marx, Marxian, Marxist, 157, 160
Mary, 73–75, 82, 180, 183, 188, 203n15, 208n9
Massachusetts, 178
Massey, Douglas, 12, 188
Matamoros, 155, 164
Matriarchal core, 35
Matrícula consular, 28, 198n8
Mayordomía (system), 9, 39, 55–56, 62–63, 197n4
McCain, John, 177
Medicaid, 198n8
Membership, 17, 21, 42, 53, 183, 197, 199n3
Merino, Joel, 150, 157
Methodologies, 14
Metropolitan Museum of Art, 66
Mexica [Aztec], 8, 180
Mexican Episcopate, 132, 188
Mexican population in New York, 11, 12, 51, 119, 125, 197n6
Mexico, Mexican, 9, 22–23, 29, 146, 162, 165, 180; government, 65; Revolution, 22–23, 75, 78, 161, 179; Conquest of, 72–75; Constitution of 1917, 161; differences from U.S., 121; Independence movement, 79; Mexican-Americans, 138, Mexican identity 115, 179
Mexico City, 11, 15, 41, 58, 65, 67, 76, 105, 144–146, 158–159, 162, 163; foundation of, 180
Mier Noriega y Guerra, Teresa de, 204n5
Migra, la, 120. 130. *See also* Border, enforcement of; Immigration and Naturalization Service (INS)

Migration, 2, 6, 12, 26–27, 198n8; accelerated, 11, 12; great Puerto Rican, 37; migration syndrome, 12; migrational city, 101; push/pull factors of, 12; theology of, 36. *See also* Puerto Rico, Puerto Ricans
Miguel, 56
Miller, Toby, 18
Minutemen, 177
Miracles, 162, 173
Mirna, 54–55, 126
Misión guadalupana, la, 15, 56, 83, 90–100, 101, 102, 181; *El Apostolado,* 205n12
Misiotes, 47
Mississippi, 154, 162; Laurel, 178
Mixteca, la (region), 5, 9, 11, 12, 22, 39, 69, 85, 142, 198n7; Mixteco language, 182
Moctezuma, 12, 80, 141
Mole, 47
Monagahan, John, 23
Montesinos, Fray Antonio de, 77
Moors, 77, 79
Morales, Estela, 64–65, 72, 78, 181
Morris, 66
Mott Haven, 46, 118, 131, 202n8. *See also* Bronx
Moynihan, Daniel Patrick, 118
Multiethnic, 123
Muslims, 101–102; Islam, 74. *See also* Pakistanis

NAFTA. *See* North American Free Trade Agreement
Nahuas, 73, 147; Nahuatl language, 73, 173, 182, 190, 198n7
Nancy, 152, 154
Narrative, 24, 130
National Parish, 35, 93
Nayarit, state of, 43

Negrete, Jorge, 32
New Jersey, 153, 167, 169; Jersey City, 170
New Sanctuary Movement, 208n10
New-York Historical Society, 207n2
Nezahualcoyotl, city of, 11
Nican Mopohua, 75, 97
Nogales, Arizona, 87
Nonprofit status, 501(c)3, 63, 71
Norget, Kristen, 23, 89
North American Free Trade Agreement (NAFTA), 12, 198n7, 200n5
North Carolina, 154, 162; Durham, 156
Novena, 39, 112
Nuevo Leon, state of, 65
Numbers U.S.A., 177

Oakland, California, 44, 103
Oaxaca, 9, 41
Obama, Barack, 177–179
"One-to-one" organizing, 44
Ong, Aihwa, 16, 19–20
Orsi, Robert, 86, 119
Our Lady of Guadalupe, 7, 25, 36, 62, 72–106, 161, 170–171; apparitions of, 72, 76, 87, 180, as arbiter of humanity, 76, 189; Basilica of, 72, 75, 81, 82, 142, 143, 144, 147, 160, 204n5; hagiography of, 72; as messenger, 149, 163–164, 167; parish of, 94, 143, 163; patronage of, 161, 180, 189; as symbol, 75, 100, 102, 161, 165; terms of endearment for, 205n14; use of, 161
Our Lady of Remedies, 76
Our Lady of Rosary Parish, 1, 14, 45, 50–59; 63, 70, 73, 90–92, 95, 104, 108, 123–129, 152, 155, 163
Our Lady of Urkupiña (Bolivia), 82

Pakistanis, 101–102
Palacios, Joseph, 103
Palestine, 108
Panethnicity, 32
Pan-Mexicanness. *See* Mexico, Mexican
Papeles, 28, 165, 201n9; *arreglar*, 22
Parish(es): 202n4; bounds, 93; urban, 93; St. Bernard, 94, 143, 162; St. Cecilia, 39, 60
Parker, Kunal, 22
Partido Revolucionario Institucional (PRI), 23, 79, 161, 179
Passion of the Christ. *See* Viacrucis (Stations of the Cross)
Passion of the Christ, The (film), 111
Patriot Act, 193, 194, 201n9p
Paz, Octavio, 178
Pease Chock, Phyllis, 18, 188
"Personhood"/"personness," 16, 20, 173, 181, 184, 185, 186, 188, 200n5
Philadelphia, 153–154
Philip II, 8
PICO, 44, 103
Pilgrimage, 108
Pinochet, General Augusto, 52
Pius XXII, Pope, 75
Planned shrinkage, 118
Polestar of America, 75
Police, 120, 144
Politics, 63, 79, 100, 185, 186; formal, 103; informal, 161; definition of 102–103; pre- or protopolitical, 102–103
Polleros. See Coyote
Poole, Stafford, 204n4
Post-secular, 36
Postville, Iowa, 178
PRI. *See* Partido Revolucionario Institucional

Priests, 99, 179; clerical presence, 24, 46–49, 63; Diocesan clergy, 46–47, 50; "red," 63; relationship with parishioners, 89; *Vicaría de la Solidaridad,* activism of, 52
Procession, 101–105, 121, 126, 164, 185
Promesa, 97, 151
Proyecto Chamba, 69
Puebla, state of, 9, 11, 14, 29, 47, 53, 87, 144, 147, 149, 155, 198n8, 205n15; Progreso, 157
Pueblo, 134, 136, 138
Puerto Rican Rights Movement, 38
Puerto Rico, 47, 51; Puerto Ricans, 39, 50–51, 60, 120, 125

Quechua, 82
Queens, 146, 155, 170, 171
Querétaro, state of, 87
Quillacollo, 82
Quintana Roo, state of, 47

Racialization, 19
Radio City Music Hall, 167
Ramírez, Daniel, 103
Rand Corporation, 118
Reagan, Ronald, 118
"Rebuke of leaders and prophets," 113–114
Reconquista, 8, 197n3
Religion, religious, 5, 16, 38, 185; affiliation, 89, 146; imagination, 79; non-Catholic, 64
Religiosity, 5, 35, 37–38, 50, 89, 111, 147, 180; of the city, 119; and community building, 89; Iberian, 8, 74, 108; indigenous, 72–74, 80, 82; Latino, 2, 94, 137, 180; popular, 37, 161
Repatriation of the dead, 69
Republican Party, 177

Right(s), 3, 4, 6, 8, 161, 173–174, 179, 183, 186; to have rights, 16
Rio Grande (Rio Bravo), 83–84
Rite of passage: border-crossing as, 85–86; running as, 142
River, as metaphor, 84, 142, 181
Rivera, Alex, 204n19
Rivera, Diego, 167
Rivera Sánchez, Liliana, 198n7
Roberto, 87
Rocío, 54
Rockefeller Center, 167
Rockettes, 167
Rodrigo, 158, 166
Romans, 123, 127, 131, 133–134
Romero, José Isaías, 146
Rosa, 36–37
Rosaldo, Renato, 18
Rosaura, 46, 116, 123, 203n13
Rouse, Roger, 27
Rubén, 54, 55, 70–71, 101, 205n16

Sacred, 82
Sahagún, Fray Bernardino de, 8
Salvation Army, 167
Sánchez, Miguel, 42, 48–49, 75, 87, 99
Santos, María, 42, 87
Santos, Raúl, 87
Sassen, Saskia, 186
Second Vatican Council. *See* Vatican II
Secularization, the secular, 36, 82
Segundo, 150–152, 203n13
Sensenbrenner, James, 176
Separation, 86
September 11, 2001, 54, 67–68, 76, 101, 167, 174–175, 193, 208n5. *See also* World Trade Center
Sergio, 141, 157, 161 166
Shrines, 8, 39, 50, 141
Sisters Luz, Gertrudis, 97
Skate Key (roller rink), 119
Skelly, Father Francis, 39, 60, 75, 94

Slavery, 77
Smith, Robert C., 29, 204n19
Smith, Timothy, 37
Sociology: of immigration, 5; of religion, 5
Solís, Jocelyn, 189
Sonidero (dj-peformer), 39
Sonora Desert, 87, 176
Sotomayor, Marcos, 147
South Bronx Churches, 44
Soysal, Yasemin, 20, 188, 200n5
Space, 92–97, 101, 105, 126–127, 142; conquest of, 101, 104–106, 129–132, 139; mapping of, 104–106, 129, 131; of the church, 182
Spanish colonial rule, 105, 197n3
Spellman, Francis Cardinal, 34, 35, 47, 142, 202n5
Spitzer, Eliot, 177
St. Bernard Parish. *See* Parishes
St. Cecilia Parish. *See* Parishes
St. John Parish, 1, 4 40–49, 63, 96, 108, 112–123, 150, 152, 153
St. Patrick's Cathedral, 142–143, 151
St. Thomas the Apostle, 77, 204n5
Staten Island, 64, 170
Stations of the Cross. *See* Viacrucis (Stations of the Cross)
Statue of Liberty, 175, 178
Stauffer, Jill, 209n13
Stevens-Arroyo, Anthony, 34, 76, 79, 137
Structural sin, 7, 127
Structures of belonging, 18
Superarse, 84. *See also* Aspirations
"Sweat equity," 22, 181; sweat tax, 185
Sweeping, 1–2, 8–10
Symbols, 72–76, 79, 161, 174

Tamaulipas, state of, 150
Tancredo, Tom, 177, 194
Tenochtitlán, 148–149, 180

Tepeaquilla. See Tepeyac, hill at
Tepeyac, hill at (*Cerro de Tepeyac*), 73, 75, 81, 141, 146, 147; *Villa* (basilica), 147; replica of, 152–153, 197
Tepeyacac, 147
Texas, 44, 84; Dallas, 176
Theology, 78, 80, 87; of liberation, 37, 46, 52, 62–63; of migration, 36; theologizing experience, 37, 205n10
Tilma, 72, 180
Tlaxcala, state of, 150
Tocqueville, Alexis de, 38
Toluca, Estado de México, 58
Tonantzin, 73
Torch, 8, 98; for carrying a message, 140–141
Transformation, 5, 10, 70, 83, 86, 105, 173–174, 181, 186; of "illegal" to "undocumented" identity, 189; into Juan Diego, 156; of relationship to Our Lady of Guadalupe, 157; of ritual significance, 90, 135–136, 137–138, 155
Transnationalism, 26, 82, 105–106, 182, 185
Turner, Victor, 79, 85–87

Undocumented, 4, 6, 10, 11, 16, 26, 181, 186, 200n8
United Farm Workers (UFW), 37–38, 78, 137, 189
United States Census, 11
United States Council of Catholic Bishops (USCCB), 132, 188
University Heights, 50, 188
Urban decay, 119
Urban religious topographies, 101
Urban renewal, 119
Urbicide, 118

Van Gennep, Arnold, 85
Vatican II, 33, 37, 63, 78, 79, 182

Vectors of identity. *See* Identity, vectors of
Veracruz, 141, 150
Viacrucis (Stations of the Cross), 15, 62, 104, 107–139, 181, *184*; in the 16th century, 110; sequence of, 110, 206n3; purpose of, 111; script of, 110, 137–139, 142; "Rebuke of leaders and prophets," 113–114; terminology of, 205n2, 206n4
Virgen de los Remedios, la, 76. *See also* Gachupines
Virginia, 154, 162

Walking, 101, 104–105
Wallace, Deborah, 118
Wallace, Rodrick, 118
Wall Street, 130, 134
Washington, D.C., 150, 176

Weber, Max, 38
Werbner, Pnina, 101, 185
White House, 150, 153, 178
Wilmington, Delaware, 155
Wood, Richard L., 45, 102–103
World Trade Center, 54, 70, 171, 202n11; disaster addressed at Asociación Tepeyac, 67–68; workers displaced from, 70

Young, Iris Marion, 199n4

Zacatecas, state of, 60
Zapata, Emiliano, 75
Zapatista movement, 115
Zapotitlán de Salinas, Puebla, 150
Zumárraga, Bishop Juan de, 141, 173, 190
Zúñiga Barba, María, 149, 156

About the Author

ALYSHIA GÁLVEZ is Assistant Professor of Latin American and Puerto Rican Studies at Lehman College/City University of New York. She is editor of the collection, *Performing Religion in the Americas* (Berg/Seagull 2007), and *Traveling Virgins/Virgenes Viajeras* (2008), a special issue of the journal *e-misférica*.